5:2

GOOD FOOD KITCHEN

More healthy and delicious
recipes for everyone, every day

KATE HARRISON

This edition first published in Great Britain in 2014 by
Orion
an imprint of the Orion Publishing Group Ltd
Orion House, 5 Upper St Martin's Lane,
London WC2H 9EA

An Hachette UK Company

1 3 5 7 9 10 8 6 4 2

A CIP catalogue record for this book is available

from the British Library.

Mass Market Paperback ISBN: 978 1 4091 5261 3

Printed in Great Britain by CPI Group (UK) Ltd, Croydon, CR0 4YY

Photographer: Andrew Hayes-Watkins
Food consultant and stylist: Emma Marsden
Prop stylist: Linda Berlin
Nutritional analysis: Fiona Hunter

The Orion Publishing Group's policy is to use papers that are natural, renewable and recyclable
and made from wood grown in sustainable forests. The logging and manufacturing processes are
expected to conform to the environmental regulations of the country of origin.

Every effort has been made to ensure that the information in the book is accurate. The
information in this book will be relevant to the majority of people but may not be applicable in
each individual case so it is advised that professional medical advice is obtained for specific health
matters. Neither the publisher nor author accepts any legal responsibility for any personal injury
or other damage or loss arising from the use of the information in this book. Anyone making a
change in their diet should consult their GP especially if pregnant, infirm, elderly or under 16.

Every effort has been made to fulfil requirements with regard to reproducing copyright material.
The author and publisher will be glad to rectify any omissions at the earliest opportunity.

www.orionbooks.co.uk

5:2

GOOD FOOD
KITCHEN

Also by the author:

5:2 Your Life

The Ultimate 5:2 Diet Recipe Book

The 5:2 Diet Book

The Boot Camp

Soul Fire

Soul Beach

Soul Storm

Old School Ties

Brown Owl's Guide to Life

The Self-Preservation Society

The Starter Marriage

The Bride Hunter

Brief Encounters

The Secret Shopper series

Important Safety Note

You should always consult a doctor before making dietary changes.

This book is written for information only and is not intended as medical advice, or as a substitute for medical advice, diagnosis or treatment.

Children, teenagers, pregnant and breast-feeding women shouldn't fast.

If you have a chronic condition or diabetes, it's particularly important that you consult your doctor, specialist or diabetes nurse, before embarking on 5:2 or any diet. Many people with Type 2 diabetes, or metabolic syndrome and pre-diabetes, have had success with this way of eating, but it's essential that you do this under supervision, especially if you are taking medication. If you have any history of eating disorders, you should also consult a doctor before making any dietary change, including 5:2.

Neither the author nor publisher or associates can be held responsible for any loss or claim resulting from the use or misuse of information and suggestions contained in this book, or for the failure to take medical advice.

Finally, never disregard professional medical advice or delay medical treatment because of something you have read in this book.

Contents

WELCOME TO THE

5:2

GOOD FOOD KITCHEN

where you eat delicious,
healthy meals for *every* day
of the week

Introduction

Dear reader,

Let's talk about good food. About making eating a pleasure, and enjoying fresh, delicious ingredients, prepared and cooked in exciting ways. About making the food we buy and eat as nourishing and tasty as it can be, and about adapting recipes and methods to suit the time we have, our dietary needs *and* the lives we lead.

That's what this book is all about.

I don't believe in additive-filled 'diet food'. Or in banning a particular ingredient, or telling you cheese or chocolate are 'sinful', or listing page after page of things you should never eat. And in this kitchen, the aim is to savour good food – and never, ever feel guilty.

This is the fourth book I've written about the 5:2 approach to food and eating, but if it's your *first* encounter with the lifestyle, then a very special welcome. Later in the book, you'll find all the information you need to make intermittent fasting – the approach of cutting calories twice or three times a week – as rewarding and enjoyable as possible.

Rewarding? Enjoyable? It may surprise you to hear those words if you're more worried that fasting means terrible hunger, or taking things to extremes. But as you'll discover, 5:2 is about liberation from feeling you *must* eat in ways or at times that don't suit you.

Welcome to my kitchen

It's warm and steamy in my kitchen because there's something delicious bubbling on the hob. If I'm honest, it's a bit chaotic, too: I don't have quite enough work surface, and the dishwasher is playing up, and

3

the pull-out larder is full to bursting. But then, how many home kitchens are all stainless steel surfaces and *MasterChef*-style machines? Cooking for friends, family and ourselves *can* involve new techniques and ingredients, but it's more about taste and mood, than technical challenge. Whether you want to feel energised, comforted, relaxed… or even seduced, there are dishes in this book that will do the trick.

I've chosen every recipe in this book by asking a simple question: does this dish make you feel good? If you have an allergy or intolerance, for example to gluten or dairy, then many of the recipes are suitable, or offer easy alternatives. And, as a vegetarian myself (though one who cooks enthusiastically for a carnivorous partner and friends), I've made sure there are lots of choices for vegetarians, vegans and pescatarians.

'Good' to me means delicious, but also thoughtful, taking into consideration where our food comes from. That's why I've added the *Making sense of…* sections to look at what's behind the eating advice we're given.

Making sense of… eating well

Our 5:2 Facebook group has over 30,000 members worldwide, and people post every day trying to make sense of how to be healthy. They ask:

- Will going without breakfast stop me losing weight?
- Are artificial sweeteners poisonous?
- Does muscle weigh more than fat?
- Should I give up wheat?
- Is it possible to lose weight without exercising?
- Will eating fat give me heart disease or protect me from it?

If *you've* ever been unsure what 'eating well' means, then you're not alone.

Taking a look behind the food scare headlines

As a former BBC and newspaper journalist, I know the same information can be 'spun' in a dozen different ways. In my previous books, I looked at the research behind intermittent fasting: now I'm taking a wider look at the most confusing issues around diet and health. I also consulted a leading nutritionist to ensure the book reflects the most up-to-date – and reliable – science.

The Internet makes life even more complicated. It's fabulous that we can search for information about anything and everything, but the web makes it just as easy for individuals to post misinformation.

My aim in the *Making sense of...* sections is to help you find answers to the questions that are most important to you. I can't answer every question, but I'll show you how I research, so you can do it yourself.

My own 5:2 journey

I've now been cutting back to 500 calories once or twice per week for more than two years. It took about nine months to lose 13kg (28 lb): more than 15 per cent of my original weight, and more importantly, I've sustained that loss. In fact, as I write, I'm 14kg (31 lb) lighter, without really trying to lose more. It's happened because I now eat when I'm hungry, stop when I'm full and don't let myself feel guilty.

More importantly, I know I've reduced many of the health risks associated with being overweight. I also believe the process of fasting twice a week is helping my body to repair itself, and potentially reducing my risk of cancer, heart disease, Type 2 diabetes and Alzheimer's disease.

A tool, not a straitjacket

The one important – and exciting – difference between 5:2 and other diets is that it's not really a 'diet' in terms of making you eat certain foods at certain times. I see it much more as a tool or a framework for helping us to understand and control our appetite and eating. Obviously, if you want to lose weight, you *will* need to consume less or use more energy, but this approach makes it easier and more flexible than 'full-time' calorie restriction.

It's also far cheaper and more sustainable than faddish diets with expensive supplements or unpalatable ingredients.

As in the 5:2 Lives sections, you'll hear from men and women who love the freedom, flexibility and healthy benefits of this approach.

Good food recipes for every day of the week

On the two days a week when you're watching what you eat, you'll be able to choose from dishes like Tex Mex Beef Salad, Summer Tomato Crumble, Chicken Chili and even Vanilla Berry Mousse.

And on the five days a week when you're eating normally, there are plenty of ideas for enjoying the same dishes, but with a little extra indulgence or a tasty side dish.

I know pre-prepared foods are a time-saver for many of us, but you'll be amazed at how quickly – and economically – you can prepare great meals.

5:2 and you

If you haven't tried 5:2, then this book contains everything you need to know. Just choose your first Fast Day, pick your favourite recipes from Part 2 and get started this week. You could even start today, if you're reading this before breakfast!

Don't forget there's a world of 5:2 support beyond the book, including the Facebook group that offers fantastic daily mutual support and success stories; find us at facebook.com/groups/the52diet, and the information on my website, the5-2dietbook.com.

I think 5:2 is the first democratic diet because we're all able to contribute our own experiences, tips and achievements to build up knowledge. And because corporations or vested interests do not control it, we're benefiting from sharing our knowledge.

Over to you

This is about *your life, your health* and *your tastes*. So, please use this book as your starting point, and share any changes and ideas you have. I'd love to hear from you, via the website, if you have new favourites.

The 5:2 kitchen is *your* kitchen. Tuck in!

Kate
December 2014

How this book works

PART 1

Eating the 5:2 Way explains the intermittent fasting approach. It summarises the health benefits, answers the questions people ask most often and offers tips and guidelines for you, whether you're new to fasting *or* have achieved your goal and now want to maintain a healthy weight and positive attitude to food.

PART 2

Good Food from the 5:2 Kitchen is the heart of this book. Life is too short for 'diet food', the kind of dishes you only eat because of their low calorie count. Instead, the recipes here are ones you'll want to eat every day.

In between the recipes, you'll find:

- **5:2 Lives** Real-life examples of how 5:2 works, including honest food diaries and success stories.

- *Making sense of…* We look at current food advice and explore how to find out what's right for us as individuals.

- **5:2 Food Heroes** The brilliant, everyday ingredients that punch above their weight.

PART 3

Resources including meal plans; recipes listed by calorie counts, a customised calorie chart, plus links to research and websites with useful information about 5:2 and eating well.

1

EATING THE

5:2

WAY

Eating the 5:2 Way

Re-discovering your appetite with the most delicious, nutritious food you can eat

What is 5:2?

5:2 is the most flexible approach to weight control and health you'll ever find.

On two days a week you cut your calorie consumption to around 25 per cent of what your body needs, and the rest of the time you eat normally.

If you think that sounds too simple – or too good to be true – that's normal. Many of us felt the same when we first heard about this way of eating. Yet, it's the simplicity and flexibility that is making this approach so popular, right round the world. It works in different cultures, different climates and with very different diets.

Why does 5:2 work?

To lose weight, you have to consume less energy through food than you're using up in your everyday life. Unlike conventional diets, 5:2 only requires calorie-counting on two days per week.

Yes, those days are stricter than most diets – 500 calories for women, 600 for men – but on the other days you have the freedom to eat out, celebrate family occasions and enjoy the foods you love.

What's interesting is that many of us find we also begin to eat more healthily without trying on the 'normal' days.

The flexibility of 5:2 or 4:3 (three Fast Days per week) means it's much more likely that you'll stick to it long-term.

And weight loss isn't the whole story; 5:2 is also different because of the potential health benefits, which are very motivating. There's more information about this on page 23.

Isn't 5:2 a fad?

Everyone who succeeds with intermittent fasting says the same thing: it feels so different to other diets. I think this is because:

1. 5:2 doesn't ban any foods, or food types, which means we're much less likely to get cravings.

2. It's flexible and empowers us to make our own decisions about when and what to eat.

3. The Fast Days re-educate us about our appetite, the energy in foods and making healthy choices.

4. Commercial interests do not lead 5:2. There are no supplements, paid-for services or branded foods.

5. There's endless support and help available online.

6. Plus fasting in itself can help the body heal.

Stage 1

PLANNING FOR YOUR FIRST FASTS

It's simple to get started with 5:2. Here's what you need to do:

1. Set your weight-loss goal
2. Pick two days to fast in the week ahead
3. Decide your Fast Day limit, and what to do on non-fasting days
4. Plan your meals
5. Find support.

1: Set your weight-loss goal

It's important to have a clear goal as you start your journey, and that means checking your current weight and measurements. I know that's hard if you feel miserable about the shape you're in, but can be motivating to see the difference as you succeed at 5:2.

First, weigh yourself, and take some measurements: hips, waist, chest/bust and, if you like, also measure your upper arms and thighs at the widest point.

Use your weight and height to calculate your BMI (Body Mass Index). There's a chart in the Resources section, or use the online calculator at www.the5-2dietbook.com/calculator.

You'll end up with a number. If it's over 25 (or 23 for some ethnic groups) you're classed as overweight. A number over 30 is classed as obese, and the higher the figure, the higher your potential risk of health problems due to your weight. It can be a huge shock to discover you're classified as overweight or obese, but remember, you *can* do something about it, and reading this book is the start.

Another important indicator that can predict your risk of cardiovascular disease is your waist measurement. The bigger you are around the waist/belly, the higher the likelihood that you've accumulated 'visceral' fat around the vital organs, which is a risk factor for heart disease and Type 2 diabetes. 'Pear-shaped' people with larger hips and thighs tend to be at lower risk than the 'apple-shaped' who store more fat around the belly.

You're at greater risk if your waist (measured round your natural waist or mid-way between the bottom of your ribcage and your hipbone) is more than half of your height.

For example, I am 64 inches tall, so my waist measurement should stay under 32 inches. As an indicator, here's how mine has changed over time:

August 2012: Waist (32 inches)÷Height (64 inches) = 0.5 (so, borderline)
January 2013: Waist (29.5) ÷ Height (64) = 0.46
April 2013: Waist (27.5) ÷ Height (64) = 0.43

One last idea: if you're feeling brave, you can also take a photo of yourself as you are now. There's no need to share it with anyone, but it can be very motivating to see the difference as you head towards your goal.

What should my goal be?

You may want to aim for just inside the 'healthy' BMI category (so, under 25 or 23) or to reach the weight or clothing size that you were when you felt happy and confident about your weight.

It's good to write down your goal, or use an app to plot your progress towards the goal, with mini goals along the way: going from Obese to Overweight, for example; hitting the 15-, 12- or 10-stone mark; or fitting into a favourite pair of jeans.

2: Pick two Fast Days for the week ahead

Look at your diary and choose two days to fast. A Fast Day lasts from the last meal the previous day, until breakfast the day after. For example:

Sunday: Eat dinner at normal time e.g. 7 p.m.
Monday: Fast – eat up to your Fast Day limit, ideally in
   3, 2 or 1 meals
Tuesday: Eat breakfast at your normal time e.g. 8 a.m.

Here are some tips on picking good days:

1. It's easier to separate your Fast Days, for example, doing Monday and Wednesday or Tuesday and Thursday. That's particularly true while you're getting used to the Fast Days. It's less difficult to keep on track when you know that tomorrow you can eat what you like.
2. Once you're used to fasting, you can choose to do the two days together. I do that occasionally, when it suits my schedule.
3. For your first fasts, choose days when you're busy, but not under serious work or family pressure.
4. Don't clear your diary completely. Staying busy is the best distraction from any hunger pangs.
5. You don't have to do the same days each week. You can fit them around work commitments or family occasions.
6. If you want to lose weight faster, you could do three fasts in a week (4:3) or try alternative day fasting (ADF) as they increase the calorie deficit, that is, the difference between what you eat and the energy you need.
7. **DO NOT DO MORE THAN TWO FAST DAYS BACK TO BACK** as it may trigger some unhelpful changes in the way your body seeks energy. It's also not always good for mental balance. For more about how our bodies respond to prolonged fasting, see *Making sense of… appetite.*

3. Decide your Fast Day calorie limit and what to do on non-fast days

Most people starting 5:2 choose to set the standard limit of 500 calories for women and 600 for men. That's based on one-quarter of the energy needs for the average female or male. If we eat no more than the Fast Day limit on those two days (and normally on the other days) we should lose around one pound (0.45kg) in weight per week.

Why the numbers matter

Dieticians estimate that to lose one pound (0.45kg) of weight, we need to have a 'deficit' of 3,500 calories over any period of time.

Any weight-loss diet aims to achieve this by cutting back on consumption so our body uses stored fat to provide the energy we need. Most diets do this by cutting back every day. But 5:2 does it by concentrating the deficit on the Fast Days.

So on non-fasting days, we can eat normally. Using the same average figures as given above, that's about 2,000 calories for a woman, and 2,400 for a man.

However if we're already overweight, we may have a skewed idea of what 'normal' is. What seems normal to us may still be too much, and overdoing it on your normal/non-fast days will slow your loss.

When I started 5:2, I very deliberately ate what I wanted on normal days, and still lost weight at one pound per week on average, and I still believe that's the ideal for most people. But it may be that if you've been over-eating for years, you need to understand better what your body needs in energy, so you can be sure you don't sabotage yourself.

How does height, weight and activity level affect what we need to eat?

Lots of factors affect what our body needs in food/energy terms. The main factors are:

- Age

- Gender

- How heavy and tall we are

- How active we are in our everyday lives.

The larger we are – and the more weight we are carrying – the more calories we need to sustain our current size.

Undersanding your Total Daily Energy Expenditure

The TDEE is an estimate of what our body needs, in calories, per day to maintain our current weight. The easiest way to work it out is by going online to www.the5-2dietbook.com/calculator – you may get slightly different results from different online calculators, but the alternative is being monitored in a lab for a few weeks so the calculator is a more practical option. They are all estimates, but the difference won't be substantial.

The TDEE is sometimes confused with the Basal Metabolic Rate, which is an estimate of what you need to eat simply to maintain basic bodily functions. It's important that you use the TDEE and not BMR to help guide your eating.

How to use your TDEE: on Fast and non-fasting Days

To personalise your Fast Day limit, **divide your TDEE by four**. For example:

My Basal Metabolic Rate: 1266.55
My Total Daily Energy Expenditure is around 1741.51

So my personalised Fast Day limit works out at 435 calories though I sometimes eat a little more.

It's more useful to know this if you are taller or heavier than average as this could give you a few extra calories to 'play with' on a Fast Day.

Your TDEE is more useful on a non-fasting day. If I used the typical calorie requirement for women of 2,000 on my non-fasting days, I'd be eating around 260 calories per day more than I need. If I did that every day, I could easily put on one pound every 13 days.

I don't believe in calorie counting all the time as I think it's tedious, but knowing the TDEE confirms what a normal, healthy calorie intake is. This applies, both to people who've been dieting for so long that they find it hard to go OVER 1,200 calories, and to people who may have lost sight of the energy content of foods.

4: Plan your meals

Pick your favourite dishes from this book, and shop in advance so you don't face temptation at the check-out on a Fast Day!

You can consume your calorie allowance in one, two or even three meals, although some researchers suspect the health benefits may be greater if you restrict it to one or two.

It doesn't matter either when you eat, though many 5:2 dieters – myself included – have found once they're used to Fast Days, it can be easiest to postpone eating until as late in the day as possible, which prolongs the fast. Some people do water-only Fast Days, which should be safe for one day at a time for people in good health and not taking medication. But do check with your doctor.

Before I started, I could never have imagined a whole day without any food. But now I frequently leave eating until the evening so I can eat the same meal as my partner. And I don't find it difficult at all.

5: Find support

If you are under supervision for any medical condition, or have any concerns, you should talk to your family doctor or specialist for advice.

For online support the 5:2 forum and the Facebook group are brilliant – I've never come across such a supportive bunch! Join us: www.facebook.com/groups/the52diet.

Checklist before moving onto Stage 2

Have you:

1. Set a clear goal?
2. Picked two days within the next week to begin fasting?
3. Decided how to handle your Fast and non-fasting days?
4. Planned your meals and shopped for the ingredients?
5. Asked for advice from any specialists/enlisted friends (or online friends) to support you?

If you can answer yes to all of those, you're ready to go.

Stage 2

THE 'FAST' ROUTE TO SUCCESS

This section is all about how to get the most from your Fast Days – and non-fasting days too.

Fast Day tips and motivations

Keep a record: Studies suggest that dieters who keep a record of what they eat tend to be more successful. You can either do that electronically, or jot it down in a notebook. An app or website like myfitnesspal.com makes it easy to record your consumption on Fast Days, and you can keep the information private or share with others to stay motivated. You simply enter the name of the food (or scan barcodes on packaging), and the app calculates the calories. It'll also keep track of weight loss over time. There's no 5:2 setting, so the easiest option is to set your membership to Maintain, but limit yourself to 500/600 on Fast Days.

Learn to handle your hunger pangs: Once you're used to Fast Days, you'll almost certainly feel energetic and positive, and you'll enjoy every mouthful of the food you prepare for yourself.

On your first Fast Day, though, you will probably feel a bit preoccupied with food, and hungry at times. 500 or 600 calories is enough to keep you satisfied, but we're so used to eating at regular times, and snacking or 'grazing' between meals, that experiencing hunger can be unsettling. Here are a few things to bear in mind:

1. Hunger tends to come in a wave. Have a hot drink, or distract yourself with a phone call, a piece of work or a *quick* check on the 5:2 groups or forums, and the wave will soon recede.
2. Watch my Top Tips for New Fasters on YouTube: http:bit.ly/1t8aBtr.
3. Remind yourself that the calorie restriction is temporary. Obviously, if you do feel really unwell or faint, as opposed to simply feel hungry, you should talk to a doctor or eat something. However, this very rarely happens.
4. Getting back in touch with your appetite is one of the best things you can do in terms of developing healthier eating habits. When you do then eat, food tastes better and you savour every bite.
5. Finally, remember the 5:2 catchphrase, 'Tomorrow you can eat what you like'. Though, interestingly, most of us find the next day, the foods we craved are no longer that desirable.

Some of the physical effects you *may* feel during your first fasts include:

- **Headaches** These are common with most dietary changes due to dehydration and/or changes to blood sugar. These should settle over time, but drinking plenty of water or taking your usual painkiller can help, too.

- **Feeling cold** This is common in winter, partly because you aren't generating heat through digesting food. Try hot drinks and wear extra socks!

- **Irritability** You may feel grumpy at first and that's the lack of blood sugar again. Try to build in another non-food treat to look forward to: a long hot bath, a hand massage, your favourite TV show.

- **Digestive changes** You may experience digestive changes as you're not eating as much. This means you may not need to open your bowels, or you may find that the next day your digestion is slower (or faster) than normal. Most people find that their digestion settles.

If you are feeling really unwell/faint – and that's extremely uncommon – then have a nutritious snack on standby on those first days, like a handful of nuts/trail mix or a high-protein cereal bar, and take medical advice before trying a second fast.

Distraction time: winning tactics for Fast Days

Finding ways to distract yourself from any unsettled feelings will help. Here are some tactics to try:

- **Drink plenty of water** or black coffee, tea or herbal teas. Diet drinks and milk *may* affect your insulin levels, which may be counter-productive, but I still have the odd diet drink on a Fast Day.

- **Move more** Once you've got your first fast under your belt, try being more active, whether that's a short walk in your lunch break, or a dance around the living room in the evening. Many of us run or go to the gym on a Fast Day with no difference in stamina or performance. Just be careful to listen to your body the first couple of times, taking a break if need be, and ensure you stay hydrated. And no, you can't earn extra calories on a Fast Day, but you will feel *very* virtuous afterwards.

- **Use the health benefits of fasting to motivate you**
  Understanding how Fast Days can help your body to repair
  itself is very motivating. Research based on humans and animal
  studies shows intermittent calorie restriction (the more precise
  term for 5:2 fasting) can reduce the risk of many cancers,
  cardiovascular diseases and Alzheimer's or other forms of
  dementia. In a nutshell, fasting triggers processes that repair the
  body's cells, to prime us for survival. It's a process that worked
  for our ancestors, who evolved to follow a feast/fast pattern.
  They took in as much energy as possible in the 'good' times,
  such as harvests, or when hunters brought back an animal to
  cook, and focused on survival in leaner times. When we fast,
  our bodies respond by trying to ensure we're in the best shape,
  a little like doing maintenance to get the house or car ready for
  a harsh winter. You can read much more about these processes
  in *The 5:2 Diet Book*, or via the research links at the end of this
  book.

- **Take advantage of the mental focus fasting can give** Fasting
  can increase mental sharpness and energy, and even have a
  positive effect on the chemicals and processes that play a part in
  depression and other mood disorders. Much of the evidence for
  long-term effects on brain function is based on animal studies
  because it's hard to do invasive tests on humans. But fasting can
  trigger neurological changes that benefit us. And anecdotally,
  many people on the 5:2 Facebook group report feeling sharper
  and more productive on a Fast Day. Again, *The 5:2 Diet Book*
  goes into lots more detail.

Mindful eating: a strategy for 7 days a week

Whatever foods you eat, and whenever you eat them, use your Fast Days to eat mindfully. The more you slow down your meals and focus on the process of eating, the more satisfying you'll find the food.

- Don't eat on the go, in front of the TV or at your desk.

- Set the table and always put your food, even if it's a snack or piece on fruit, on a plate.

- Remember, your sense of smell plays a huge part in how things taste, and even sets off the digestion process before you take a single bite.

- Eat slowly.

It takes time for the stomach to send signals to the brain to indicate it's full, so taking your time over meals on both fasting and non-fasting days will help you feel satisfied by your meals.

The other five days: how to make them work for you

Fast Days are simple and enjoyable, as you give your body and mind a break from overload! But some of us find the other five 'normal' days harder to manage because there are no rules.

Far fewer people binge-eat than the critics feared when 5:2 began to take off, but it's useful to have some guidance to help make good choices. Even what you call your non-fasting days can play a part. I call mine 'feast' days because everything feels like a feast when your senses are heightened the day after fasting, but some dieters see that as encouragement to overdo it. So pick a word you find the most motivating: non-fasting, healthy or normal.

The calorie-count question and combining 5:2 with other diets

On page 16, I explained why calorie counting isn't necessary but can be a useful tool. The same is true of combining this tool or way of eating with other diet plans, which offer valid information on balanced eating, but there are some aspects that don't 'sit' with 5:2. Be wary of meal replacements as they don't re-educate our taste buds or appetite to look for 'real' food.

If you *do* choose to calorie count, or use guidance from another diet, calculate your TDEE and make *that* your goal. Or plan a few non-fasting days based around the TDEE and use those to get a sense of portion size and range. Above all, don't ban any foods; try to set positive goals, not negative rules. I enjoy chocolate, cheese, treats, celebratory meals and wine, and I've lost 20 per cent of my body weight, *and* maintained that loss.

Research has shown that ICR (intermittent calorie restriction) doesn't lead to binge eating. In one study of people following a 4:3 plan, dieters ate between 95 per cent and 125 per cent of their TDEE on the day after a fast. Yet even the higher figure wasn't enough to cancel out the Fast Days. If you're doing two Fast Days, not three, there's a little less room for error, but for most of us, calorie counting and limited eating on Fast Days is more than enough to help us make better choices all of the time.

Aiming high on non-fasting days

Instead of focusing on calories, why not set other, more positive objectives? For example:

1. **Fresh tastes** Buy one or two ingredients each week to experiment with, and widen your food repertoire.
2. **10-a-day** How many portions of vegetables can you manage on a non-fasting day? (The Vegelicious chapter is a great start.)
3. **Meat-free days** You don't have to become a vegetarian to see the health (and budget) benefits of basing meals for one day around non-meat alternatives.
4. **The rainbow on your plate** The eating process begins with our eyes, and aiming for a rainbow of colours of natural produce will whet your appetite *and* ensure you get a range of nutrients.
5. **Special delivery** Order a veg box from a local farm and make seasonal soups, salads and sides from the lucky dip of ingredients.

If you do get cravings, there are tips that may help on page 89.

How fast will I lose weight when I fast?

In our group, most people lose .45–1kg (1–2 lb) per week. Some lose a lot more, especially in the first few weeks. Others find they hit a plateau at times, perhaps a week or two when they don't lose. Then, for no apparent reason, they find they have lost weight the next time they weigh in.

If you're more of a tortoise than a hare, you're in good company because I was the same. But now I am very happy with my weight. In general, people with more weight to lose are likely to see more rapid losses, and the last few pounds to your target can be the toughest to shift.

What if I'm not losing?

Our bodies also vary day by day depending on what we've been eating, and in the case of women, hormonal changes can add 2.2–2.75kg (5–6 lb), or in some cases even 4.5kg (10 lb) or more at different times of the month. So avoid weighing more than once a week!

If after a couple of weeks of following this plan, you're not losing weight, then consider adding up the calories you're eating on an average non-fasting day, and check they're not way over your TDEE. You could either consider switching to 4:3 or ADF for a little while, or see if there are ways to cut back on consumption to closer to the TDEE without losing the pleasure in food.

Certain medical conditions including thyroid and hormonal imbalances can make it harder to shift weight; so if you are confident you are following the plan, it's worth discussing it with your GP.

When life gets in the way ... T.I.T.S.-U.P. Days

We've all had them. Days when you get bad news, or lots of stress, and your planned fast goes out of the window.

I came up with a name for these: Temporary Interruption To Scheme, Un-Planned. The most important word there is temporary – 5:2 is flexible and one day won't make a difference if you're in this for the long haul. A T.I.T.S.-U.P. day could also be about good news, or a sudden celebration. We need to recognise that food can be a comfort and a pleasure. By keeping a sense of perspective – and sense of humour – you are in a better place to start again tomorrow!

Stage 3

5:2 FOR LIFE – MAINTAINING A HEALTHY LIFESTYLE

When I first decided to try 5:2, I didn't think about what the future held. I'd lost weight in the past on other diets, but never kept it off.

So I reached and then exceeded my original goal after six months, I felt nervous.

Every dieter knows that losing the weight is one thing but that keeping it off can be even harder. So being aware of how to manage this next stage is really important.

You've hit your goal – now what?

Congratulations! Celebrate, of course! Buy yourself something you love to mark this moment, and maybe raise a glass to your achievement, with friends and family who've helped you.

When the celebrations are over, begin to plan how you're going to sustain your achievement for the months and years ahead.

Maintaining the balance: 6:1, flexi-fasting and other scheduled eating approaches

For many of us, Fast Days become a habit we definitely *don't* want to break even after we've met out goal because the sense of doing something good for our bodies, and reminding ourselves how satisfying healthy food can be, is powerful.

So here are some of the ways you can keep fasting in your life:

- **6:1** Fasting one day each week is the most obvious way to do it because it will help you stay aware of the benefits of fasting and of how you can learn to trust your appetite. It will also help smooth over any days when you might overdo it, such as holidays or special events.

- **Flexi-fasting** This is what I do. I trust my instincts on how

29

much I've eaten out and exercised the previous week, and then I adjust my number of fasting days accordingly. Mostly I'll do one Fast Day, but if I've been over-indulging, I switch to two until my clothes are looser. I never fast on holiday!

- **Other scheduled eating approaches** (e.g. 16:8) Since 5:2 has taken off, lots of other approaches have appeared that use time as a diet tool, such as limiting when we eat. See page 148 in *Making sense of… when to eat* for more information.

Weighing in vs. the Jeans of Truth

So what about monitoring your weight maintenance?

It's up to you whether you want to weigh yourself weekly. On the plus side, it means you can't be in denial if the weight begins to creep back on.

The other option is keep an eye on how your clothes fit. We all have a pair of jeans or outfit that fits us perfectly when we're at our ideal weight. Trying on your Jeans of Truth is a good gauge of whether it's time to take action.

Coping with challenging times

Stress, life change of even the good times can make maintaining good habits a challenge. The key is not to see minor deviations as a huge setbck. For me, the summer of 2014 was difficult: after a very stressful winter, I found myself tired and demotivated, and tempted to over-eat again.

I decided to be kind to myself, to forgive the couple of weeks where my treats became everyday events, and to get back to 5:2 and I also laid off weighing myself while I got back on track. When I did step back on the scales, I was lighter than I thought, bringing my total loss to 14kg (31 lb). I'd faced the 'two-year diet itch' and won! By seeing 5:2 as a flexible strategy, instead of a punishment or restriction, I am happy to embrace it for life.

For more tools to help you deal with any blips, see *Making sense of... emotional eating,* page 240. My book, *5:2 Your Life,* also has a lot more information on applying 5:2 to other aspects of your life, including exercise and relationships, and can help with goal-setting and motivation.

Fastiversaries: something to celebrate

I have one final tip for making this a life change and not just a quick fix. Make a note of when you have your first fast – and then celebrate your *Fastiversary!* It's the name I've given to the anniversary of your first fast, but you can also give yourself a pat on the back at one, two, three or six months.

With every other diet I've ever tried, the idea of *celebrating* being on it after a year or more would have seemed crazy. But the health and mindful-eating benefits of 5:2 mean every Fastiversary marks another year of doing something proactive for your health and future.

2

GOOD FOOD FROM THE

5:2

KITCHEN

We're all on a journey when it comes to food. I went from being a veg-phobic, fussy eater in my teens, to a vegetarian food-lover as an adult. However, my new enthusiasm for cookery and eating meant I also put on weight. I tried every diet going, succeeding and then failing, because my inner glutton always won out. And then I found 5:2 and everything changed.

Food advice changes all the time, too. We're told full-fat foods like cheese may not be the threat to health we'd been told they were, while the carbohydrates we were encouraged to use to bulk out our diet may not be the whole answer after all. You can read more about how to make sense of so much contradictory information in the *Making sense of …* sections at the end of each recipe chapter.

There are also truly inspiring stories from people whose lives have been changed in 5:2 Lives, and we profile some of the best value and useful ingredients for healthy cooking in Food Heroes.

5:2 Good Food Kitchen cooking tips

Calorie awareness

Weighing and measuring food may seem boring, but you only have to do it on two days a week.

- I use a small digital scale on the worktop, ready to use.

- The **calories listed in this book** *actually* **refer to kilocalories** (nutrition labels use the abbreviation kcal), but the word calorie is what most people use so we've stuck to that. Some countries use kilojoules on food labels: one kJ is just under one-quarter of 1 kcal, so multiply the kJ on the label by four to get an equivalent.

- **Weighing your food brings lots of surprises**, for example, the serving size recommended on a cereal packet is probably much less than you usually pour. Weighing will help you discover where you might be adding 'hidden' calories.

- **Weighing will affect how you eat on non-fasting days too.** You don't need to weigh all the time to be more aware of what a portion size is, and which choices offer the most filling food for fewer calories.

- Our **calorie count list at the end of the book** includes most ingredients, though we haven't listed every herb or spice. Some ingredients you buy have higher or lower counts than our list, so check labels. We've checked many times, but with so many numbers, there may be occasional mistakes.

- The **energy/calorie content of fresh produce depends on size** but rather than weigh every carrot or onion, we've given averages. Most vegetables are low in calories, but watch out for the exceptions like: avocado and potato both need to be measured carefully if you're eating them.

- Some products like grated Italian cheese (Parmesan or the slightly lower calorie Grana Padano) and desiccated coconut should be weighed on scales as measuring spoons give a slightly inaccurate reading.

- Where there's a range of calorie counts in a recipe or the counter, we've used the lower count to calculate the dish.

Cooking methods

- **Steam, poach or boil** for flavourful fresh foods with no added fat.

- **Roast or fry, but with the minimum of fat** If carefully measured you can often get great results with ½ a teaspoon or less of fat (when you realise a teaspoon of fat has 45 calories, you'll understand why this matters).

- **Use non-stick frying pans and saucepans** These allow you to use higher temperatures without food sticking or burning.

- **Try coconut oil or butter for frying** Both work well, can add flavour and are more stable at high temperatures than olive oil, too. Coconut oil is solid at room temperature and has potential health benefits so is worth experimenting with. Sesame oil is good for stir-fries.

- **Experiment with low-calorie cooking sprays** These sprays are emulsions of oil, water and a few other ingredients, including alcohol, which, the makers say, evaporates completely during the cooking process. They can be used to fry or roast. Calorie counts for these are not given in recipes, as it depends how many sprays you use.

- **You can make your own cooking spray** Use a mixture of 50% water and 50% oil (rapeseed or olive) in a pump bottle. It's a little harder to be certain about the calorie count, so use sparingly.

- **Don't add more oil** If something sticks or burns, use water, stock or lemon juice to cool things down!

- **Avoid cooking at high temperatures if you're not using any fat.**

Brunch-time

FEEL GOOD FOOD FOR A GREAT START

Brunch is one of my favourite words – and favourite meals. Yet it's not an invention of the laid back 1960s or hippy 1970s. In 1895, a writer in *Hunter's Weekly* suggested, 'a new meal, served around noon, that starts with tea or coffee, marmalade and other breakfast fixtures before moving along to the heavier fare? By eliminating the need to get up early on Sunday, brunch would make life brighter for Saturday-night carousers.'

Bravo! But why save it for Sundays? Brunch is actually the perfect meal for 5:2 fasters, especially if you can't face breakfast first thing. Many of us have found our eating patterns have changed since starting this plan, and that's true for me. On fasting *and* non-fasting days, I now mostly have a protein-rich dish around midday to keep me full, and a bigger meal later in the evening. And if you hate breakfast but are worried about skipping it, then I look at the research in *Making sense of … breakfast* at the end of this chapter.

Of course, these dishes are good served any time of day: tuck in!

EGGS 'BENEFIT' WITH MUSTARD SAUCE

NOOSA-STYLE MUSHROOMS AND GOAT'S CHEESE
WITH LEMON PESTO DRESSING

BAKED HADDOCK SMOKIE POT

CHEDDAR AND APPLE 'PLOUGHMAN'S BRUNCH' MINI-MUFFINS

MEDITERRANEAN-STYLE QUINOA CAKES
WITH HOME-MADE KETCHUP SALSA
VEGAN OPTION: PORTOBELLO MUSHROOMS WITH MEDITERRANEAN QUINOA
STUFFING

PICK 'N' MIX CHILLED-OUT MAGIC MUESLI

APRICOT AND COCONUT ENERGY BITES

THE WORLD'S EASIEST CHOCOLATE AND ALMOND PANCAKES

PLUS …

MAKING SENSE OF … BREAKFAST

5:2 FOOD HERO: THE EGG

5:2 Lives

4 STONE LIGHTER, INSPIRED FOR LIFE

'I have lost 4 stone, I'm the same size as I was on my wedding day in the 1980s, and I feel the happiest that I've ever felt!' Pippa, 53

Pippa Cotton's 5:2 journey began in the cold, snowy January of 2013 as she was recovering from an exhausting chest infection.

'I felt very unwell. I had also been diagnosed with high cholesterol and had been advised to look at my diet. My weight was 80kg (176 lb) and I was a size 18 at 160cm (5ft 3in). My BMI was classed as obese. I found it hard to walk up stairs and was breathless, which was not a good state to be in.'

Pippa had watched the BBC *Horizon* programme the previous summer, but didn't feel fasting was right for her, until she got hold of a copy of *The 5:2 Diet Book*. 'I'd felt trapped in the cycle of yo-yo dieting and then eating poorly. But after reading the book, I decided to start this way of life, as I was all fired up.'

Pippa's determination paid off, with impressive results right from the beginning. 'I found that the weight loss was steady at 1kg (2 lb) a week and within a month I had lost half a stone, taking me to 76kg (168 lb), which felt like a milestone. I continued with two days fasting a week until July 2013 when I reached 67kg (148 lb), a 12.7kg (28 lb) loss and normal BMI, which had been my original goal weight.'

But it didn't stop there for Pippa, whose whole life was undergoing a 5:2 style revolution.

'I was exercising by walking, running and Zumba, and also doing the Jillian Michaels *30 Day Shred* DVD, which helped me tone and lose more inches from my tummy, waist and thighs.'

And lose she did: 19cm (7.5 in) from her waist, 20cm (8 in) from her hips and 20cm (8 in) from her tummy. Once she'd reached her original goal, she maintained by fasting once week, but combined with the exercise, the pounds kept falling off. 'By August 2013 I was maintaining on one Fast Day a week and trying the odd 16:8, which means restricting when I ate to an eight-hour window in the day.'

Her list of fitness challenges makes energising and slightly exhausting reading, as she completed the 5K Colour Run around Wembley Stadium, tried out classes like Parkfit and Fitsteps dance classes, and even became a Simply Walk Leader for Buckinghamshire, leading walks to improve other people's fitness. She also does HIIT interval training, and is aiming to do a park run race this year and keep reducing her time.

Pippa's achievements mean she's now eight and a half stone. But the biggest change is to how she feels. 'I have so much more energy than ever before, fewer menopausal symptoms, and lower cholesterol, which was my main reason for starting this way of life.'

Pippa's Fast Day diary

Breakfast: 1 large portobello mushroom grilled with a poached egg, black coffee or decaffeinated Earl Grey tea/or no breakfast and a soup based on vegetables and beans for lunch.

Lunch or dinner: a large salad with some protein either 50g (1.75 ounces) of prawns or some chicken with a tablespoon of balsamic vinegar.

If I can fit it into the calorie allowance, I'll add the occasional Options hot chocolate too.

Pippa's non-fasting day diary

Breakfast: Poached egg on wholemeal toast with butter or full-fat yoghurt with a handful of almonds or a bacon sandwich.

Lunch: Large salad with protein or a vegetable-based soup with a roll with some sort of protein.

Dinner: A roast with vegetables and a glass of merlot.

Favourite foods

Chicken roast dinner, and chocolate, though I find that two small squares of plain dark chocolate are more than enough to satisfy me now.

Best thing about 5:2

I am so much more positive and joyful around food and life in general. I also use some of the techniques from Kate's *5:2 Your Life* book, and have tried out mindfulness. I actually feel the happiest that I have felt, and really like the new me, not the one who did not like herself!

Pippa's top tip

Have a small intermediate goal, for example, to get to your first half stone, and then treat yourself with a non-food gift. Then focus on the next small goal.

EGGS 'BENEFIT' WITH MUSTARD SAUCE

Calories per 1-egg serving: 189 for Florentine; 193 for Benedict;
220 for Royale (add 78 for a second poached egg)

---

*Vegetarian/nut free/gluten free and low carbohydrate when served
without toast*

My favourite brunch dish is Eggs Florentine, a vegetarian variation
on Eggs Benedict. It's a toasted English muffin, topped with wilted
spinach, two poached eggs and LOADS of sunshine yellow hollandaise sauce. But hollandaise is fiddly to make at home and *very* heavy
on the butter. So I thought I'd invent a Fast Day version, using simple
mustard cream.

I call it Eggs 'Benefit', because eggs are great for keeping you full
during the day and have numerous nutritional benefits.

Serves 1
Preparation time: 5 minutes
Cooking time: 7 minutes

For the sauce

1 tsp Dijon mustard 5 cals
2 tbsp half-fat crème fraîche 52 cals
fresh herb leaves, such as chives, parsley or dill, plus extra to garnish
pinch sugar (optional)

For the 'Benefit' layer

50g fresh or defrosted frozen spinach 13 cals (or 20g smoked salmon 44 cals
    or 20g slice of ham 17 cals)
squeeze lemon juice, if using spinach
1 very thin slice of sourdough bread weighing 15g 41 cals
1 medium egg 78 cals
splash vinegar
salt and pepper

1. Make the sauce by heating the crème fraîche and mustard gently in a small saucepan for 2 minutes. Use scissors to snip the herbs directly into the saucepan, reserving a few leaves for garnish. Season to taste. If it's too sharp for you, add a pinch of sugar or sweetener.

2. For the 'Benefit' layer, microwave or pan cook the spinach with a little water and a squeeze of lemon juice until wilted. Season with pepper then drain through a sieve. When cool enough to handle, carefully squeeze out as much of the water as possible and set aside.

3. Toast the sourdough bread lightly under the grill or in a toaster.

4. For the egg(s), bring a medium saucepan of water to the boil with a splash of vinegar. Break your egg onto a small plate. Create a whirlpool in the water with a fork or whisk and, with your other hand, slip the egg into the middle of the saucepan as gently as possible. Turn off the heat and set a timer for 3 minutes. After that time, check that the egg white has set before removing from the saucepan using a slotted spoon. Place gently onto a plate lined with kitchen paper to absorb the excess cooking water.

5. Set the toast on a warm plate, lay the spinach, ham or salmon on top then add the egg(s) and finally the sauce. Season, and garnish with the reserved herb leaves and serve immediately.

More ideas from the 5:2 Kitchen Sautéed mushrooms are a tasty and gluten-free alternative to spinach. On a non-fasting day, double up on the eggs, and butter your toast. A few pumpkin seeds scattered on top add extra crunch and nutrients.

NOOSA-STYLE MUSHROOMS AND GOAT'S CHEESE WITH LEMON PESTO DRESSING

Calories per serving: 178; 247 with bread

Vegetarian/low carbohydrate and gluten free if served without bread

While I was writing this book, we achieved a life-long dream of travelling to Australia where brunch is an art form. One of the most memorable was a platter of pan-fried mushrooms with pesto and cheese, served at a beachside café in Noosa, a very foodie resort on the Sunshine Coast, Queensland.

I experimented with a 5:2-friendly version back in my own kitchen, creating an intense oil-free pesto. If you don't want to make your own pesto, use shop-bought sparingly.

You can use 1-cal cooking spray for the mushrooms, but olive oil adds flavour.

Serves 1
Preparation time: 6 minutes
Cooking time: 8 minutes

> ½ tsp olive oil 22 cals
> pinch dried chilli flakes
> few black or pink peppercorns, lightly crushed
> 3 portobello or field mushrooms, weighing about 150–200g 44–52 cals
> squeeze lemon juice
> a little water or vegetable stock
> 25g soft goat's cheese, plain or with garlic and herbs 68 cals

For the dressing

> 5–6 fresh basil leaves, plus extra to garnish (optional)
> juice and zest of ¼ lemon 5 cals
> 1 clove garlic, roughly chopped 4 cals
> 5g pine nuts, reserving 3 for garnish 35 cals
> pinch sea salt

Garlic Toast (Optional)

1–2 thin slices, weighing about 25g, sourdough or ciabatta bread 69 cals
½ clove garlic, for rubbing the toast

1. Heat the oil, chilli flakes and peppercorns in a medium non-stick saucepan and add the mushrooms, stalk-side down. Cook for 4 minutes over medium heat. If the mushrooms burn or stick, add 1 or 2 teaspoons of water or vegetable stock. After 4 minutes, turn them over and add the lemon, and more water or stock, if needed. Cook for another 4 minutes, or until the mushrooms are tender.

2. Meanwhile, make the dressing. Place the basil, lemon juice and zest, garlic and sea salt in a pestle and mortar or mini food processor and add the pine nuts. Grind together until you have a light green paste. Add more salt or lemon juice, to taste.

3. If using bread, toast lightly under a grill or in the toaster. Rub the cut edge of the halved garlic clove over the toasted bread for an intense garlic hit.

4. Spoon the mushrooms onto the bread, if using, or serve them on their own in a warmed serving dish. Crumble over the goat's cheese, and drizzle the pesto over the top. Finish with the reserved pine nuts, a grinding of black pepper and a few small basil leaves, if using.

More ideas from the 5:2 Kitchen Double up on the pesto ingredients, and keep the extra portion covered in the fridge for 1–2 days. It goes well with chicken and many vegetables. Try sun-dried tomatoes, whipped with a little ricotta, for a lighter pesto.

BAKED HADDOCK SMOKIE POT

Calories per serving: 205; 285 with Scottish oatcakes

Nut free/gluten free*/low carbohydrate without oatcakes

This version of the classic Scottish dish was inspired by my friend's wide smile when she had this for lunch in a local pub, the Sussex Yeoman in Brighton. Their version was much richer, but this is just as tasty and super satisfying. The oatcakes are optional, but seem to fit perfectly if you're using true 'smokies' from Arbroath. Oatcakes are lower in carbohydrates than wheat-bread, and take more time to digest, meaning you stay feeling fuller for longer.

Serves 1
Preparation time: 5 minutes
Cooking time: 12–15 minutes

75g fresh or frozen spinach 19 cals
squeeze lemon juice, plus a lemon wedge, to serve
85g smoked haddock fillet or chunks, flaked 99 cals
handful fresh chives or dill, snipped, plus a few left whole to garnish 5 cals
2 tbsp reduced-fat crème fraîche 52 cals
10g mature low-fat cheddar cheese, grated 22 cals
2 rough oatcakes 80–90 cals
30g watercress, baby spinach or other salad leaves, to serve 8 cals
salt and pepper

1. Preheat the oven to 190°C/375°F/Gas mark 5. Microwave or pan-cook the spinach with a little water and a squeeze of lemon juice until wilted. Season with pepper then drain through a sieve. When cool enough to handle, carefully squeeze out as much of the water as possible and place in a large ramekin or small ovenproof dish.

2. Scatter the haddock flakes evenly over the spinach and set aside.

3. Mix the snipped herbs with the crème fraîche then spoon the mixture onto the fish. Scatter the grated cheese over the top along with another good grinding of black pepper and a little sea salt, if you like it.

4. Bake for 12–15 minutes then remove from the oven and sprinkle over the reserved herbs. Serve with the oatcakes, green leaf salad and a lemon wedge on the side.

* Most oatcakes are gluten-free, but it's best to check the label. Oats contain avenin, a protein that causes allergies in 5 per cent of coeliacs (people whose digestive system is damaged by gluten, see page 213). In addition, there is a small risk of cross-contamination in mills where wheat and oats are processed. See www.coeliac.org.uk for more details.

More ideas from the 5:2 Kitchen For more protein, you can add 1 medium egg (78 extra calories) by breaking it carefully onto the fish at the end of step 3. For a Mediterranean twist, add sun-dried tomatoes or a few chopped capers to the crème fraîche. On a non-fasting day, add more cheese, and serve with crusty seeded bread and farmhouse butter.

CHEDDAR AND APPLE 'PLOUGHMAN'S BRUNCH' MINI-MUFFINS
Calories per muffin: 44

Vegetarian/nut free

Cheese and apple are my favourite parts of a Ploughman's lunch, and these bite-size mini-muffins are just the thing for a Ploughman's brunch on the go. One mini-muffin makes a good snack (perfect if you're starting out and want something in reserve) while two or three will fill you up. For a sit-down brunch, serve alongside two grilled tomatoes and some spinach wilted in a saucepan, plus a pickled onion or two.

Makes 24 mini-muffins
Preparation time: 20 minutes
Cooking time: 15–20 minutes

    225g wholemeal flour 698 cals
    2 tsp baking powder 10 cals
    1 Cox apple, grated 60 cals

50g reduced-fat extra-strong Cheddar, grated 108 cals
leaves picked from 3 sprigs thyme
175g fat-free natural or 0% fat Greek yoghurt 96 cals
1 medium egg 78 cals
2 tbsp semi-skimmed milk 14 cals
salt and pepper

1. Preheat the oven to 200°C/400°F/Gas mark 6. Line a 24-hole mini-muffin tin with mini-muffin paper cases.

2. Sift the flour and baking powder into a large bowl. Stir in the grated apple, grated Cheddar and thyme leaves. Mix well.

3. Whisk together the yoghurt, egg and milk and season well. Make a dip in the middle of the dry mixture and pour the wet mixture into it. Stir quickly with a table knife until the mixture is just folded together.

4. Divide the mixture evenly across the muffin cases, and bake in the oven for 15–20 minutes, or until risen and golden.

5. Cool on a wire rack for 10 minutes and serve warm or leave to cool completely.

More ideas from the 5:2 Kitchen Add crushed walnuts or a pinch of dried mixed herbs, to the muffin batter. On a non-fasting day, use the muffins instead of bread for a full ploughman's lunch or dinner, complete with a chunk of cheese, some pickles and a half pint of bitter. Freeze in a re-sealable bag for up to three months. Thaw at room temperature for about an hour

MEDITERRANEAN-STYLE QUINOA CAKES WITH HOME-MADE KETCHUP SALSA

Calories per serving: 214; 249 made with pre-prepared quinoa; with ketchup add 14

Vegetarian/nut free

With lots of protein and nutrients, quinoa is one of the goodies of the grain world (see page 246 for more on whole grains), with lots of protein and nutrients.

These little cakes are ideal for breakfast. You can use ready-to-serve quinoa, but that pushes the calories up a little because olive oil is added. The ketchup salsa is a tangy, smoky alternative to sugary bottled versions. It'll keep for 4–5 days in the fridge, covered.

Serves 4 (3 cakes per serving)
Preparation time: 20 minutes
Cooking time: 6 minutes

For the ketchup salsa

150g ripe tomatoes, chopped 30 cals
1 large spring onion, chopped 4 cals
1 tbsp cider vinegar 2 cals or balsamic vinegar 5 cals
1 tbsp tomato purée 10 cals or sun-dried tomato purée 20 cals
½ tsp sweet paprika or cayenne pepper 3 cals
sea salt and black pepper
¼ tsp honey (optional) 5–6 cals

For the cakes

100g uncooked quinoa 365 cals or 250g pack ready-to-serve quinoa 505 cals
1 courgette, grated, liquid squeezed out 34 cals
3–4 sun-dried tomatoes (not in oil), weighing about 15g, snipped with scissors 24 cals
leaves picked from 3 sprigs oregano or small handful fresh chopped basil leaves 5 cals
6 pitted black olives, sliced into rings 40–50 cals

2 medium eggs, beaten 156 cals

1 red onion, finely diced 38 cals

75g reduced-fat feta-style cheese, crumbled 135 cals or 75g smoked tofu 129 cals

25g breadcrumbs 60–80 cals

1. To make the ketchup, place all of the ingredients in a food processor, season well and blend until smooth. Or, chop the mixture finely by hand for a more salsa-like texture. Place in the refrigerator, covered, until ready to serve. This will keep for up to 2 weeks in the fridge.

2. Make the cakes. If using uncooked quinoa, rinse very well, then boil for 15–20 minutes in 300ml water (or check pack instructions) then leave to cool slightly. You can use ready-to-serve quinoa straight from the pack.

3. Place the quinoa in a large bowl with all of the cake ingredients except the breadcrumbs. Mix well then leave to rest for a couple of minutes.

4. Drain off any liquid in the bottom of the bowl then stir in the crumbs. Leave to rest for 5 minutes (or up to 48 hours, covered, in the fridge) to soak up any moisture. When you are ready to make the cakes, divide the mixture into quarters and use each quarter to form 3 round cakes with wet hands. Squeeze out any excess moisture.

5. Spray a non-stick frying pan with 1-cal cooking spray and fry the cakes over a medium heat for 4–5 minutes, then turn and fry for 4–5 on the other side. They may break up a little, but just push them back together with the spatula! Alternatively, bake them in an oven at 200°C/180°C fan oven/Gas mark 6 for around 15 minutes.

6. Serve with a good tablespoon of the ketchup.

To freeze, place the cooked cakes between sheets of greaseproof paper and store in an airtight container in the freezer. When ready to use them, thaw then microwave for 30–40 seconds per serving to reheat. The cakes will keep for up to 2 months in the freezer.

More ideas from the 5:2 Kitchen Add your own favourite flavours and vegetables to the cakes. Try curried quinoa cakes (use curry powder or garam masala, 1 grated carrot, spring onion and a few sultanas). Or, 'Mex it up' by stirring a chopped jalapeño pepper, cooked black beans and cumin into the cake mixture and serving them with avocado slices.

Vegan option:

PORTOBELLO MUSHROOMS WITH MEDITERRANEAN QUINOA STUFFING

Calories per serving: 229; with ketchup add 14

The vegan version leaves out the egg. This makes for a crumblier filling, which is ideal for stuffing vegetables like mushrooms, courgettes or peppers.

Make as with main recipe until the end of stage 3, leaving out the egg and using tofu instead of feta. Preheat the oven to 180°C/350°F/ Gas mark 4. Use 3 large portobello mushrooms per person (54 calories), pull out the stalk, and heap one-third of the mixture each into the caps. Place in a baking tray and cook for 10–12 minutes then serve with the salsa. You can freeze the stuffing in single portions and defrost it before using.

PICK 'N' MIX CHILLED-OUT MAGIC MUESLI

Calories for base: 85–108; with Pick 'n' Mix option, up to 190

Vegetarian/vegan option/gluten free/nut free (depending on options chosen)

I call this magic muesli becasues it takes just a few moments at bedtime to prepare for the morning.

Chilled 'bircher muesli' is less gloopy than hot porridge. Just pick and mix the flavours you fancy, or invent your own. (My favourites are Apple Pie and Cherry Bakewell.) You can make two or three portions in one go and keep, covered, in the fridge.

Serves 1
Preparation time: 3–5 minutes

20g rolled or jumbo oats 72 cals
100ml almond milk 13 cals or skimmed milk 35 cals or apple juice 36 cals

1. Place the oats in a bowl. Add the milk or juice and any flavourings, cover and leave to sit overnight or for a couple of hours in the fridge. Use a plastic container if you want a takeaway.

2. In the morning, add fresh fruit, nuts, and other ingredients suggested below. You may need an extra splash of liquid to get the consistency you like. Brands of oats vary so you may need another 25ml to avoid heaviness. Stir well then tuck in!

Pick 'n' Mix options

CHERRY BAKEWELL
Calories per serving: 47 (plus muesli base)

¼ tsp ground cinnamon 2 cals
50g cherries, pitted 30 cals (frozen cherries are good value)
½ tsp almond extract negligible cals
2.5g ground almonds or flaked toasted almonds 15 cals

1. Add the ground cinnamon to the juice or milk. Stir the mixture into the oats and place in the fridge to chill overnight.

2. In the morning, stir the cherries and almond extract into the muesli and top with the ground or flaked almonds to serve.

'MOM'S' APPLE PIE
Calories per serving: 77 (plus muesli base)

Try doubling up on the apples, with apple juice to soak the oats, and grated apple on top.

¼ tsp apple pie spice or ground cinnamon 2 cals
5g sultanas 15 cals
squeeze fresh lemon juice
small dessert apple around 60 cals

1. Add the pie spice or ground cinnamon and the sultanas to the juice or milk. Stir the mixture into the oats and place in the fridge to chill overnight.

2. In the morning, grate the apple (skin on) over the mixture, and give it a stir. Squeeze over a little fresh lemon juice to serve.

MIDDLE EASTERN YOGHURT PARFAIT
Calories per serving: 30–57 (plus muesli base)

Pomegranate molasses has a slightly sweet-and-sour taste and adds a fruity, subtle tang.

few drops orange flower water, negligible cals
2–3 ready-to-eat dried apricots, chopped 10–20 cals
1 tbsp fat-free Greek yoghurt 8–10 cals
1 tbsp pomegranate seeds 12 cals
1 tsp pomegranate molasses (optional) 15 cals

1. Add the orange flower water and chopped apricots to the juice or milk. Stir the mixture into the oats and place in the fridge to chill overnight.

2. In the morning, top with yoghurt, pomegranate seeds and molasses, if using.

STICKY TOFFEE PUDDING
Calories per serving: 82 (plus muesli base)

Blackstrap molasses is treacly in taste and it contains the nutrients and minerals removed from white sugar in the refining process. Use sparingly, though, because it's still high in calories.

20g medjool date, stoned and chopped 58 cals
½ tsp vanilla extract 3 cals
½ tsp honey or blackstrap molasses (optional) 10 cals
3g crushed walnuts 21 cals

1. Add the chopped date and the vanilla extract to the juice or milk. Stir the mixture into the oats and place in the fridge to chill overnight.

2. In the morning, stir in the honey or molasses, if using, and top with the crushed walnuts to serve.

APRICOT AND COCONUT ENERGY BITES
Calories per energy bite: 73–80

Vegetarian/vegan/gluten free*

Cereal bars are another supposedly 'healthy' option but that are often overly sweet and highly processed. These are different: nuts help balance out the sweetness of the dried fruits. Processing affects the calorie count of dried apricots, so check the label and adjust the count if need be.

Energy Bites are particularly brilliant if you can't face breakfast first thing, but get peckish later at work. Freeze a batch, each wrapped individually in non-stick baking paper, then take one to work, ready for when you need a boost.

Makes 12
Preparation time: 15 minutes

25g jumbo oats 89 cals
50g whole almonds 305 cals
10g desiccated coconut 62 cals
150g dried apricots 270–350 cals (depending on brand)
50g stoned ready-to-eat dates 144 cals
½ tsp ground cinnamon 2 cals

1. Whiz the oats in a blender until roughly chopped, then place in a bowl and set to one side. Do the same with the almonds and coconut.

2. Return oats and nuts to the processor with the apricots, dates, cinnamon and 1 tablespoon cold water. Pulse until the mixture becomes a paste.

3. Scoop up a large teaspoon of the mixture and weigh it (you want 25g) then squeeze together and shape into a ball. Do the same with the rest of the mixture until you have 12 balls.

4. Wrap each bite separately in non-stick baking paper or cling film and add to an airtight container, then freeze. Take out as needed, and leave to thaw for half an hour before eating.

*see note, page 48.

More ideas from the 5:2 Kitchen Keep the apricots as the base, but ring the changes with different nuts and fruits, for example cashew nuts or dried cranberries would both work well.

THE WORLD'S EASIEST CHOCOLATE AND ALMOND PANCAKES
Calories per pancake: 109; plus topping: 125

Vegetarian/gluten free

These are so quick to make, and you're likely to have the ingredients at home. A banana eaten on its own isn't a great diet choice because the sweetness can give you a sugar rush that makes you hungry again very quickly. But combining the fruit with protein from an egg or nuts slows down your digestion, so you feel energised for longer. This recipe makes two servings, and the batter will keep for 24 hours in the fridge in a covered plastic container.

The batter is easy to make, but flipping the pancake can take practice. If it breaks, don't worry. It'll taste just as good!

Serves 2
Preparation time: 3 minutes
Cooking time: 6 minutes

1 medium banana, weighing about 110g with the skin on 90–110 cals
1 medium egg 78 cals
1 tsp ground almonds 32 cals
1 tsp unsweetened cocoa powder or raw cacao powder* 18–19 cals
½ tsp almond extract 0–3 cals
30g fat-free Greek yoghurt 16 cals
100g fresh strawberries, hulled and halved (or thawed frozen raspberries, blueberries or mixed berries) 16 cals

1. Peel the banana, add to a bowl and mash with a fork. Add the egg, ground almond, cocoa and almond extract. Mix well to form a batter.

2. Spray a small non-stick frying pan with 1-cal cooking spray, and place over a low heat. Pour half of the batter into the pan distributing it evenly across the surface. (Depending on the size of your pan, it might not quite cover the bottom). Cook for 3 minutes.

3. Loosen the underside of the pancake with a spatula and use a second spatula or a palette knife to turn the pancake over. Cook for a further 3 minutes.

4. Slide the pancake onto a small serving plate. Place the yoghurt and then the fruit in the centre then roll the top of the pancake forward to create a 'clamshell'. Serve warm.

*Raw cacao is available from health food shops, and *may* be nutritionally superior to normal (unsweetened) cocoa powder, though that's open to debate. Both are rich in anti-oxidants and some minerals, but cocoa, which has been roasted in processing, gives a slightly sweeter result.

More ideas from the 5:2 Kitchen Try vanilla extract instead of the almond, or leave out the cocoa and almonds, and add 1 teaspoon of sesame seeds (32 calories) for a nuttier version that would be lovely served with a peach or apricot instead of the berries.

Making sense of... breakfast

The 'Making sense of . . . ' sections are all about helping us navigate our way around food scares, myths and contradictions. So for our first, we're tackling the first meal of the day.

Will skipping breakfast make me ill – or fat?

The saying goes 'Breakfast like a king, lunch like a prince, and dine like a pauper' – and the message that going without breakfast is a Very Bad Idea has been hammered home for decades by fitness trainers, nutritionists and, um, cereal manufacturers.

I never challenged this until I started doing 5:2. Then I realised that, with a daily limit of 500 calories, what suited me on Fast Days was to delay eating until lunchtime or later, so I could enjoy one or two larger meals. I found that I felt a lot hungrier on the days I *did* take breakfast.

Many people in our Facebook group have had similar experiences. When I asked members when they ate, only 65 of the 344 who answered always had breakfast. The rest often skipped it and, like me, had two meals or only one on a Fast Day.

It seems to work for many of us. But are we putting our weight loss – even our health – at risk?

The case for breakfast

It's not just proverbs that tell us skipping breakfast – or any meal – is a bad idea. Various studies appear to back it up.

- Men over 45 who skip breakfast may be at 27 per cent higher risk of heart attack (2013 study by researchers at Harvard School of Public Health)

- Breakfast 'makes you brainy', and reduces stress and anxiety levels (Cognitive Effects of Breakfast study in 2012)

- *Not* eating breakfast may prime your brain to seek out fatty foods later in the day (2012 report from scans of 21 people at Imperial College London).

Worrying stuff. Yet I still happily skip breakfast on my Fast Days, and sometimes on other days each week. Am I crazy?

You always need to read between the headlines.

Factor 1: Confounders (or why breakfast-skippers might have lots of bad habits)

If we've been told since we were children that skipping breakfast is bad for us, then those of us who want to live a healthy lifestyle are likely to toe the line.

This means that people who ignore the conventional wisdom and skip breakfast may ignore other health warnings. These invisible factors are often known as 'confounders'.

Take the Harvard study. The diet writer Zoe Harcombe (who is notoriously sceptical about a lot of health advice, including 5:2!) analysed it and found that breakfast skippers were three times as likely to be smokers than the breakfast eaters – a sign of those 'bad habits' perhaps? On average, breakfast skippers also drank a bit more alcohol, watched more TV, exercised less, weighed a bit more and were slightly less likely to be married – all factors that other studies have suggested can contribute to heart disease risk.

She also found that though heart 'incidents' were higher in the skippers, the numbers for both were very low. Of course, Harcombe has her own views and books on nutrition but one of the key things about reviewing evidence is to look at critical points of view.

The best policy? Go to the original report, and check out the critics, too, before drawing your own conclusions.

Factor 2: Research motives (studies can be a way of selling us stuff)

How about the Cognitive Effects of Breakfast study – the one that says you're smarter and less anxious if you've eaten breakfast? The research was carried out by Mindlab, which describes itself on its website as, 'the UK's only laboratory devoted to communications and PR related research'.

So who funded the breakfast research? It was Warburton's, the UK's 'leading independent baker', which produces two million loaves, rolls and crumpets every day. In fact, I'm a fan of those crumpets, not to mention their flatbreads and sandwich thins.

Still, just because they funded it, doesn't mean it's wrong. Their press release explains that the 25 subjects ate breakfast one day, and skipped it on the other. Their results in reasoning and reaction-time tests were better on the day they consumed a 'traditional bakery breakfast' than on the day they skipped it. But I also wanted to know:

- In their normal lives, did the participants usually skip breakfast, or usually eat it? If they did usually eat first thing, then changing their routine probably would make them anxious or edgy the first time.

- How soon after the breakfast did the subjects take the tests, and what exactly did they eat? Baked goods, especially refined carbohydrates, can give you a rush of energy at the time, but leave you edgier later in the morning due to the effects on insulin.

I decided I didn't want to change my habits based on results from 25 people, tested over two days. But the Imperial College brain scan research was more interesting.

Factor 3: Interesting research that needs follow-ups

Dr Tony Goldstone, a highly respected obesity researcher, conducted the brain scan research. In the study, 21 people of normal weight skipped breakfast one day, and on another they had a 730-calorie breakfast. That's a pretty big breakfast.

Their brains were then scanned in a magnetic resonance imaging machine as they looked at pictures of calorie-dense foods. On the day they skipped breakfast, the orbitofrontal cortex area of the brain became much more active when the people were shown pictures of high-calorie foods. The same didn't happen with low-calorie foods. And when the participants were offered lunch after the scans, they ate on average one-fifth more calories on the day they skipped breakfast.

But while the headline, 'Skipping Breakfast Primes the Brain to Seek Out Fat', is accurate, does that mean we breakfast skippers *will* put on weight? If I ate one-fifth more calories at lunch than normal, I'd still be unlikely to eat as many calories as the participants did when they had a 730-calorie breakfast. Plus, as with the second study, we don't know if the participants were usually eaters or skippers, which might have had an effect on their brain's response.

It's interesting research, and I am sure is being followed up, but I know from experience that missing breakfast doesn't make *me* eat the 'wrong things', if, indeed, high-fat foods are 'the wrong thing' (see *Making sense of… carbohydrates, fats and proteins*, page 271).

Overall, maintaining weight is about matching our energy consumption to our energy expenditure in daily life. Some people find breakfast gets them off to a good start, others may prefer to wait for lunch and eat fewer, but bigger meals. And age is a factor, too. There is some data that children and teenagers do, in fact, perform better when they've eaten before school, hence the rise in breakfast clubs, but for adults it's not clear-cut.

How to break your fast – at any time of day

There's a wider issue that none of these studies address, and that's *what* to eat.

We know that foods high in sugar give us an energy boost, but that's often followed by a 'crash' as blood sugar levels drop, and we feel hungrier, sooner (see page 303). So, ideally, breakfast would consist of foods that are lower in sugar, and higher in foods that keep us satisfied for longer (like eggs and fish). Yet an independent overview from the consumers' association *Which?* in 2012 showed 32 out of 50 cereals were high in sugar, almost all because of *added* sugar, with one well-known brand aimed at children containing 37 per cent sugar.

Cereal bars, promoted as a filling option for breakfast on the go, are no better. In the same year *Which?* found that 29 out of 30 bars analysed were high in sugar, with just over half containing more than 30 per cent. Only one (coincidentally, it's one I like, hoorah!) contained no added sugar.

You can find analysis of many health stories, including the *Which?* reports, via the NHS Behind the Headlines site www.nhs.uk/news. It tends to take a conservative approach, however. For example, the suggested 'healthy alternative' to sugary cereals was 'scrambled eggs on wholemeal toast with a glass of orange juice', even though many doctors are now suggesting that juice is *not* the best way to consume fruit.

Kate's Verdict

Skipping breakfast works for me, but you may prefer more frequent meals. And the research into children does suggest breakfast is beneficial for them.

When it comes to *making sense of how to eat well*:

- **Work out what suits you best** If you **love breakfast**, and find it stops you eating processed or higher calorie foods later, then stick with it. But if you **don't enjoy eating first thing**, and feel more able to eat nutritious meals by delaying eating until later, then follow your appetite.

- **Take your food news with a pinch of salt – and always go back to the source** Follow links on news stories online to the **institution** that produced the report, or search the **title** of the study itself, to read the **original report** and what others have to say about it, **critics as well as supporters**. For example, the most recent research from the University of Bath, involving 38 people of a healthy weight, showed eating breakfast had no significant effect on metabolism or eating patterns compared to fasting till midday. Those who did take breakfast had more stable blood sugar levels later in the day, however.

- **Whatever time of day you're eating, focus on making good food choices** Aim for fresh produce with minimal processing or additives.

5:2 Food Hero

THE EGG

Eggs are often taken for granted, and sometimes even labelled as being bad for you. Yet I feel the humble egg is a true 5:2 hero, offering high quality protein and other nutritional benefits in a very versatile, good-value package.

Time for the egg to come back out of its shell!

All about eggs

Eggs are designed to sustain the embryo of the chicken (or other bird) through its development, which is why they're so packed with nutrients.

Nutrition

Chicken eggs are a 'complete protein' with all the essential amino acids the human body needs, plus vitamins and minerals that aid health, including Vitamin D, which helps with the growth and repair of bones and teeth. They're also rich in protein, which helps keep us feeling fuller, for longer. The diet a chicken is fed *will* affect the vitamin content, which is why it makes sense to buy eggs from producers with the highest welfare standards you can afford.

The colour of the shells has no impact on the taste of the egg – it's caused by diet – but different countries have different preferences. The Brits prefer brown while Japanese shoppers prefer white.

Calories: Hen's eggs contain from 55 to 90 calories depending on size.

The yolk: This yellow sphere contains almost three-quarters of the calories in the egg, and all the fat (up to 5g depending on the size), plus choline, a nutrient important in brain development, plus significant amounts of cholesterol.

The white: Egg white is mainly water, with some protein. It contains no cholesterol and little, if any, fat.

Downsides

- **Salmonella in eggs** In the 1980s, when a British minister had to resign after saying most eggs were contaminated by the salmonella bacteria, something farmers strenuously denied. But salmonella infection can cause nasty food poisoning, and is dangerous to the very young, old, or unwell. Now different countries take different approaches to reducing the incidence. In the US, eggs are washed before they are allowed to be put on sale whereas in the UK flocks are vaccinated against salmonella, which means outbreaks are much rarer.

- **Cholesterol** Eggs *do* contain cholesterol but recent studies of moderate egg consumption by humans (up to one per day) don't seem to show any additional risk of heart disease in most people. A small number of people with a condition called hypercholesterolaemia *are* more susceptible to cholesterol from all sources in their diet and should take advice from their doctor.

- **Allergies to eggs** These are more common in very young children than in adults: avoiding eggs increases the chances of a child 'growing out of it'.

Animal welfare

Battery farming, where hens are kept in unnatural conditions to increase maximum egg production is cruel and inhumane. In fact, many supermarkets in the UK now refuse to sell anything but free-range eggs, but even their welfare standards vary. Buy the best you can afford. Approved organic farms tend to have the best standards, or check the standards for own brands on your supermarket's website. When hens are pasture-fed, which means they spend all or most of their time feeding outdoors, their eggs tend to have higher vitamin content and omega-3 fatty acids, and lower levels of cholesterol. Buying locally at a farm or farmers' market allows you to ask the producer directly about their welfare standards and freshness of the eggs.

How to buy and store

- It's best to keep eggs in your fridge, in their box, not in the racks in the fridge door where the temperature is inconsistent and the eggs rattle every time you open the door. Keeping them on the worktop is usually safe, but the fridge may stop the growth of salmonella in the very unlikely event an egg *is* contaminated: you can also buy pasteurised egg whites in a carton.

- You can use eggs a couple of days past their sell-by date for most cooking purposes.

- To check for freshness, place the egg in a bowl of water – the more it floats, the less fresh it is. That's because as the egg ages, the air sac inside grows larger as the yolk and white deteriorate.

- For a change, try richer duck eggs, which contain higher levels of omega-3 fatty acids and other nutrients, or little quail's eggs, which contain more phosphorous.

Getting the best out of your egg

The best way to preserve the nutrients is to poach or soft-boil your egg. Due to the small risk of salmonella, however, pregnant women, babies and toddlers, elderly people and anyone whose immune system is compromised, should only eat eggs that have been well cooked or use pasteurised eggs (most are not, so check the label).

Recipe Ideas

Souped Up:

DELICIOUS, NUTRITIOUS MEALS IN A BOWL

Soup is pure magic. Not only does it keep you fuller for longer (read *Making sense of… your appetite* at the end of this chapter to understand why), but it also makes you feel *extremely* accomplished in the kitchen. The results always seem so much more than the sum of the ingredients and effort involved.

Soups are brilliant for Fast Days. And they are so versatile. Almost all freeze incredibly well, they're warming in winter, refreshing in summer, and equally at home on the kitchen table or at the most fancy dinner party. The recipes that follow really are souper heroes.

FRESHLY MINTED GREEN SOUP WITH GOAT'S CHEESE FLOATS

SPEEDY VIRGIN MARY SOUP
(WITH BLOODY MARY OPTION FOR NON-FASTING DAYS)

COCONUT AND CHICKEN THAI BROTH

CREAMY CHICKEN AND TOMATO SOUP

MEXICAN TORTILLA SOUP

MULLIGATAWNY WITH SHREDDED BEEF (WITH VEGAN OPTION)

CAULIFLOWER AND MUSTARD SOUP WITH
MELTED CHEESE CRISPY CRUMBS

FENNEL-AND-TOMATO-FLAVOURED FISH BROTH

CALMING APPLE AND CELERY SOUP WITH WALDORF TOPPING

PLUS …

MAKING SENSE OF… APPETITE

5:2 FOOD HERO: CHICKEN

5:2 Lives

FROM OBESE AND IN DENIAL
TO A STUNNING SIZE 8

'I'm happy, more confident and just feel well.
5:2 has brought the real me back.'
Elaine, 42

When it came to her weight, Elaine Stockwell was in denial.

'I had avoided weighing myself for years (and I do mean years). I knew I was overweight and that I needed to do something but the question was what. Weight has always been a very personal and private thing for me, so much so that I wouldn't even tell my husband what my weight was when I finally did step on the scales. I was horrified that I weighed more than him.'

It's a pattern familiar to so many dieters. Elaine's weight had crept up over the years, 'and I had not got in control and stopped it. Each visit to the doctor, whatever it was for, resulted in him asking to weigh me and then telling me I needed to look at my weight. My BMI was considered obese at 31.6. Yet I knew that Weight Watchers and Slimming World were really not my kind of thing.'

The crunch came in January 2013. Elaine picked up a copy of *The 5:2 Diet Book*, and 'I started fasting the next day. Emotionally I was finally ready to confront my weight and I just knew that for me fasting was the way to go.'

And her instinct has been proved right. Elaine achieved an impressive loss of 26kg (57 lb), and went from UK dress size 16 to an 8. Her BMI is now 22.

'My diet had always been pretty healthy with lots of fruit or vegetables and salad; the issue was portion sizes.

'Once I started fasting I became aware of what I was eating, when and why. I also found that I became more educated on the calorific value of food. Instead of just having what I wanted, when I wanted it, I found myself questioning if I really needed to eat. I also stop eating when I'm full now, not when the plate is empty.'

Elaine, who lives in North Wales, has ditched the 'diet' products and buys real food instead. 'I now only buy full-fat foods. I've always preferred butter but do so guilt-free now. As a family we eat far less meat than we used to. We do eat fish regularly. The shopping bill is cheaper!'

'I'm much more active. I walk between six and ten miles a day and am just about to complete my first half-marathon. I'm happy, more confident and just feel well. People have commented how well I look, as in healthy glowing skin, great weight loss.'

Elaine's Fast Day diary

I keep my Fast Day meals simple. Vegetable soup then eggs on toast or fish with boiled vegetables.

Elaine's non-fasting day diary

I start my Feast Days with toast and marmite with avocado on top and coffee. For us, breakfast is the family meal of the day, so I don't skip it when I'm not fasting. It's the one time of the day we can all share time over a meal.

Lunch I can take or leave, and dinner is fish with vegetables and potatoes, vegetable curry with rice or pasta with salad. If we've had a roast at the weekend it's often leftovers!

71

I don't calorie count at all, though I did find checking portion sizes and calories per portion useful at the beginning.

I like to bake and cook and have not stopped since doing 5:2. Overall, I do eat less cake, but that is because smaller slices are sufficient!

Favourite food and drink

Pho: a complete meal in a bowl. I lived in Vietnam for a while and it reminds me of being there. Champagne, because who doesn't like a glass of bubbles?!

Best thing about 5:2?

The weight loss bringing 'me' back.

Elaine's top tip

You need to commit to the fast and stay strong. I cannot count the number of times I hear people say they have failed a fast and will try again tomorrow. It's two days a week! Dig deep, commit to the fast and do it!

FRESHLY MINTED GREEN SOUP WITH GOAT'S CHEESE FLOATS

Calories per serving: 70; 84 with goat's cheese topping

Vegetarian/vegan and dairy-free option/gluten free/low carb

Mid-way through shelling the peas for this, I was thinking, 'Never again!'

Then I tasted the finished dish and it was the MOST delicious soup I have ever made. Seriously, if you like spring fresh flavours, this is for you. Of course, it still tastes good made with *frozen* peas, but fresh ones elevate it to a whole different level.

Plus, with a little time on your hands, shelling peas is a bit like popping bubble-wrap; the perfect distraction on a Fast Day.

Makes 4 servings
Preparation time: 5–20 minutes
Cooking time: 15 minutes

½ tsp of butter or olive oil 19 cals or 1-cal cooking spray oil

3 spring onions, chopped 6 cals

600–700g fresh peas in their pods (around 250g after shelling) 200 cals or 250g frozen peas 175 cals

170g courgette, diced 34 cals

4 pods from the fresh peas, if using 0 cals

600ml fresh vegetable stock 15 cals or water and 2 tsp Marigold bouillon 24 cals

Good handful fresh mint, thicker stalks removed, reserve 5–6 tiny leaves, to garnish 5 cals

20g soft goat's cheese 54 cals (vegans can use a heaped tablespoon of non-dairy yoghurt to add creaminess, e.g. soya yogurt, 10 cals)

salt and pepper

1. Heat the butter or oil in a non-stick saucepan over a medium heat. Add the spring onions and cook gently for 2 minutes, then add the peas and courgette, and cook in the saucepan for a further 2 minutes.

2. Add the reserved pods and 500ml of the vegetable stock. Bring to the boil then reduce the heat simmer for 8–10 minutes, or until the vegetables are tender.

3. Add the mint. Stir the soup for 1 minute, then fish out and discard the four pods. Blend with a stick blender. If it is too thick, use the remaining vegetable stock to thin it down to your preference. Taste and season well.

4. Just before serving, divide the goat's cheese into four equal-sized portions then shape them into small balls using a spoon or your fingers and flatten them. Divide the soup between four bowls. Gently set one piece of cheese onto the surface of each to float on the soup, garnish with the reserved mint leaves and serve.

More ideas from the 5:2 Kitchen This is also delicious served cool on a hot summer's day. Or, for a fancy dinner party starter, boil two little quail's eggs per person, peel off the shell, halve the eggs, and float them, yolk-side up.

SPEEDY VIRGIN MARY SOUP (WITH BLOODY MARY OPTION FOR NON-FASTING DAYS)
Calories per serving: 44

Vegetarian/vegan/dairy-free/gluten-free/low-carb

This great soup has all the freshness and savoury tang of an expertly made Virgin Mary cocktail, and it's so adaptable. It's at its absolute best in summer using the ripest tomatoes you can get, especially the ones that are a bit too juicy for salad. But, if you're craving the taste of sunshine on a wintry night, tinned Italian plum tomatoes are a good option.

Makes 4 servings
Preparation time: 5 minutes
Cooking time: 12–13 minutes

  2 small celery sticks, leaves still attached, weighing about 60g 6 cals
  ½ tsp olive oil 22 cals
  1 red onion, chopped 38 cals
  ½ tsp fennel seeds (optional) 3 cals
  400g ripe tomatoes or 400g tin plum tomatoes 80 cals

1 tbsp tomato purée 10–20 cals
few black peppercorns, crushed, or pink peppercorns, left whole
800ml fresh vegetable stock 20 cals or water and 2 tsp Marigold bouillon
    24 cals
salt and pepper

To serve

small section of celery sticks
pinch celery salt
1 tsp Worcestershire sauce 5 cals
1 tsp Tabasco sauce, less than 3 cals

1. Reserve four small celery slices, ideally with leaves attached, as garnish. Chop the rest of the celery and set aside. Heat the olive oil in a saucepan over a medium heat and add the onion, chopped celery and fennel seeds, if using, for 3 minutes.

2. Add the tomatoes, tomato purée and the peppercorns and cook gently. After 5 minutes, add the stock. Stir everything together then increase the heat and bring to the boil. Reduce the heat and simmer for 5 minutes, or until the celery is tender.

3. Blend the soup in the saucepan using a stick blender (it's normal for some of the celery fibres to stay whole and give the soup texture). Season to taste, remembering you'll be adding more flavourings later.

4. Serve hot, or chilled, with your choice of as much and as many or few of the flavourings as you like from the list, garnished with the celery.

More ideas from the 5:2 Kitchen For a party, serve in shot glasses, with a stick of celery to stir, and a selection of flavourings for guests to mix their own perfect Virgin Mary soup at the table. For a grown-up version, add 10ml of Vodka per serving, which adds 21 calories.

COCONUT AND CHICKEN THAI BROTH

Calories per serving: 179

Gluten free/dairy free/vegan option/low-carb

This is stunning to look at – a translucent emerald broth with jewelled vegetables and fresh chicken – and even more stunning in fragrance and taste. Instead of adding coconut milk, which is high in fat and can be cloying, this lighter alternative takes its flavour from coconut oil and the delicious Thai spices.

Makes 2 servings
Preparation time: 15 minutes
Cooking time: 15 minutes

> 30g bunch coriander 15 cals
> 1 shallot, roughly chopped 7 cals
> 1 garlic clove 4 cals
> ¼ tsp each coriander and cumin seeds 5 cals
> 2cm-piece peeled ginger weighing 5g, finely chopped 4 cals
> 1 medium fresh green chilli, weighing about 25g, halved and deseeded 10 cals
> ½ tsp coconut oil 22 cals
> ½ red pepper, thinly sliced 15 cals
> 100g sugar snap peas, halved 35 cals
> 1 medium carrot, weighing about 100g, thinly sliced or cut into batons 34 cals
> 400ml hot chicken stock 16 cals
> 150g fresh chicken breast, thinly sliced 180 cals
> ½ lime cut in half again, to serve 10 cals

1. Add the fresh coriander to the bowl of a food processor (reserve 2 sprigs for the garnish) along with the shallot, garlic, spices, ginger and chilli. Add 50ml water and blend to a paste.

2. Heat the coconut oil in a saucepan over a very low heat. Stir in the blended spice paste and cook for 2–3 minutes, or until some of the water has evaporated and it has the consistency of a sauce.

3. Stir in the vegetables and cook for about a minute, then add the stock. Bring to the boil and add the chicken, then cover and reduce the heat to a simmer and cook for 15 minutes, or until the chicken has cooked through.

4. Divide between two bowls (or reserve one portion for your next Fast Day; it will keep in the fridge for up to three days). Garnish with a sprig of coriander and serve with a wedge of lime.

More ideas from the 5:2 Kitchen On non-fasting days, serve this as you would a curry. Sprinkle with chopped salted peanuts and serve, with jasmine or basmati rice to soak up the broth. Vegans and vegetarians can make an equally delicious and even lower calorie version of this dish using vegetable stock and replacing the chicken with thinly sliced firm tofu (around 128 calories for 150g). Reduce the cooking time to 10 minutes. The tofu version works out at 170 calories per portion.

CREAMY CHICKEN AND TOMATO SOUP
Calories per serving: 135

Gluten free/nut free/dairy free

This is soothing, warming and has a Fast Day cooking secret of its own. Yes, it's super creamy, but the wonderful velvety texture comes from a sprinkling of red lentils stirred in at the beginning of cooking.

Makes 2 servings
Preparation time: 15 minutes
Cooking time: 15 minutes

½ tsp olive oil 22 cals
1 shallot, finely chopped 7 cals
1 medium celery stick, finely chopped 6 cals
1 medium carrot, finely chopped 34 cals
15g red lentils 51 cals
¼ tsp paprika 3 cals
200g plum tomatoes, chopped 40 cals
300ml hot chicken stock made with water and 1 chicken stock cube 12 cals
75g skinless, boneless chicken breast, chopped 90 cals
2 tbsp freshly chopped parsley 5 cals

1. Heat the oil in a saucepan and add the shallot, celery and carrot with 1 tablespoon water. Cook over a medium heat until the shallot has softened.

2. Stir in the red lentils, paprika, plum tomatoes and hot stock. Season well then cover and simmer for 15 minutes. Stir in the chicken then blend everything together until smooth.

3. Reheat over a very low heat and stir in the parsley then serve.

More ideas from the 5:2 Kitchen If you're not fasting, a spoonful of soured cream and a little grated Cheddar on top make a delicious addition.

Kate's cooking tip This is a great way to use up chicken left over from a roast. Just weigh out the cooked chicken (removing any skin) and add to the soup at the end of the cooking time.

MEXICAN TORTILLA SOUP

Calories per serving: 127

Vegetarian/vegan and dairy free (without crème fraîche)/gluten free*/ nut free

I love Mexican food; the flavours and colours are so vibrant and satisfying. Here, I've made a rich, smoky tomato soup, added black beans and then topped it with crunchy vegetables and tortilla chips. If you're short of time, you can skip the griddling stage: the soup will still be delicious. *Ay caramba!*

Makes 4 servings
Preparation time: 5 minutes
Cooking time: 16–19 minutes

1 red pepper and 1 green or yellow pepper, cored and quartered 60 cals
4 spring onions, a little of the green tops snipped off for the topping 8 cals
2 cloves garlic, crushed 8 cals
1 whole fresh jalapeño pepper, deseeded, pith removed, finely chopped 5 cals
1 dried chipotle pepper rehydrated in hot water 20 cals or use 1 tsp chipotle paste 2–8 cals depending on brand

½ tsp each ground cumin and dried chilli flakes 5 cals

100g frozen or canned sweetcorn kernels, drained 90 cals or 1 whole fresh
   corn on the cob 120 cals

100g canned black beans, rinsed and drained 100–110 cals

400g can chopped tomatoes 72–100 cals

300ml vegetable stock made with water and 1 tsp Marigold 12 cals or water

juice of ½ lime, to taste 10 cals

1 corn tortilla 117 cals or 25g tortilla chips 120–145 cals*

2 level tbsp 0% fat crème fraîche, to serve (optional) 12 cals

salt and pepper

1. Cut and reserve 2 narrow strips from each of the peppers for the topping and set aside.

2. Spray a griddle with 1-cal cooking spray and chargrill the peppers and whole spring onions
   for 6–8 minutes, turning halfway through, until the skins are softened and ridged with
   black. (You can also do this under the grill but don't allow the whole surface to turn black or
   the flavour will be overpowering.)

3. Spray a large non-stick saucepan over a low heat with 1-cal cooking spray. Snip the spring
   onion, chipotle and peppers into the pan then add the chilli, cumin and dried chilli flakes and
   cook gently for 2–3 minutes.

4. Add the sweetcorn kernels, black beans, chopped tomatoes and the stock or water to the
   onion mixture. Cook over a medium heat for 8 minutes, or until the peppers have softened,
   stirring occasionally and adding a little water if the mix begins to stick or dry out.

5. Turn off the heat, and season, adding lime juice, to taste.

6. If using whole tortilla, brown under grill till crispy then cut into strips or triangles.

7. Just before serving the soup, swirl 1 tablespoon of the crème fraîche, if using, onto the
   surface of each portion. Divide the reserved pepper strips and spring onion tops, tortilla (or
   tortilla chips) between the four bowls as a garnish.

*Check label to ensure these are gluten free if you are avoiding gluten.

More ideas from the 5:2 Kitchen Not fasting? Add shredded cooked
chicken or chopped avocado, and serve with a warmed corn tortilla!

Kate's cooking tip This soup is also delicious blended until smooth. Reserve a tablespoon each of black beans and sweet corn kernels at step 4, then at the end of step 5, after seasoning, just whiz with a stick blender. Use the reserved beans and corn kernels as part of the topping.

MULLIGATAWNY WITH SHREDDED BEEF
Calories per portion: 253

Gluten free, nut free, dairy free (vegan option)

This is the ultimate winter warmer – rich, spicy and satisfying. It's perfect for those days when it's cold outside and you need something to fill you up. For a vegan version, just leave out the beef and use a hearty homemade vegetable stock. Meat-free mulligatawny is only 164 calories a bowl.

Makes 2 servings
Preparation time: 15 minutes
Cooking time: 1 hour 10 minutes

    1 tsp olive oil 45 cals
    1 small red onion, finely chopped 38 cals
    1 medium stick celery, finely chopped 6 cals
    1 medium carrot, finely chopped 34 cals
    100g braising beef, chopped 177 cals
    ½ tsp each curry powder, ground coriander and ground cumin 9 cals
    1 tbsp tomato purée 10–20 cals
    400ml hot beef stock 20 cals
    25g red lentils 86 cals
    50g canned chickpeas, rinsed and drained 64 cals
    60g baby leaf spinach 16 cals
    salt and pepper

1. Heat the oil in a pan over a low to medium heat and stir in the red onion, celery and carrot. Cover and cook over a low heat for 3 minutes. Add a splash of water if the mixture looks as if it might stick.

2. Stir in the beef and season well. Continue to cook for 3–5 minutes, or until the beef has seared on each side.

3. Stir in the spices and tomato purée and cook for 1–2 minutes, then pour in the hot stock. Cover and bring to a simmer, then turn the heat down low and cook for around an hour until the beef is tender.

4. Stir in the lentils, chickpeas and 300ml boiling water and continue to cook for 15–20 minutes, or until the lentils have softened.

5. Lift the beef out onto a cutting board and shred with two forks. Whiz half the soup mixture in the pan with a stick blender. Return the shredded beef to the pan along with the spinach and serve.

More ideas from the 5:2 Kitchen For an Indian meal in a bowl to enjoy on non-fasting days, serve with warmed naan bread, with a spoonful of creamy yoghurt added to the soup.

CAULIFLOWER AND MUSTARD SOUP WITH MELTED CHEESE CRISPY CRUMBS

Calories per serving: 53 made with almond milk; 71 made with semi-skimmed milk, plus 30 with topping

Cauliflower cheese is the ultimate comfort food, but making a proper cheese sauce involves lots of calorific ingredients like flour, butter and whole milk – not recommended on a Fast Day. So here, I've made a tasty, luxuriously creamy textured soup with cauliflower and mustard then added a cheese crumb topping at the last moment to maximise the Cheddar taste. All the comfort at around 100 calories per bowl.

Makes 4 servings
Preparation time: 8 minutes
Cooking time: 25 minutes

½ tsp butter or olive oil 19–23 cals
1 white onion 38 cals
1 medium cauliflower, florets only 100 cals

600ml homemade vegetable stock 15 cals or water and 2 tsp Marigold
   bouillon 24 cals
2–3 tsp Dijon mustard 15–30 cals
200ml almond milk 26 cals or semi-skimmed milk 98 cals
30g reduced-fat mature cheddar cheese 65 cals
20g breadcrumbs 55 cals
salt and pepper

1. Add the butter or oil to a large non-stick saucepan over medium heat. Add the onion and fry for 2 minutes then add the cauliflower and let it brown lightly for 3 minutes.

2. Add the stock and bring to the boil. Simmer for 18–20 minutes, or until the cauliflower is soft enough to blend.

3. Add 2 teaspoons of Dijon mustard and the almond or semi-skimmed milk and blend using a stick blender, or move the mixture to a blender goblet to blend, until smooth. Season with salt and pepper to taste. If you like more mustard, add it now.

4. To serve, preheat the grill to medium. Divide the soup between heatproof bowls. Gently sprinkle over the cheese and breadcrumbs so they don't sink. Place the bowls under the grill and cook until the crumbs are brown and the cheese has melted.

More ideas from the 5:2 Kitchen This soup freezes well (but without the cheese and crumb topping). Add the topping after defrosting when you re-heat the soup to serve. As a variation, you can use blue cheese in place of cheddar in the cheese crumb topping. If you have different mustards (I got a gift set for Christmas!), it's a great way to use up the different flavours. Ale mustard would be delicious here. Or use wholegrain mustard in an alternative topping: simply mix together 1 level tablespoon 0% fat crème fraîche (6 calories) and 1 teaspoon wholegrain mustard (8 calories) and swirl into each portion just before serving.

FENNEL-AND-TOMATO-FLAVOURED FISH BROTH

Calories per serving: 148

Gluten free/nut free/dairy free

Blending the mixture halfway through cooking produces a really hearty texture, so this nourishing, delicately scented broth becomes half soup, half stew. Try it with different types of white fish (check out what's on special offer).

Makes 2 servings
Preparation time: 10 minutes
Cooking time: 15 minutes

½ tsp oil 22 cals
2 spring onions, chopped
pinch fennel seeds, crushed 3 cals
½ bulb fennel, chopped, fronds roughly chopped and reserved 31 cals
150g celeriac, chopped 44 cals
200g canned chopped plum tomatoes 36–50 cals
150g white fish, such as cod, pollock or haddock, cut into large chunks
    144 cals
2 tbsp chopped fresh chives 10 cals
2 cocktail gherkins, chopped 5 cals
salt and pepper

1. Heat the oil in a saucepan and sauté the spring onions, fennel seeds, fresh fennel and celeriac over a low to medium heat for 5 minutes. Cover the pan with a lid and stir every now and then for 5 more minutes. Add a splash of water if the vegetables start to stick to the bottom of the pan.

2. Add the tomatoes and 300ml water and season well. Cover and bring to the boil then reduce the heat and leave to simmer for 5 minutes. Turn off the heat and, using a stick blender directly in the saucepan, blend about one third of the mixture.

3. Turn the heat back on to medium and add the fish. Cover and leave to simmer for 5 minutes, or until the fish is cooked through.

4. Spoon into bowls, and sprinkle over the chives, gherkin and the reserved fennel fronds to serve.

More ideas from the 5:2 Kitchen On non-fasting days, this is truly delicious with cheesy toasts or (croûtes) on top. Pile some grated Cheddar or Gruyère onto a few thin slices of baguette, set them on the surface of the soup then toast under the grill until bubbling to serve.

CALMING APPLE AND CELERY SOUP WITH WALDORF TOPPING
Calories per serving: 52 with almond milk; 76 made with semi-skimmed milk, plus topping 15

Vegetarian/vegan option/gluten free

The sweetness of the apple and the mildness of the almond milk combine to give a really pure-tasting, delicate soup – even if, like me, you're usually a bit unconvinced by celery. I experimented with lots of different versions, and if you want to cut the calories even further, use water in place of the almond milk and serve chilled.

Makes 3 servings
Preparation time: 5 minutes
Cooking time: 15 minutes

2 medium dessert apples, peeled, and cored 95–120 cals
lemon juice, for sprinkling
5g butter or ½ tsp olive oil 19–22 cals
3 spring onions, trimmed and snipped, green parts reserved for topping 6 cals
2 small sticks celery, weighing about 80–100g, chopped 8–10 cals
½ tsp fennel seeds 3 cals
500ml filtered water
200ml almond milk 26 cals or semi-skimmed milk 98 cals
1 level tbsp 0% fat crème fraîche or 0% fat Greek yogurt 9 cals
5g chopped walnuts 35 cals

chopped celery leaves, tops chopped from the spring onions or a few snipped
    chives
celery salt and black pepper

1. Cut 6 very thin slices of apple for the garnish. Place in a dish and sprinkle with lemon juice to stop them turning brown and set aside. Chop the rest of the apple flesh.

2. Place the butter or olive oil in a saucepan over medium heat. Add the onion, celery, and fennel seeds and fry for 3 minutes. Stir in the chopped apple and fry gently for 2 more minutes.

3. Add the water and leave the mixture to simmer for 5–10 minutes, or until the apple is soft.

4. Add the milk and, using a stick blender, blend in the pan until smooth.

5. If serving warm, heat the soup gently. Otherwise, remove from the heat, pour into a large bowl and chill, covered, in the fridge. You can also serve this at room temperature, if you prefer.

6. To serve, pour soup into a bowl, add 1 teaspoon crème fraîche to each serving and swirl with a spoon. Float apple slices on the top of the soup, sprinkle over the walnuts and garnish with the chopped leaves. Season with black pepper or celery salt.

More ideas from the 5:2 Kitchen On a non-fasting day you can be more generous with the walnuts, and serve with brown soda bread on the side.

Making sense of... appetite

When I was growing up, Milky Way bars were advertised as 'the sweet you can eat between meals without ruining your appetite'.

When was the last time *you* heard anyone worrying about ruining his or her appetite? These days, we're told instead to snack or 'graze' to 'keep blood sugar levels stable', and food manufacturers have changed their ads to reflect that. Companies now focus on 'eating occasions' or 'missed snacking opportunities', instead of meals. Apparently we *never* need to get peckish ever again.

Before starting 5:2, I was anxious about how it would feel to go hungry, even for a day, and whether that would affect my health or concentration. Yet very soon I realised that appetite and hunger are not frightening. In fact, they're the opposite: they're vital signals, telling us when to eat – and when to stop.

I also realised that the grazing had been one of the reasons I'd put on weight. What worked for Stone Age woman, surviving on the odd foraged berry or seed, did not work for twenty-first-century Kate, surrounded by chocolate and crisps.

Fasting turned out to be the most brilliant tool to help me listen to my appetite, on fasting and non-fasting days. But what exactly *is* appetite? And what techniques can we use to stay in control of hunger, one of our most powerful urges?

The digestive *system* and the digestive *process*

You know the basics: we put food in our mouth, chew and swallow it. Acids, enzymes and bacteria in the mouth and intestines break food down to fuel our bodies. Fat, protein and carbohydrates are broken down by different processes, and digested at different rates. And then anything the body can't use, comes out the other end! If we're healthy and lucky, the whole process happens without us having to think too much about it.

But the 'moving' parts of the system – the waste disposal functions that fascinate small children and are not discussed in 'polite' conversation – are only part of the story. The role of the brain in telling us when to eat, and when to stop, is critical, too.

The digestive *process* begins even before you take a single bite. As soon as you smell something appetising, the brain tells glands in your mouth to start producing saliva, ready to begin breaking down your food as you chew.

Hungry like the wolf?

But what makes us feel hungry? You might think the feeling is triggered once your stomach empties, but it's not that simple.

To explain, let me tell you a story about soup – let's make it the delicious Mexican Tortilla soup from page 78.

Let's say you're cooking it for lunch on a Fast Day. Because you haven't eaten since the previous night, the smell and colours are making your mouth water as you prepare it (the saliva will help start the digestive process as you eat).

Your stomach is growling a bit too: that's ghrelin, a hormone released by cells in the wall of the stomach when it is empty. But your stomach isn't in control – your *brain* is. Ghrelin, nicknamed 'the hunger hormone', reaches your brain via the bloodstream. In response, you become conscious of the need to eat. You may 'feel' that in your stomach, but a whole range of hormones and processes are at work to create that urge.

Hooray. The soup is ready! You sit down, and savour every delicious spoonful. As you swallow, the soup travels down to your stomach. As it fills, the stomach walls stretch, so the cells stop producing ghrelin. The enzymes and acids get to work on the carbohydrate in the vegetables, the proteins in the beans and, as you've added a nice swirl of crème fraîche and some avocado, there's fat there, too. You won't feel hungry again until the stomach empties and those cells begin to release ghrelin again.

But it's not *just* the calories or nutrient type (protein vs. carbohydrate for example) that affects how long it'll be before you're hungry again. It's also how it's been prepared: and soup is one of the good guys for keeping you full (scientists call this satiety). In two different experiments, people who ate soup stayed full for between an hour and 90 minutes longer than people who ate *exactly the same ingredients*, but in solid form. In another study, people who were given soup, solid food or liquid shakes on different days ate the fewest calories in other meals on the days they'd had soup.

But why is this? One theory about this is that soup stays in the stomach for longer because it has a larger volume when it's blended with water. Another theory is that it's more of a mental response: our brains interpret the soup as soothing, warming and satisfying and we 'feel' fuller mentally.

If finding an answer to such an apparently simple question – why does soup keep us full? – is so hard, it's no wonder controlling our appetite is even tougher.

The brain's appetite control centre

Many weight-loss researchers focus on the hypothalamus, the part of the brain that also regulates other essential functions, like thirst, body temperature and the immune system.

The processes controlling appetite are known as the 'appestat' which regulates hunger and fullness via hormones like ghrelin and leptin. Leptin, which is produced in the fat cells, helps to signal when the body is full and it's time to stop eating.

Leptin and ghrelin were discovered in the late 1990s, and were hailed as having great potential to fight obesity. Yet there's no magic bullet: while ghrelin and leptin do help signal hunger or fullness, neither can be made to work as simply as an on/off switch. Leptin's main role, for example, may be more about keeping body fat percentages high – and sounding the alarm when they're not – than it is about telling us when to stop eating. We do know that both

Eggs 'benefit' with mustard sauce (page 61)
189–220 calories

Noosa-style mushrooms and goat's cheese
with lemon pesto dressing (page 45)
178 calories

Cheddar and apple 'ploughman's brunch'
mini-muffins (page 48)
44 calories

Coconut and chicken Thai broth (page 76)
179 calories

Mexican tortilla soup (page 78)
127 calories

White bean and spinach salad with pecorino pesto (page 111)
120–200 calories

Smorgasbord of home-cured fish, salad and rye (page 139)
333 calories

Vegetarian Thali (page 141)
241 calories

Great big veggie burrito bowl (page 163)
262 calories

Home-made pizza with cauliflower base and blue cheese topping (page 165) *296–326 calories*

Lemongrass and ginger pork with noodles (page 206)
356 calories

Smoky Spanish mussels (page 205)
287 calories

Chilli-spiced chicken burger on a mushroom 'bun' (page 231)
150 calories

Rich pork lasagne with lucky-seven vegetables (page 267)
289 calories

Whipped vanilla mousse with
red fruit ripple (page 299)
52 calories

Mango
smoothie
(page 292)
*171–207
calories*

Black forest
yoghurt drink
(page 290)
92 calories

Berry mint
smoothie
(page 289)
31 calories

hormones are affected by bariatric surgery, designed to reduce weight by changing how the digestive system works. But it's early days.

The brain and the body have the same goal: to keep us alive, ideally long enough to reproduce and raise our children. Starvation is a huge threat to that survival so, to maintain our body weight, the brain wants us to seize any opportunity to eat.

For most of us, the threat of starvation has passed – but our bodies are still primed to make us eat. The food supply has changed, but our basic evolution hasn't caught up. No wonder obesity is a problem.

Emotions, environment, epigenetics

Our Emotions

In a crisis, many of us find ourselves reaching for sweet or fatty foods as a source of comfort. Often the cravings are as powerful, we feel out of control , even 'addicted'. And that's not surprising: the brain wants to reward us with 'pleasure chemicals' for doing the things we need to survive, including eating high-energy foods like cake or chips. And those pleasure chemicals also play a part in addiction. But often there's little pleasure when we eat due to emotional triggers. We may eat so quickly that we barely taste the food – and guilt kicks in the moment we're finished. Read more about how to deal with it on page 240, *Making sense of… emotional eating*.

Our Environment

Our eating is strongly affected by where and how we live. The habits we learned as children, the people we know, the location where we live or work all make a difference. Do your local shops sell fresh produce, or long-life, highly processed meals? Do you sit down at the table to eat, or grab something on the go or while watching TV? That will influence how fast you eat. And how many of us have had a dessert or an extra glass of wine during a night out to keep a friend company?

Our Epigenetics

Epigenetics is the 'hot' area of medical research right now. It's the study of how our body's cells respond and adapt to experiences and environment.

Nearly all the cells in our body contain an 'instruction manual', the DNA, which tells the cell what to do. This DNA is passed down from parents to children – in other words, 'in the genes'. Genes influence why food tastes different to me than it does to you, why some of us love sweet and some love savoury dishes, the level of cravings we experience, and even how quickly we feel full after eating.

But *epi*genetics is about how our genes are not our destiny. It turns out our cells change their behaviour, depending on what's happened to us, including our upbringing, what we eat, how much exercise we take, and countless other factors. It may even be affected by what our parents ate *before* we were conceived.

The idea that we may be able to influence how our cells respond, has potential in many areas of medicine – and weight control is no exception. These changes in cell behaviour may also reveal why someone who has yo-yo dieted may find it harder to keep the weight off than someone of the same weight who has stayed the same all their life. And, in future, it may help us learn how we can resist one of our strongest instincts in this post-starvation world of temptations.

Kate's verdict

What can we do to make these theories useful to us in real life?

Here are my tips:

- Use 5:2 as a tool to help you understand not only your appetite, but how much food you need to eat to feel full.

- Control your eating environment. Sit down at the table to eat your meals rather than eating in front of the TV or while travelling.

- If snacks are contributing to weight gain, then on a non-fasting day, try sticking to three meals a day, using the same distraction techniques we use on Fast Days (see page 22).

- Read more about *when* to eat, and meal frequency, in *Making sense of… when to eat,* page 148.

- Eat soup or always eat carbohydrates with proteins and a little fat to stay fuller for longer.

- If you *do* occasionally find yourself eating more than you intended, be kind to yourself. Our environment puts pressure on us, and willpower alone isn't always enough to resist temptation. After all, an occasional celebration meal, or one-off low-energy day when you break your no-snacking intentions won't derail your attempts to lose or maintain weight. Focus on the future, not the past.

5:2 Food Hero

CHICKEN

There are more chickens on Earth than any other bird, with more than 50 billion reared worldwide each year for eggs and meat. Chicken contains no carbohydrate, is high in protein and low in fat (if the skin has been removed). It's the most popular meat in both the US and the UK.

Nutrition

Chicken offers all the amino acids the human body needs, making it a 'complete protein'. And the breast, without the fatty skin, is the lowest in fat and calories: the darker the meat, the higher the fat content.

- **Calories** A small piece (100–110g) of lean, raw, skinless chicken breast is around 120–130 calories. One area of confusion can be the difference between raw and cooked. Raw chicken appears to be lower in calories than cooked, simply because cooking removes water and makes it denser. So, the same piece of chicken breast has the same number of calories before and after cooking, so long as no fat was added during the process.

- **Vitamins** Poultry is one of the best sources of B6, which aids the function of the immune system, the brain and red blood cells, as well as helping the body process carbohydrates.

- **Minerals** It's also rich in phosphorous, which helps cell and bone growth and repair, and selenium, which supports the immune system and helps regulate the thyroid.

Downsides

- **Food poisoning** Poor handling or cooking of chicken can lead to food poisoning.

- **Factory farming** Poultry production can be intensive and unpleasant, so welfare issues are worth considering if that concerns you (see box).

Animal Welfare

- If you're concerned about welfare, look for the RSPCA Freedom Food labels, which mean minimum standards for chickens and other farmed animals are met. For example, birds must be allowed to mature at a normal rate, they must have free access to outdoor pastures, and they must be fed a suitable diet.

- Consider organic or free range, if you can afford it (using smaller cuts or portions can make this more affordable). Or shop at farm shops or markets and ask questions.

- Corn-fed chicken is a different colour, but the taste is rarely significantly different.

How to handle raw chicken

- Refrigerate chicken as soon as possible after buying it, and always follow the 'Use by' dates.

- Always wash your hands before and after preparing chicken (and

other meats). Use separate cutting boards and utensils for raw
chicken and wash them well afterwards.

- Do NOT rinse raw chicken under the tap before preparing or
cooking. This can spread any bacteria present all over your kitchen,
increasing the risk of food poisoning. Instead, wipe the chicken with
kitchen paper.

- Check all the meat is opaque, with no hint of pink meat, before
serving. When pierced with a skewer or sharp knife, the juices
should run clear.

Recipe Ideas

Salad Days and Picnic Feasts

This is not a chapter about limp lettuce leaves, half a celery stick and cloying, artificially sweetened dressing. It's about salad days to celebrate with recipes that make the most of truly tasty, fresh ingredients in exciting combinations. The dishes are great for taking to work in packed lunches or even spontaneous, 'it's sunny, let's eat in the park' picnics. But these portable feasts aren't just for summertime. When the weather's cooler, the warming spices in the Tex Mex and Quinoa salads are satisfying and nourishing.

Be creative. Mix and match the dressings, add other ingredients from the calorie counter list (see page 358) and feast on freshness.

TEX-MEX BEEF SALAD

'CORONATION' QUINOA WITH ASPARAGUS AND ALMONDS

CRUNCHY CHICKEN SALAD WITH PARMESAN AND MUSTARD DRESSING

WARM PRAWN COCKTAIL SALAD

ROMAINE 'TACOS' WITH FRESH SPROUTS, AVOCADO AND CHEESE

MUSHROOM AND HERB PATÉ WITH MELBA TOAST

QUICK AND EASY CHILLI OMELETTE ROLL WITH TOMATO
AND RICOTTA FILLING

SMOKED MACKEREL WITH CRISP VEGETABLE REMOULADE

WHITE BEAN AND SPINACH SALAD WITH PECORINO PESTO

CROSTINI WITH FRESH TOPPINGS: MELON AND GOAT'S CHEESE/
BROAD BEAN AND FETA/PEAR AND BLUE CHEESE

PLUS …

MAKING SENSE OF… 5-A-DAY AND HEALTH BY NUMBERS

5:2 FOOD HERO: THE TOMATO (AND PEPPERS AND AUBERGINES)

5:2 Lives

IT TAKES TWO TO 5:2 – LOSING SEVEN STONE BY DIETING TOGETHER

'5:2 is definitely our way of life now and in the future! We now eat to live, not live to eat and food is not the be all and end all of our days.'
Carol and Peter, 64 and 66

Husband and wife Carol and Peter Chapman have lost seven stone between them in *their* 5:2 journey – proof that two can be better than one when it comes to revitalising your life and health.

Both were overweight and suffering the consequences before they tried intermittent fasting: Carol had needed knee replacements at the age of just 53, and Peter had high blood pressure and been diagnosed with 'pre-diabetes'. The physical effects were only part of the picture though. Carol says, 'I was a size 22/24 bottom and 18/20 top and felt really frumpy. I had always been a skinny child and teenager, actually only weighing 6st 12 when I got married in 1971. I hated being so overweight.'

The couple, from Worthing in West Sussex, started fasting twice a week in autumn 2012, after the *Horizon* programme explored the potential health benefits. At that stage, there were no books about 5:2 and Carol remembers feeling nervous – but had run out of other options. 'I was worried about the actual fasting aspect, but we thought we would give it a try. My husband was much keener than me as he had been told he was pre-diabetic. I was just over 17 stone and my BMI was over 40.

'I then joined Kate's 5:2 Facebook group and bought her book when it came out, which set me on the right path and gave support and inspiration when needed.'

It was a voyage of discovery for both of them: Peter, who is 66 and works part-time as an examiner and author, found it hard to stick to the 600-calorie limit for men when he tried to fit in three meals a day, so he switched to eating a single evening meal. He says 'I have learned to quite enjoy the hungry feeling rather than be agitated by it. I just know that people weren't designed to eat whenever they felt like it.'

And the result? Peter has lost over 25.5kg (56 lb) in weight, more than his initial target, and has kept it off. Plus he lost an impressive 25 centimetres (10 in) from his waist alone. His doctor also monitored him: Peter's blood sugar reverted to normal within three months of starting, and his cholesterol went down by a level his GP said was unprecedented.

Carol lost three stone (19kg or 42 lb), around four dress sizes, and had to go out and buy a completely new wardrobe! 'I still feel I have a way to go weight wise but I can now go shopping and find clothes that are flattering and fit. My mood was greatly improved through being happier in myself. I used to suffer migraines, which I think were hormonal. Now, although I still get a few headaches, I rarely get a full-blown migraine.'

But it's the extra energy that stands out for Carol, who took up exercise once she began to feel better about herself: 'Before 5:2 I despaired as to ever being able to move about easily again, which was frustrating as I used to enjoy sports and I just love to dance! When I first started it was hard to do a 45-minute class, which left me out of breath and bright red in the face. Now I go to classes three times a week. I can put so much more effort in without gasping for air.'

Peter and Carol's Fast Day diary

Peter and Carol love red bush or green tea during the day, plus a hot Bovril drink in winter, and they wait till after 5 p.m. to have dinner. Carol says: 'It can be a prawn stir-fry, large salad with chicken, tuna or salmon, a Quorn chili or a recipe from Kate's 5:2 or Hairy Bikers' recipe books. I have always exercised on a Fast Day without any problems. In the winter I do feel quite cold, but that is when I try to save a few calories for a warming chocolate Options, fill a hot water bottle and have an early night with a good book!'

Peter and Carol's non-fasting day diary

Carol says, 'I have never been a breakfast person and always felt guilty as I have always been told this was the most important meal of the day to kick-start your system. Now, if I don't feel like breakfast I don't have it.'

'We also do have a dessert on the weekend as a treat or maybe some chocolate, chocolate peanuts or nuts, but never as many as we used to have. Most of our desserts are fresh fruit – strawberries, raspberries or grilled pineapple with cinnamon served with Greek yoghurt.'

Peter has cut out most bread and potatoes, and aims to have two days of vegetarian eating per week, while Carol has cut out fizzy drinks, and most snacks. And they both still like to have an alcoholic drink now and then, as Peter explains. 'Carol drinks the odd glass of wine and I tend to finish the bottle! However, I don't drink anywhere near as much as I used to as my capacity has decreased with my weight loss, saving me a fortune!'

Favourite foods

Peter says, 'Now I really enjoy fish and many vegetarian options. I much prefer quality to quantity now.'

Carol says, '5:2 has awakened my taste buds. I never used to like steak but now I have learnt to cook it properly and enjoy a nice rib-eye or venison steak on a Saturday night.'

Best thing about 5:2?

Peter: 'I don't have to count calories. I weigh in each week and modify my lifestyle accordingly.

Carol: '5:2 has given me confidence in my life. I can also join classes at the gym without feeling that people are looking at "that old fat woman". I am me, and I am beginning to like myself again. 5:2 is definitely our way of life now and in the future!'

Carol and Peter's top tip

Only keep clothes that fit you, then you become aware of any weight gain at an early stage and can solve the problem quickly.

TEX-MEX BEEF SALAD

Calories per serving: 246

Nut free/gluten free/dairy free

This is the *ultimate* in satisfying salads – hearty, spicy and, yes, meaty. It is very popular with men and any cowboy or cowgirl who needs a fast, sustaining dish at lunch or dinner! It's also a great one to make for anyone who says 'Oh, you're doing that *starvation* diet, are you?', though, luckily, they're getting fewer these days!

Serves 1
Preparation time: 15 minutes
Cooking time: 6 minutes

pinch each smoked paprika, dried thyme and dried chilli flakes
50g lean sirloin steak 100 cals
1-cal cooking spray
¼ red onion, thinly sliced 10 cals
4 cherry tomatoes, halved 12–20 cals
¼ red pepper, sliced 7 cals
50g canned kidney beans, rinsed and drained 55 cals
1 tbsp sherry vinegar 2 cals
1 tsp extra virgin olive oil 45 cals
½ red gem lettuce, weighing 60g, leaves separated 10 cals
small handful coriander leaves 5 cals
salt and pepper

1. Put all the spices into a pestle and mortar, pound them to a powder and then rub them all over the steak. Spray a pan thoroughly with the 1-cal cooking spray (using up to 5 sprays) and place over a high heat. Add the steak and cook for 3 minutes on each side, or until just pink in the middle. Set aside to rest.

2. Put the red onion, cherry tomatoes, red pepper and kidney beans into a bowl. Whisk together the sherry vinegar and olive oil, season well and toss it with the bean mixture to coat.

3. Place the gem lettuce leaves on a plate and spoon the bean mixture on top. Slice the steak thinly then arrange the slices on top of the salad and serve.

More ideas from the 5:2 Kitchen The Tex-Mex spices are great with any meat, so you can try this with cooked chicken left over from the Sunday roast. And, on a non-fasting day, maybe have a nice cold beer, cowboy-style, with a slice of lime.

'CORONATION' QUINOA WITH ASPARAGUS AND ALMONDS
Calories per serving: 285

This dish was inspired by a delicious lunch overlooking the sea at the Byron Beach Café in Australia. My partner had never tried quinoa and this dressed the grains in a curry oil along with puy lentils, vegetables and halloumi. This version takes the main flavours and gives them a Fast Day makeover. The sweet and spicy 'coronation' flavours are loosely based on Coronation Chicken. You can save half the dressed quinoa, covered, in the fridge, to eat the next day. For a tangier version, omit the crème fraîche.

Serves 2
Preparation time: 7 minutes
Cooking time: 15 minutes

  100g uncooked quinoa 365 cals or 1 pre-packed 250g quinoa pouch 505 cals
    (due to added oil)
  200g asparagus 50 cals
  2–3 tbsp cider vinegar 4–6 cals
  1 tsp garam masala 5 cals
  ½ tsp turmeric 3 cals
  15g mango chutney 30 cals
  30g 0% fat crème fraîche (optional) 18 cals
  1 spring onion, finely chopped 2 cals
  10g sultanas 30 cals
  10g flaked almonds, toasted 63 cals
  fresh coriander, chopped, to garnish
  salt and pepper

1. If using dried quinoa, rinse well to get rid of any bitterness, and cook in 200ml of water for around 15 minutes, till water is absorbed. Drain and rest back in the pan for a few minutes to keep it fluffy. Steam or boil the asparagus for 3–8 minutes, depending on thickness, and set aside.

2. Prepare the dressing. Mix 2 tablespoons of the vinegar with the spices in a small dish. Chop any chunks in the mango chutney finely and add to the dish, with the crème fraîche, if using. Mix well and taste – if you like a tangier flavour, add a little more vinegar.

3. To assemble, mix the quinoa with chopped spring onion and the dressing, reserving a little to drizzle over the top. Spread quinoa over a plate, top with the asparagus then scatter over the sultanas, flaked almonds and coriander on top. Drizzle with the reserved dressing, season to taste and serve.

More ideas from the 5:2 Kitchen You could use long-stemmed broccoli in place of the asparagus. On a non-fasting day, double up on the dressing, and add a pouch of pre-cooked puy lentils to the dressed quinoa. For a very satisfying and delicious salad for four, thinly slice a pack of halloumi cheese and pan-fry it with a little oil to serve on top of the salad.

CRUNCHY CHICKEN SALAD WITH PARMESAN AND MUSTARD DRESSING
Calories per serving: 271 (including dressing)

Nut free

Do you like Caesar salad? You'll *love* this Fast Day alternative. It's a truly satisfying main meal dish, with lots of crunchiness from the croutons and the raw vegetables. Sliced raw asparagus is delicious, but if you prefer, blanch the stalks in a pan of boiling water for 2 minutes until just tender.

Serves 1
Preparation time: 20 minutes
Cooking time: 10–12 minutes

100g skinless chicken breast 120 cals
small slice wholewheat bread, weighing about 25g, cut into cubes 55–70 cals
4 spears of asparagus 13 cals
½ cos lettuce, chopped or separated into leaves and torn 10 cals
¼ cucumber, sliced 8 cals
1 medium celery stalk, thinly sliced 6 cals
black pepper

For the dressing

10g Parmesan, finely grated 42 cals
1 tbsp low-fat natural yoghurt 8 cals
1 tsp white wine vinegar 1 cal
1 tsp wholegrain mustard 8 cals

1. Preheat the grill to medium. Thickly slice the chicken, place on a baking sheet and season. Grill for 10–12 minutes, or until golden then turn over and cook the other side. Cut one of the thicker slices in half to check it's cooked. There should be no pink juices or fleshy parts inside. Place the chicken in a large bowl.

2. Add the bread cubes to the baking sheet and grill until golden on both sides then add to the chicken in the bowl.

3. Slice the asparagus diagonally along the stalk, or use a vegetable peeler to create thicker shavings. Put in the bowl with the chicken and bread then add the lettuce, cucumber and celery.

4. Mix together the Parmesan, yoghurt, vinegar and mustard and season with black pepper. Drizzle the dressing over the salad to serve.

More ideas from the 5:2 Kitchen On a non-fasting day, add olive oil to the salad just before serving, and maybe place a few extra shavings of fresh Parmesan on top.

WARM PRAWN COCKTAIL SALAD

Calories per serving: 217

Nut free

You might notice a bit of a 70s vibe in parts of this cookbook. Don't worry! No flares or Blue Nun wine required, but I definitely wanted to revisit some of the classics, like this one. I promise you won't miss the mayo. The prawns are warmed through in the pan with punchy spring onion and a dash of hot Tabasco, then coated in yoghurt.

Serves 1
Preparation time: 15 minutes
Cooking time: 5 minutes

1 Little Gem lettuce, cut into wedges or chopped 20 cals
½ baby avocado, around 40g 60–65 cals
½ cucumber, diced 15 cals
1 tsp sun-dried tomato paste 5–10 cals
1 spring onion, sliced 2 cals
juice of ½ lime 10 cals
couple dashes Tabasco sauce 3 cals
100g cooked prawns 80 cals
2 tbsp fat-free yoghurt 16 cals
25g pea shoots 6 cals
salt and pepper

1. Arrange the lettuce wedges in a bowl, then top with the avocado and cucumber.

2. Put the sun-dried tomato paste into a frying pan with 2 tablespoons of water. Add the spring onion and cook over a low heat for 1–2 minutes, or until it starts to wilt.

3. Stir in the lime juice and Tabasco and bring to the boil, then add the prawns and season well. Toss everything together then remove from the heat and stir in the yoghurt.

4. Spoon the prawns over the salad, top with the pea shoots and sprinkle over some freshly ground black pepper.

More ideas from the 5:2 Kitchen On non-fasting days, serve with crunchy croutons and swap the yoghurt in the dressing for soured cream for a slightly richer, but still tangy, cocktail sauce. Use the leftover avocado in the following recipe.

ROMAINE 'TACOS' WITH FRESH SPROUTS, AVOCADO AND CHEESE
Calories per serving: 122; 152 with sunflower or pumpkin seeds)

Vegetarian/gluten free

This was a spur-of-the-moment invention that tastes so much more indulgent than the ingredients suggest and is incredibly quick to make. Grow your own sprouts (see the instructions on page 337) and you will feel like Barbara from *The Good Life*.

Serves 1
Preparation time: 5 minutes

> fresh lemon juice for sprinkling
> ½ baby avocado, weighing about 40g, chopped 60–65 cals
> 2 large romaine lettuce leaves, weighing about 30g 5 cals
> 4 cherry tomatoes, quartered 12–16 cals
> 1 sliced spring onion or a few slices red onion 2–4 cals
> 30g fresh sprouted seeds and beans, such as mung bean 10–15 cals
> sea salt and black pepper
> ¼ tsp balsamic vinegar 1 cal
> 15g reduced-fat Cheddar cheese, grated 32 cals
> 5g sunflower or pumpkin seeds (optional) 30 cals

1. Sprinkle lemon juice over the unused half of the avocado and reserve it for another dish.

2. Arrange the lettuce leaves on a plate and place some chopped avocado in the centre of each then add the tomatoes, onions and sprouts. Season, drizzle over the vinegar then top with the grated cheese and seeds, if using.

More ideas from the 5:2 Kitchen Use romaine lettuce this way with any cold or warm taco filling (avoid getting it too hot so the lettuce doesn't wilt), from black bean stew to cold cooked chicken. Top with chilli sauce, jalapeño peppers, fresh sliced chilli or crème fraîche.

MUSHROOM AND HERB PATÉ WITH MELBA TOAST
Calories per serving: 54 plus 18 for two melba toast triangles

Vegetarian/gluten free served with gluten-free bread

First prawn cocktail; now this. It makes me come over all 'Abigail's Party'. But paté with melba toast is due a revival, and this paté is amazingly tasty for such a low calorie count. I love it even more than I love pineapple and cheese cubes on sticks.

Makes 4 servings
Preparation time: 10 minutes
Cooking time: 15 minutes

    5g dried porcini mushrooms 12 cals
    10g butter 74 cals
    2 cloves of garlic, crushed 8 cals
    1 red onion, chopped 38 cals
    200g mixed mushrooms, such as chestnut, button or shiitake, roughly
        chopped 26–40 cals
    2 tbsp half-fat crème fraîche 52 cals
    1 good handful fresh herbs, such as tarragon or thyme 5 cals
    2 slices of white or multi-grain bread, crust removed 70 cals
    salt and pepper

1. Soak the porcini in a couple of tablespoons of boiling water for at least 10 minutes. Heat the butter in a small saucepan over medium heat, add the garlic and red onion and cook gently for 5 minutes.

2. Snip or chop the soaked porcini into the pan, along with the soaking liquid and the chopped fresh mushrooms. Cook for 5–7 minutes, or until the liquid has evaporated.

3. Remove from the heat and season. Allow the mixture to cool a little then place in the bowl of a food processor with the crème fraîche and herbs (reserve a few for the garnish). Process until smooth, season and then spoon into 4 small ramekins or 1 larger bowl. (If you don't have a processor, chop all the ingredients very finely and mix in a bowl for a slightly rougher-textured pate.) Top with the reserved herbs. Cover dish with cling film and refrigerate until needed.

4. For the melba toasts, toast lightly in a toaster or under the grill. Use a very sharp, serrated knife to slice right through the middle of the bread, so you end up with 2 very thin slices for each original slice of bread. Cut each slice in half diagonally to form 8 triangles and grill, toasted-side down, for 3–4 minutes, or until the slices curl up.

More ideas from the 5:2 Kitchen This also makes an excellent topping for crostini (see page 112). On a non-fasting day, add a tablespoon of port, sherry or red wine to the saucepan and serve with lots of crusty French bread.

Melba toast tips Use a gentle sawing action to cut the bread rather than pressing hard. The toasts are very delicate (that's part of the appeal) but will keep for about seven days in a sealed plastic box (not in the fridge).

QUICK AND EASY CHILLI OMELETTE ROLL WITH TOMATO AND RICOTTA FILLING
Calories per roll: 83 plus 56 for filling

Vegetarian/low carb/gluten free/nut free

This is *so* easy, handy and adaptable it's no wonder this kind of egg roll is so popular in Japan and Korea. It's actually a one-egg omelette, flavoured and filled with your favourite ingredients and rolled up like a mini savoury Swiss roll – and it takes less than five minutes to make. Serve with a salad (the Chilli Beetroots from page 333 are excellent with this).

Serves 1 (1 for a good snack; 2 make a nice lunch or supper)
Preparation time: 5 minutes
Cooking time: 4 minutes

1 medium egg 78 cals
½ tsp dried chilli flakes (or, for a stronger flavour, use a few finely chopped
    slices from a fresh red deseeded chilli) 3 cals
1 small spring onion, snipped 2 cals
1-cal cooking spray
30g tbsp ricotta cheese 40 cals
3–4 sun-dried tomatoes, weighing about 10g, (not in oil), snipped 16 cals
salt and pepper

1. Break the egg into a mug or bowl, beat lightly, then season and whisk in the chilli and the
   spring onion.

2. Spray 1-cal spray on a small non-stick frying pan over high heat and pour in the egg mixture
   to cover the surface. Cook for 1–2 minutes then check with a spatula to see when it's
   brown underneath. If so, flip it over and cook for a further 1–2 minutes.

3. Transfer to a plate lined with a piece of kitchen paper to absorb any moisture and leave it to
   cool for a minute while you prepare the filling. Place the ricotta in a small bowl and stir in
   the tomatoes.

4. Spread the filling over the cooled omelette. Either eat as a roll with your hands, or cut into
   pinwheel slices.

More ideas from the 5:2 Kitchen Simply fill the roll with whatever
you'd put in a flour wrap. The egg roll has fewer calories and is high
in protein and low in carbohydrates, so will keep hunger pangs at
bay for longer. The homemade Kimchi from page 175 is fantastic in
this. Or, try a ham and cheese version, with a slice of each rolled up in
the pinwheel. You could also use smoked salmon with a little cream
cheese, or horseradish and thinly sliced beef. Vary the flavour of the
omelette itself with herbs like dill or basil to replace the chilli.

SMOKED MACKEREL WITH CRISP VEGETABLE REMOULADE

Calories per serving: 223

Gluten free/nut free

Remoulade, a fresh-tasting but satisfying salad with crunchy carrot and cabbage plus earthy celeriac, is a French classic. Rich, nutritious mackerel is the traditional accompaniment but here we've tweaked the recipe so the dressing is lower in fat, but still seriously creamy and luxurious.

Serves 1
Preparation time: 10–15 minutes
Cooking time: 3 minutes

    1 tbsp fat-free Greek yoghurt 8 cals
    1 tsp low-fat mayonnaise 13 cals
    juice of ¼ lemon 5 cals
    ½ celeriac, finely chopped into batons 22 cals
    1 carrot, finely chopped into batons 34 cals
    3 leaves sweetheart cabbage, finely chopped 5 cals
    ¼ tsp paprika 1 cal
    50g smoked mackerel 130 cals
    1 tbsp finely chopped fresh chives, to garnish 5 cals
    salt and pepper

1. Put the yoghurt, mayonnaise and lemon juice into a bowl. Whisk in 1 teaspoon cold water to loosen and season well. Add the celeriac, carrot and cabbage then toss everything together and set aside while you prepare the mackerel.

2. Preheat the grill until hot. Sprinkle the paprika all over the mackerel then grill until golden.

3. Spoon the remoulade onto a plate, top with the mackerel and serve sprinkled with the chives.

More ideas from the 5:2 Kitchen If you're not a fan of mackerel, the remoulade is equally delicious with three slices of Parma ham (93 calories). Or, it makes a great side dish for any grilled meat, a slice of quiche or a vegetable tart.

Kate's tip If raw vegetables are not your thing, blanch the vegetables first for just a few seconds to take the edge off the rawness but leave them wonderfully crunchy. Just fill a small pan with water and bring to the boil. Add the vegetables, cover and bring back to the boil, then drain immediately. Put in a bowl and stir in the dressing.

WHITE BEAN AND SPINACH SALAD WITH PECORINO PESTO
Calories per serving: 120; 200 with dressing

Nut free/vegetarian option

This is so colourful and tempting it disappeared in the blink of an eye at our photo-shoot, which is always a sign of a winning recipe! It's much more filling and generous than the calorie count would suggest, too.

Serves 1
Preparation time: 15 minutes
Cooking time: 5–10 minutes

4 cherry tomatoes, halved 12–15 cals
¼ small head broccoli, cut into florets 16 cals
5g pecorino cheese, grated 20 cals
1 tsp olive oil 45 cals
12 fresh basil leaves, finely chopped 5 cals
juice of ½ lemon 10 cals
50g canned butter beans, rinsed and drained 54 cals
25g cooked chicken breast, shredded 30 cals
30g baby leaf spinach 8 cals
salt and pepper

1. Preheat the grill until hot. Put the cherry tomatoes on a baking sheet and season well then grill, cut-side up, until just golden. Steam the broccoli florets and steam until just tender and set aside.

2. Make the dressing by whisking together the grated pecorino, olive oil, basil and lemon juice. Alternatively whiz all the ingredients together in a mini food processor.

3. Put the beans in a bowl and stir in the chicken breast, broccoli, tomatoes and spinach.

4. Spoon over the dressing, mix gently to coat and serve.

More ideas from the 5:2 Kitchen Vegetarians can simply leave out the chicken, and the salad with the dressing will come in at 170 calories. Or, add 25g reduced-fat feta cheese (45 calories) or fresh mozzarella (around 60 calories). The pesto works brilliantly on all kinds of dishes: add a clove of garlic if you like it, and make double to use on the salad for lunch, and with Courgetti Pasta (page 322) in the evening.

CROSTINI WITH FRESH TOPPINGS

Melon and Goat's Cheese/Broad Bean and Feta/Pear and Blue Cheese
Calories per 2 crostini: 86 (plus toppings, 82–156)
Vegetarian/nut-free options

Crostini are those lovely Italian toasts with tasty toppings, and here I've combined fresh vegetables or fruit with cheese. Some people would say it's cheating to eat something as carbohydrate-heavy as bread on a Fast Day, and it's certainly not compulsory. But if you cut bread very thinly (see cook's tips below), you can still get that satisfying crunch. Or simply use the same toppings on the lovely cup-shaped leaves of a Little Gem lettuce. I've listed the toppings and crostini separately. Each topping is enough for two sourdough or baguette crostini.

Makes 1 serving
Preparation time: 5–10 minutes
Cooking time: 3–5 minutes (broad beans only)

For the crostini

2 x 15g slices day-old sourdough or ciabatta bread 74 cals
30g rocket or peppery salad leaves 7 cals
1 tbsp balsamic vinegar or a little lemon juice 5–15 cals
sea salt and black pepper

1. Slice bread as thinly as possible with your sharpest serrated knife, using a soft sawing action without too much pressure. Toast under the grill or in a normal toaster. Toss the leaves with either the balsamic vinegar or the lemon juice.

2. Cover the bread with your choice of topping (see below) and place a few dressed leaves on top.

MELON AND GOAT'S CHEESE TOPPING
Calories per serving: 82

1 slice of peeled watermelon, weighing about 80g 28 cals
20g soft goat's cheese, without rind 54–83 cals
a few whole pink peppercorns and a few basil leaves, to garnish

1. Make the crostini as above and spread with the cheese. Top with the diced melon and a scattering of peppercorns and the basil.

BROAD BEAN AND FETA
Calories per serving: 94

50g fresh or defrosted frozen broad beans 44 cals
30g reduced-fat feta 48 cals
few mint leaves or whole chives, snipped 2 cals
salt and pepper

1. Boil the broad beans for 3–5 minutes (more for frozen). Drain in a sieve under cold water and then slip the thicker skins off each pod, revealing the bright green bean.

2. Mash the cooked beans and feta gently together in a bowl and spread onto the prepared crostini. Top with a few snipped herbs and season to serve.

PEAR AND BLUE CHEESE
Calories per serving: 123–156

½ a ripe pear, very thinly sliced, skin on 45 cals
25g blue cheese, such as dolcelatte or gorgonzola, very thinly sliced, or
  crumbled 78–100 cals
level tsp honey 23 cals or 5g crushed walnuts (optional) 33 cals

1. Layer pear and blue cheese in alternate layers on top of the crostini. Drizzle with the honey or scatter over the crushed walnuts, if using.

More ideas from the 5:2 Kitchen On a non-fasting day, you can make crostini crunchier by toasting them in the oven, drizzled with olive oil or spread them with a little butter.

Kate's tip Day-old bread makes good crostini. It is easier to slice than freshly baked, and toasting it takes away any stale taste. You can also freeze the slices, untoasted, in freezer bags and take them out, as you need them. It's a great way to use up bread that's too hard to eat untoasted!

Making sense of... 5-a-day (and health by numbers)

When so much health advice is controversial, isn't it nice to have a simple health goal everyone can agree on? Like 5-a-day: just eat five portions of fruit and vegetables every day (like the yummy salads in this chapter), and you'll be healthier and happier.

Except as we'll see, not everyone *does* agree. And, as for simple, if it's that straightforward, how come only one in five Britons manage to hit the target?

Health advice by numbers – does it add up?

5-a-day isn't the only health advice that we're given by numbers. There's also:

- 14–21 units: the weekly limit on alcoholic drinks

- 2 litres: the minimum amount of water we should be drinking each day

- 10,000 steps: the number we should be walking every day for good health

- 0.5 or below: what you should get when you divide your waist measurement by your height

Giving health advice as numbers is quick, memorable and clear. But just because it *sounds* definite, it doesn't mean it's always good advice.

The 5-a-day story

5-a-day was launched in the UK in 2003, which was 11 years after the first campaign in the USA. It started as a partnership between a cancer charity and fruit and vegetable growers, and since then, the campaign has spread to over 25 countries world-wide.

But the US has turned its back on 5-a-day, in favour of the Fruits and Vegetables More Matters campaign (fruitsandveggies morematters.org), with different portion guidelines depending on age, gender and activity level. For example it recommends up to nine portions for adult men.

Meanwhile, in Australia, where obesity is rising at a faster rate than anywhere else in the world, the advice is to have two portions of fruit and five of vegetables daily (gofor2and5.com.au).

So what is a portion? And does a potato count as a vegetable?

The guidelines on what counts as a portion *and* a vegetable vary country by country, too. Starchy vegetables like white potatoes don't count, but sweet potatoes often do. Legumes like baked beans or hummus *can* be a yes (watch out for added sugar, salt and fat) in some countries, while portion sizes could be anything from a tablespoon of pulses to 150g of fresh fruit. The World Health Organisation recommends 400g in total.

Despite the simple slogan, '5-a-day' can be complicated, and that's before we even look at the research.

Is five the magic number for improved health?

I've no idea. And neither do government advisors, nutritionists or scientists.

The reason the original campaign chose five portions is not clear, but studies reported since show mixed results. A review of 16 different studies involving 830,000 people (published in 2014 by Chinese and American universities) *did* conclude that consuming fruit and vegetables reduced the risk of dying from premature death and heart disease, though it didn't seem to make a difference with cancer. Each 'dose' of vegetables or fruit led to a 5 per cent cut in the risk of early death, and a 4 per cent cut in the risk of heart disease. However, that 'benefit' stopped once a person had consumed five portions. In other words, '5-a-day' would be about right.

Yet another reputable study earlier in 2014 by University College London found that there was no limit to the benefits from eating more fresh produce. People who ate seven or more portions a day had a 33 per cent reduced risk of death compared with people who ate less than one portion. The study looked at 65,000 people aged over 35 and living in England, and found that consuming vegetables appeared to be significantly better than consuming fruit. Oddly, consumption of tinned or frozen fruit seemed to show an *increased* risk of death.

Remember the confounders in the breakfast chapter? Studies don't always reflect bad *or* good habits. If four out of five of us don't manage to consume 5-a-day portions, then it's likely the minority who do are pretty health-conscious. In the UCL study, people who consumed more fruit and vegetables were likely to be older, be women, be of a higher social class and been educated for longer, and they were also less likely to smoke. Plus, we all have a habit of telling people, including scientists, what they want to hear rather than the whole truth.

One final study found that consuming fruit and vegetables doesn't make you lose weight if you eat them on top of your usual diet. A review by the University of Alabama at Birmingham confirmed that you do have to reduce what you eat, or use more energy, to lose weight. Eating a salad won't undo the effects of chocolate cake.

Kate's verdict

Exactly how *much* fruit and vegetables can protect our health isn't clear, but boosting our intake of vegetables in particular *is* a great plan for most people. When combined with proteins and a little fat, vegetables will help keep you full and support the body's functions, especially the immune and digestive system.

However, our knowledge has changed since 1991, and I feel the advice should reflect that. Drinking five glasses of fruit juice in a day would be a bad idea from a blood sugar/hunger point of view (see more about fruit sugars in *Making sense of... sugar and sweeteners*, page 302), so only whole fruit should 'count', and we should understand that variety brings the best mixture of nutrients.

KATE'S 5-A-DAY TIPS

- Aim for a 'rainbow' of at least five differently coloured vegetables and pulses per day.

- Enjoy fruit in moderation, and choose berries when you can. Eat whole fruit, and do not drink juice.

- Eat vegetables to replace over-processed starches, instead of having them in addition to white bread or white pasta, and so on.

Making sense of... units of alcohol

Trying to make sense of the advice about drinking alcohol is enough to, well, drive you to drink. A study by psychologists at the University of Sussex in England found a huge variation in drinking guidelines in 57 countries. There was disagreement about how much was safe for men and women, whether to have an alcohol-free day during the week, and even what a standard drink or unit of alcohol was.

In many cases, the guidelines seem to have been made up on the spot: one of the members of the UK team has been quoted as saying they were based, not on evidence, but 'an intelligent guess'! More significantly, most guidelines take no account of a person's overall size, which will affect how the body responds to alcohol. And while the UK recommendation of a maximum of 14 units of alcohol for women and 21 for men sounds clear, 77 per cent of Britons didn't know that there are 2.5–3 units of alcohol in a large glass (250ml) of wine!

Alcohol *is* a big concern, with rates of death due to alcohol-related liver disease increasing by 18 per cent in 2012 in the UK. That's not counting the rise in accidents and domestic incidents caused by excessive drinking.

Yet at the same time, we're given mixed reports about the possible health benefits of red wine, versus the high sugar content. It's no wonder we're so muddled.

Kate's Verdict

Moderate drinking *may* reduce the overall risk of premature death, according to one 2006 review of studies involving over a million people. But again, it could be about lifestyle: people who drink, but not to excess, are likely to be in control of their lifestyles generally.

My own guideline is to aim for three or four alcohol-free days per week. If I'm celebrating something, I do sometimes exceed the advice that women shouldn't drink more than 2–3 units in one day, but I'm particularly aware that alcohol increases the risk of breast cancer in women. With my family's history of the disease, it makes sense to be conscious of what I drink.

How much alcohol you drink is a very personal decision and I am absolutely *not* recommending you do the same as I do. To help you make *your* mind up, download *What's Your Poison?* from the NHS website. And don't overlook the *calorie* content of booze, either: a small glass of wine contains the same number of calories as a slice of Madeira cake, while a pint of lager is around 180 calories – more than many of the full meals in this book!

Making sense of... 'Drink 2 litres of water per day'

This advice dates back to 1945, but the evidence is hard to find. Yes, we need fluids to keep our body functioning, but we're actually pretty good at absorbing them from what we eat. Vegetables and fruit have a high water content, and even pizza contains 40–49 per cent water. Tea and coffee contribute to hydration too, despite the long-standing belief that they don't.

So why is the advice repeated so often? One report, by doctor and broadcaster Margaret McCartney, points out that – surprise, surprise – many of the messages about the dangers of dehydration come from organisations funded by companies producing bottled water.

But it's good for your skin, right? Well, maybe. It might increase blood flow to the capillaries (small blood vessels) in the skin, but the effect lasts for thirty minutes or fewer. So, you'd have to keep on sipping to stay dewy.

Kate's verdict

Do drink water throughout the day if you enjoy it – it's good to avoid dehydration, which can be uncomfortable. Being properly hydrated helps with weight control, as many people confuse thirst with hunger.

Personally, I don't stress about whether or not I am meeting the daily two-litre target. The exception to this advice would be people, such as those with a history of kidney stones, who are advised by a specialist to keep their water intake high.

Making sense of... 10,000 steps

Pedometers, which you wear on your body to keep track of every step you take, are the must-have gadget. I have a passionate love affair with my FitBit, and have even written about it in *5:2 Your Life*. But where does the advice to do 10,000 steps come from, and is there any science behind it?

The guidance is from Japan. The Japanese pedometer craze originated back in the 1960s and now every average Japanese household has 3.1 pedometers. But I couldn't find any *actual* evidence that 10,000 is a magic number, versus say, 9,000 or 11,000. In fact, 10,000 is said to come from the *name* of one of the pedometers first marketed in Japan.

There *is* evidence from some studies that owning a pedometer can increase the exercise you take by around 2,000 steps per day, though it's not clear if that change is permanent. However many steps you take, the evidence that being less sedentary can have very beneficial effects on overall health is growing and walking can be the easiest, cheapest way to achieve that.

Kate's verdict

Step on it! 10,000 is an easy number to remember and I know my pedometer definitely motivates me to be more active. But if you can't always meet the target, or prefer to swim or go to the gym, don't get stressed out. It's spending less time sitting down and more time being active that counts for most of us.

Making sense of... 0.5 or below

Slipping a tape measure round your waist could be the best way to discover your health destiny.

It's quick and easy, and may be much more reliable than the BMI, because being wider around the waist is an indicator of 'visceral fat' around your vital organs, which can be particularly dangerous.

You divide your waist measurement in centimetres or inches by your height, and if your number is above 0.5, then your risk of cardiovascular disease is high and may be lowered by losing weight. Take the measurement either around your natural waist (the slimmest part), or midway between the bottom of the ribcage and your hips.

Kate's verdict

As a quick measurement, this is extremely useful, and it is backed up by science. It's worth doing this every year or so, to keep on track.

5:2 Food Hero

THE TOMATO (AND PEPPERS AND AUBERGINES)

Many people know that the tomato is a fruit, not a vegetable, and this is because tomatoes grow like berries on the plant. There are more than 7,500 varieties of tomato worldwide, but they were originally found in South America. The tomato is part of the Nightshade family, which also contains goji berries, paprika, chilli peppers, potatoes – and tobacco.

Facts about the Med Three

- **Lycopene** is a substance found in tomatoes, and some other produce, which may protect against cancers *and* skin damage caused by the sun or inflammation. Cooking and canning tomatoes helps make this more available to the body.

- **Solanine** All three contain a compound, solanine, which is poisonous to insects that try to eat the stems and leaves (solanine is also what makes potatoes go green). This compound can cause inflammation and aggravate joint pain in a *very* small number of people who are sensitive to it. If your diet is rich in these ingredients, and you have arthritis, it may be worth talking to your doctor about whether excluding them from your diet may help.

- **Antioxidants** The capsicum (or bell) pepper is very closely related to chilli peppers or hot peppers but it is the larger peppers most commonly seen in the produce section, in green, yellow, orange or red, with the green the least ripe, and the red the most: red ones are also richer in antioxidant properties.

- **Vitamins** Tomatoes and peppers are rich in vitamins A and C.

How to buy and store

All three fruits are at their most flavoursome in the summer and autumn, though supermarkets usually stock them all year round.

- Look for taut, highly coloured examples with no wrinkling.

- Go to farmers' markets or local growers for the tastiest and widest variety of tomatoes in the summer, or grow your own cherry tomatoes on a sunny windowsill.

- Keep tomatoes out of the fridge in a bowl on the counter, but out of direct sunlight.

- Peppers and aubergines can be kept in a paper bag in the salad drawer.

- Deliciously chewy and savoury sun-dried tomatoes are useful in cooking. For Fast Days, choose those not preserved in oil.

How to cook

- Cooking tomatoes can increase the level of lycopene and roasting or grilling concentrates the sweet flavour, but raw tomatoes contain more vitamin C.

- Most aubergines no longer need salting to remove bitterness. Just stew, grill or roast them to make the most of them. They're great sliced thinly, and griddled, which emphasises the smokiness. Or, like red peppers, aubergines are great stuffed.

- Roasting or grilling really brings out the flavour of peppers. The skins are quite indigestible, so if you scorch them during the cooking process, place the peppers in a bowl covered with cling film. The steam will make it easier to remove the skins once cool.

Recipe Ideas

One-plate Feasts

FANTASTIC FLAVOURS FROM AROUND THE WORLD

Every dish in this chapter is a feast offering a generous collection of exciting flavours, each one adding up to a complete, satisfying meal. Some are higher in calories for when you want a single dish for lunch or dinner on a Fast Day, others are remarkable 'calorie value' for the portion size. The recipes are ideal for cooking when you're expecting family or friends: they'd never guess you were fasting unless you told them!

In this chapter you will find the whole world on a plate, from the Moroccan Lamb with Cauliflower 'Couscous' to the Asian-inspired Fish Parcels. Or enjoy tasting plates of antipasti, mezze, smorgasbord, thali or tapas, from Italy, the Middle East, northern Europe, India and Spain.

SUNSHINE MEZZE: FETA DIP, AUBERGINES WITH TAHINI, PITTA CHIPS

SPANISH TAPAS: ASPARAGUS TORTILLA, CATALAN ROAST VEGETABLES, NIBBLES

ITALIAN ANTIPASTI PLATTER: FIERY MOZZARELLA, TOMATO AND COURGETTE BRUSCHETTA, SALAD

SMORGASBORD WITH HOME-CURED FISH, SALAD AND RYE

VEGETARIAN THALI: MUSHROOM AND GREEN BEAN KORMA, RAITA, PICKLES

ASIAN SPICED FISH PARCELS WITH FENNEL, ONION AND CELERY, WITH RICE

MOROCCAN LAMB WITH CAULIFLOWER COUSCOUS AND HUMMUS DRESSING

RICH SALMON AND GNOCCHI BAKE

VEGETARIAN OPTION: VEGETABLE AND MOZZARELLA GNOCCHI BAKE

PLUS ...

MAKING SENSE OF... WHEN TO EAT

5:2 FOOD HERO: FISH

5:2 Lives

BACK IN THE SWIM OF THINGS, THANKS TO 5:2

*'It's wonderful to look forward to my summer
holiday without that dreadful feeling of
"what am I going to wear?"
I am in love with 5:2.'
Nicky, 39*

Like many women, midwife Nicky Wasawo was keen to get back into shape after the births of her two children, Noah and Millie. What she didn't know was *how* to lose the 16kg (35 lb) she'd put on since becoming a mum.

Nicky had tried conventional full-time dieting but 'I found it thoroughly miserable as you must diet day in day out. When I had a treat I would fall off the wagon for the rest of the week and literally eat as much as I could, as you can only start back on your diet on a Monday, can't you?'

Fed up with the yo-yo cycle, Nicky, who lives in York, heard about 5:2 in February 2013 and downloaded *The 5:2 Diet Book* the same day.

'I was on a mission that this was it: the plan for me!'

And Nicky was right: 'I lost 13kg (28 lb) in the first ten weeks just by doing 5:2 with no extra exercise. I never counted on feast days and just naturally ate more sensibly, but I certainly enjoyed my treats and meals out/takeaways. I always ate my full 500 calories on Fast Days.'

Her confidence growing, Nicky then felt ready to go back to one of her favourite forms of exercise. 'Before 5:2 there was no way I would be seen in a swimming costume now I go twice a week and just feel generally fitter and better for it. Swimming helped me lose the last 3kg (7 lb) and I finally achieved my pre-pregnancy target!'

Her husband Steve has benefited, too: 'He has also lost weight just by having the same evening meal as me on Fast Days.'

All dieters find that maintaining can be the tricky bit, and Nicky is no exception. But one blip and she was back on track. 'The only time I put weight on was over Christmas 2013. I had carried on with 5:2, but the treats were obviously a little too many and I ended up with a 4kg (9 lb) gain.

'I gave myself a bit of a talking to when I got to the beginning of Feb 2014 and all I did was cut back the treats on the feast days and I lost that 4kg (9 lb) in 2–3 weeks. I have maintained ever since.'

A slimmer body was the target, but Nicky says she's gained so much more, 'The main improvement for me has been confidence and positive outlook on life. Losing weight has affected my energy levels too: as soon as you add in exercise too, you feel so much better about yourself which in turn improves your mood and total outlook on life, which has a positive knock on effect to your family.'

Nicky's Fast Day diary

On my Fast Day I save all my calories up for my evening meal (around 8 p.m.). I often have a three-course meal on 500 calories. It's amazing how far you can stretch 500 calories when you need too.

If I struggle on my Fast Days I will have a coffee with skimmed milk or make a beef Oxo drink. My favourite hot drink is Mocha and if I really am missing one of these on a Fast Day I just make one with a spoonful of coffee and mix with a low-calorie hot chocolate and I have Mocha for 40 calories.

I often just tweak family meals so that we can all eat the same thing but I just skip the potatoes and have a side salad or a few new potatoes instead. That way my children don't know that I am eating any differently to them.

Nicky's non-fasting day diary

My whole attitude to food has changed. I find myself sometimes glancing at calories in something and when it is a little high you automatically think, "Wow I managed the whole day yesterday on less calories than that wrap. Do I really want it?" It really is amazing psychologically to think I only have to diet or fast two days a week.

Favourite foods

Lasagne, lamb, any meat in a nice creamy sauce, pizza and, of course, fish and chips! I love stodgy filling food. Sticky toffee pudding and cream is one of my favourite puddings and I am quite partial to a bit of pink champagne or a cocktail!

Best thing about 5:2?

I have the best of both worlds. Gone are the days of me feeling miserable when we get invited to a last-minute BBQ when I have to restrict what I eat and not drink alcohol. I just think, 'Right. I will fast the next day and enjoy the BBQ. Plus, no embarrassing weigh-ins, hanging your head in shame when you are told you have put weight on. However, be warned the only expense is buying new clothes as the weight drops off, but there is nothing more exciting than having to take smaller clothes into the changing rooms. I seriously just want the world to know how amazing it is. I regularly try to spark up conversations with random overweight strangers just in case I can steer the conversation to include chatting about 5:2.

I am totally in love with 5:2 it has changed my attitude to food in a great way.

Nicky's top tip

If you are struggling on a Fast Day have a large drink, such as water, sugar-free squash, flavoured water, a diet drink, coffee or flavoured tea. Look at the clock and give yourself twenty minutes and I guarantee you that in twenty minutes you will really feel so much better and are not as hungry.

SUNSHINE MEZZE: FETA DIP, AUBERGINES WITH TAHINI, PITTA CHIPS

Calories per mezze plate: 303

Vegetarian/vegan (aubergine dish only)/gluten free (served without pitta)

This is a mixture of my favourite flavours from Greece, Turkey and the Middle East: lemon, thyme, garlic, sesame and pomegranate. And if that sounds like a messy mezze, it isn't, the cuisines blend brilliantly on the plate.

Serves 2
Preparation time: 20 minutes
Cooking time: 5–6 minutes

Feta dip
Calories per serving: 52

    70g 0% fat Greek yoghurt 39 cals
    30g lower fat feta-style cheese 54 cals
    leaves from two sprigs thyme
    pinch dried chilli flakes, to taste
    juice of ½ lemon, zest from ¼ lemon 10 cals

Aubergine and chickpeas with tahini
Calories per serving: 152/145

    150–175g aubergine, trimmed and sliced into 16–20 discs 35 cals
    1-cal cooking spray
    ½ red onion, chopped 19 cals
    1 tsp ground cumin 5 cals
    120g cooked chickpeas or ½ 400g can chickpeas, rinsed and drained 130 cals
    2 tsp tahini and 2 tsp hot water 60 cals
    1 tsp sesame seeds 32 cals
    finely chopped fresh parsley, to serve 2 cals
    2 tsp pomegranate molasses 20 cals or 1 tsp ground sumac
        5 cals
    salt and pepper

Crudités and wholewheat pitta dippers
Calories per serving: 108

150g cherry tomatoes, halved 30 cals
75g radishes, halved if large 8 cals
1 medium cucumber, cut into sticks 30 cals
2 mini wholewheat pitta breads, grilled 148 cals

1. Combine all the ingredients for the Feta Dip except the lemon juice and chilli flakes in a small bowl. Add chilli flakes to taste, drizzle over the lemon juice and sprinkle the zest on top. Sprinkle over a few more chilli flakes, if you like, and set aside.

2. Spray 1-cal cooking spray onto a griddle and heat to high. Add the aubergine discs and cook for 4–5 minutes on each side, until wilted and charred with griddle lines.

3. Meanwhile spray a small saucepan over a low heat with 1-cal cooking spray. Add the onion and cumin and cook for 2 minutes then add the chickpeas and heat through for 2 more minutes.

4. Place the grilled aubergine discs round the edge of a platter or two serving dishes and tip the warm chickpea mixture into the centre and set aside. Combine the tahini and hot water in a small dish, mix vigorously with a spoon till emulsified. Pour across the dish, sprinkle over the sesame seeds and parsley, drizzle with the molasses or sprinkle with sumac. Season at the table and serve with the Feta Dip, pitta chips and crudités.

More ideas from the 5:2 Kitchen Sumac is a delicious red spice with a lemony, peppery flavour. It works well on Middle Eastern salads, dips and meat dishes, but you can use lemon juice and black pepper if you don't have sumac. For tastier sesame seeds, toast them gently in a dry pan and remove as soon as they begin to brown.

SPANISH TAPAS: ASPARAGUS TORTILLA, CATALAN ROAST VEGETABLES, NIBBLES

Calories per serving: 340; plus choice of side nibbles: 44–52

Vegetarian (tortilla and roast vegetables only)

The word tapa means 'cover' or 'lid', as, originally, these dishes began as little pieces of bread given to drinkers to stop flies landing in their sherry. Escalivada is the Catalan version of French ratatouille, with much less chopping involved. Traditionally, the vegetables would be cooked in the embers of a fire to give the smokiest flavour. *Buen provecho!*

Serves 2
Preparation time: Escalivada 15 minutes; Tortilla 5 minutes
Cooking time: Escalivada 50 minutes; Tortilla 25 minutes

Escalivada roast vegetables
Calories per serving:129

  2 peppers (red or yellow) 60 cals
  200g aubergine (1 large or 2 small) 40 cals
  2 white or red onions, peeled and halved 76 cals or 1 bunch chunky spring
     onions 50 cals
  175g ripe tomatoes (about 3) 35 cals
  1 tsp olive oil 45 cals
  1 tbsp sherry or red wine vinegar 2–5 cals

Asparagus tortilla
Calories per serving: 211

  1 small white onion, chopped 38 cals
  2 cloves garlic, chopped 8 cals
  150g fine asparagus or green beans, cut into 2cm pieces
     41 cals
  ½ tsp olive oil 22 cals
  4 eggs, beaten 312 cals
  salt and pepper

Nibbles
Calories per serving: 44–52

50g anchovies in oil, drained 88 cals or 6 thin slices of cooked chorizo sausage 102 cals or 100g pimento-stuffed olives, drained 103 cals

1. To make the escalivada, preheat the oven to 180°C/350°F/Gas mark 4 and line a roasting tray with foil. Smear a little oil on both your hands, then rub them all over the vegetables (except the tomatoes) to coat, then place them on the roasting tray.

2. Roast for 25–30 minutes, or until the peppers are charred, then turn the vegetables over and roast for another 25 minutes or so, and add the tomatoes. If the onions start to burn, cover with a little foil.

3. After roasting, place the vegetables in a bowl and cover with cling film. Leave for 10 minutes so the skins can steam, making them easier to remove. When just cool enough to handle, remove the stalks, seeds and any skin that slips off easily (I don't mind some remaining).

4. Cut the vegetables into chunks. Add a little of the 'juice' from the serving pan and use a fork to mash the vegetables up to form a loose purée. Add the oil and the vinegar, if using, and stir it through the mixture. Season well with salt and pepper and set aside.

5. Make the tortilla by gently frying the onions, garlic and asparagus or green beans in the olive oil in a small non-stick frying pan over a low heat for 5 minutes, or until cooked but not browned.

6. Tip the fried vegetables in a bowl, stir in the beaten eggs and season well. Increase the heat under the frying pan to medium and add a few drops more oil if needed. Pour in the egg mixture, making sure the vegetables are distributed well in the mixture. Cover with a lid and cook for 9–10 minutes. After a few minutes, check the underside of the tortilla by lifting up the edge with a spatula. If there are any signs of burning, reduce the heat.

7. To turn the tortilla, remove the lid and place a large plate on top of the pan. Holding the plate and pan together firmly, flip both over so the tortilla lands on the plate, uncooked-side up. Then slide the uncooked side down onto the hot surface of the frying pan. Don't worry if a little of the egg slides off, just add back to the pan and cook for another 8 minutes till lightly caramelised.

8. Cut the tortilla into four wedges and place two on each plate: heap the escalivada alongside it, along with the olives, anchovies or chorizo.

More ideas from the 5:2 Kitchen Try red peppers or par-boiled sliced potatoes in the tortilla. On a non-fasting day, serve with crusty bread and a little tomato rubbed onto the cut bread first in place of butter, and maybe a glass of chilled Manzanilla sherry and some almonds. The tortilla will keep in the fridge for 24 hours, and the escalivada for 2–3 days.

ITALIAN ANTIPASTI: FIERY MOZZARELLA, TOMATO AND COURGETTE BRUSCHETTA, SALAD
Calories per serving: 319

Italian food is much more than pasta and pizza. At its best, it's about the kind of naturally tasty produce that this colourful plate provides. The recipes are simple, but buying the best ingredients pays off in fresh, zesty flavour.

Makes 2 servings
Preparation time: Mozzarella 15 minutes; Bruschetta: 8 minutes

Fiery marinated mozzarella
Makes 2 servings (but easy to halve)
Calories per serving: 185

  1 pack buffalo milk mozzarella, torn into small pieces 360 cals
  1 tbsp capers, chopped 3 cals
  ½ small fresh red chilli, deseeded, finely chopped around 2 cals
  1 tbsp lemon juice 4 cals or juice of ½ lemon 10 cals
  few oregano leaves (optional)
  salt and pepper

1. Place all of the ingredients into a shallow dish and toss lightly to coat. Leave to marinate for at least 10 minutes, turning halfway. You can leave this to marinate for longer in the fridge, but remove it 10 minutes before serving to return to room temperature.

Rocket and olive salad
Calories per serving: 22

40g rocket or mixed leaves 10 cals
10g pitted black olives, rinsed if brined or packed in oil, finely chopped 33 cals

1. Combine the rocket with the olives. Season and set aside.

Tomato and courgette bruschetta
Makes 4 servings
Calories per serving: 112

120g mixed ripe tomatoes (including yellow if available), finely diced 24 cals
½ red onion, finely diced 18 cals
1-cal cooking spray
1 medium courgette, sliced very thinly lengthways 34 cals
60g ciabatta bread, cut into 4 slices 148 cals or 2 small crusty rolls weighing
    30g each, halved 180 cals
1 clove garlic, halved

1. Place the diced tomatoes and onions on a plate lined with kitchen paper to absorb any
   excess liquid. Spray a griddle or frying pan with 1-cal cooking spray, place on a medium
   heat and cook the courgette slices for 4 minutes. Turn them over and add the bread to the
   pan. Cook bread and courgettes for 4 more minutes.

2. Rub the halved garlic onto the grilled bread then top with the tomato, red onion and then
   the courgettes. Divide between 2 plates, and serve immediately with the cheese and salad,
   seasoning everything to taste.

More ideas from the 5:2 Kitchen The second portion of mozzarella
is delicious melted on the pizza on page 165.

SMORGASBORD WITH HOME-CURED FISH, SALAD AND RYE
Calories per serving: 333 calories

Nut free

Scandinavian cuisine has a healthy, tasty reputation and this dish lives up to that: two piquant salads, home-cured fish and dark nutty rye bread squares. Strictly speaking a 'smorgasbord' is a buffet table, but I think this almost fits the bill! You need to cure the fish the day before, but it's so much nicer to pickle your own fish than buy ready-prepared rollmops.

Serves 1
Preparation time: 20 minutes, plus overnight marinating

For the pickled herring or mackerel
Calories per serving: 179/174

  3 tbsp white wine vinegar 6–9 cals
  1 tsp golden caster sugar 15 cals
  pinch mustard seeds
  100g very fresh herring 158 cals or mackerel fillet 153 cals

For the beetroot salad
Calories per serving: 40

  1 cooked beetroot, quartered or chopped 35 cals
  1 tbsp freshly chopped dill 5 cals
  squeeze lemon juice

For the cucumber salad
Calories per serving: 21

  ¼ cucumber, sliced into long fingers 7 cals
  1 tsp capers 3 cals
  2 cocktail gherkins, chopped 3 cals
  1 tsp wholegrain mustard 8 cals

For the rye squares
Calories per serving: 93

1 tbsp quark 10 cals
thin slice dark rye bread weighing 40g 80 cals
3 radishes, sliced 3 cals

1. Mix together the vinegar, sugar and mustard seeds in a shallow sealable container. Add a pinch of salt and stir everything together. Place the herring or mackerel fillets flesh-side down in the liquid and chill overnight.

2. When you're ready to eat, toss the beetroot with the dill and squeeze over the lemon juice. Spoon the mixture onto the side of a large plate.

3. Arrange the cucumber on the plate. Mix together the capers, gherkins and mustard and spoon on top of the cucumber.

4. Spread the quark over the rye and cut in half. Top with sliced radishes and add to the plate.

5. Lift the herring or mackerel out of the cure, roll it up and secure it with a wooden cocktail stick. Set it onto the plate to serve.

More ideas from the 5:2 Kitchen If you make double quantities, you can create a deli-style sandwich for the day after your fast, wrapping the fish and salads together in a wrap or linseed roll.

VEGETARIAN THALI: MUSHROOM AND GREEN BEAN KORMA, RAITA, PICKLES

Calories per serving: 241 for thali

Vegetarian/vegan/gluten free

I love all kinds of curry, but have a very soft spot for korma. The richness of the sauce seemed to make it a no-no for Fast Days, until I decided to try using almond milk in place of cream and full-fat yoghurt. That swap, plus cutting right down on the nuts, makes for a deliciously creamy sauce that is still light and fragrant. Served with the raita, plus the crunchy pickles on page 331, you have a fast-day thali that's a true feast. Or make cauliflower rice (see page 320) to soak up the sauce.

Serves 2
Preparation time: 5 minutes
Cooking time: around 20 minutes

Mushroom, almond and cashew korma with apricots
Calories per serving: 173

½ tsp coconut oil 22 cals
1 small red onion, sliced 38 cals
1 clove garlic, crushed 4 cals
2cm-piece peeled ginger, weighing 5g, grated 4 cals
1 small green chilli, finely chopped 5 cals
½ tsp garam masala, ¼ tsp each cinnamon and ground cardamom 5 cals
150ml almond milk 20 cals
10g cashew nuts 59 cals
10g flaked almonds, reserving a few for garnish 63 cals
200g mushrooms 26 cals
100g fine beans or sugar snap peas 27–42 cals
40g dried apricots, snipped 72–90 cals

1. Heat coconut oil in a non-stick saucepan over a low heat. Add the onion, garlic, ginger, chilli and spices and fry very gently for 3 minutes. Then add the almond milk, and the nuts. Simmer gently for 7 minutes. Blend with a stick blender, pour into a cup and set aside.

2. Fry the mushrooms in the same pan for 3 minutes over medium heat. Don't move them around too much, so they brown nicely. Add the beans or peas and the snipped apricots then return the spiced sauce to the pan. Simmer for 6–8 minutes, or until the beans or sugar snaps are tender.

Pomegranate and mint raita
Calories per serving: 43; 98 with vegan coconut yoghurt

> 100g 0% fat yoghurt 55 cals or coconut yoghurt 185 cals
> few fresh mint leaves, chopped
> 30g pomegranate seeds 30 cals
> Instant Pickles (see page 331), to serve 25 cals

1. Combine the yoghurt with the chopped mint leaves and top with the pomegranate seeds.

2. Serve the korma in one bowl, sprinkled with the reserved nuts, with the raita and pickles in separate dishes on the side.

More ideas from the 5:2 Kitchen The second portion of korma will keep in the fridge for a day. Reheat it gently and, on a non-fasting day, serve it with a chapatti or naan to scoop up all the sauce.

ASIAN-SPICED FISH PARCELS WITH FENNEL, ONION AND CELERY
Calories per serving: 374

Gluten free/dairy free

Steaming fish in a parcel is so easy and makes the most of all those delicate flavours. Here the fish is topped with an amazingly zingy Thai-inspired pesto, plus there's nutritious brown basmati to soak up every drop of the juice from the parcel.

Serves 2
Preparation time: 15 minutes
Cooking time: 20 minutes

Rice
Calories per serving: 166

> 100g brown basmati rice 332 cals
> pinch salt

Fish parcels
Calories per serving: 146

> ½ fennel bulb, thinly sliced 31 cals
> 1 medium stick celery, thinly sliced 6 cals
> ¼ red onion, thinly sliced 9 cals
> 2 x 150g Pollock fillets 243 cals
> 3 radishes, halved 3 cals
> salt and pepper

Coriander pesto
Calories per serving: 62

> Small handful coriander leaves and stalks 5 cals
> ½ lemongrass stalk, chopped 5 cals
> 2 tsp grated fresh root ginger 4 cals
> 15g toasted cashew nuts 88 cals
> juice of ½ lime 10 cals
> ¼ tsp sesame oil 11 cals
> 1 tsp Chinese rice vinegar 1 cal

1. Preheat the oven to 200°C/400°F/Gas mark 6.

2. Put the rice in a pan and cover with 250ml water. Add a pinch of salt then cover with a lid and bring to the boil. Turn the heat right down low and simmer for about 20 minutes, or until all the liquid has been absorbed. Fluff up with a fork and set aside but keep warm.

3. Make the fish parcel. Divide the fennel, celery and onion between 2 large squares of non-stick baking paper and season. Place the fish on top and scatter over the radish halves. Spoon 1 tablespoon of water over the top of each. Fold over the baking paper and twist each end to make a parcel. Put on a baking sheet and bake in the oven for 20 minutes.

4. Make the pesto by adding all of the ingredients to a food processor. Season with a pinch of salt, and then process to make a paste.

5. Take the fish out of the oven and put each parcel on a plate. Open up each parcel and serve half the pesto on top of each portion of fish with half the rice.

More ideas from the 5:2 Kitchen Make extra pesto to serve with any plain fish or poultry, or use it to top stir-fried vegetables and sesame-smoked tofu.

MOROCCAN LAMB WITH CAULIFLOWER 'COUSCOUS' AND HUMMUS DRESSING
Calories per serving: 337

Gluten free/dairy free

As richly fragranced as a Moroccan spice bazaar, this dish is fantastically satisfying. The 'couscous', made from cauliflower, does a terrific job of soaking up the sauce and the hummus dressing, with just a fraction of the calories of real couscous. This is a meal for sharing, but the lamb will freeze in individual portions.

Serves 4
Preparation time: 30 minutes
Cooking time: around 1 hour

1 tsp olive oil 45 cals
300g diced lamb 864 cals
2 whole garlic cloves 8 cals
4 shallots, peeled 28 cals
2 carrots, chopped into chunks 68 cals

2 medium celery stalks, chopped into chunks 12 cals
½ fennel bulb, chopped into chunks 31 cals
½ red pepper, chopped into chunks 15 cals

¼ tsp each cayenne, paprika and
    turmeric 3 cals
½ tsp each ground cumin and
    coriander 5 cals
½ cinnamon stick
4 dried apricots 20–35 cals
200g tinned tomatoes, chopped
    36–50 cals
300ml hot chicken stock 11 cals

½ cauliflower, broken into florets 50
    cals
50g canned chickpeas, drained and
    rinsed 54 cals
juice of ¼ lemon 5 cals
1 tbsp tahini 90 cals
pinch paprika
salt and pepper

1. Heat the oil in a flameproof casserole and brown the lamb quickly. Lift out and set aside.

2. Add the garlic, shallots, carrots, celery, fennel and pepper and cook in the pan for about
   3–5 minutes until starting to turn golden. Stir in the spices and cook for 1–2 minutes.
   Return the lamb to the pan with the apricots, tomatoes and stock. Cover and bring to a
   simmer. Turn the heat right down low and simmer for 45 minutes to an hour, or until the
   lamb is tender.

3. Meanwhile, place cauliflower florets in a food processor. Blitz to break down the florets until
   it looks like couscous. Put in a pan with 100ml water, cover and bring to the boil. Cook for
   5 minutes, or until tender, stirring from time to time. Season well and set aside but keep
   warm.

4. Make the hummus dressing. Put the chickpeas in a food processor or blender with the
   lemon juice, tahini and paprika. Pour in 50ml cold water and whiz until smooth.

5. Divide the cauliflower rice among four bowls, followed by the lamb tagine. Drizzle over the
   dressing and serve.

To freeze the lamb, spoon it into a freezer-proof container and leave
to cool. Seal the containers then freeze for up to three months. To
use, thaw overnight in the fridge then reheat in a pan with a splash of
water to loosen the sauce.

More ideas from the 5:2 Kitchen The hummus dressing is also
terrific on steamed vegetables like broccoli, carrots or green beans.

INDULGENT SALMON AND GNOCCHI BAKE

Calories per portion: 449; Vegetarian option: 432

Vegetarian Option: Vegetable and Mozzarella Gnocchi Bake

Nut free/vegetarian option

This Italian-inspired beauty is higher in calories than many recipes in the book, but many of us do find it more convenient to have a single nutritious dinner at the end of a Fast Day. And you'll be looking forward to this one with its healthy but hearty salmon, its great flavours and the pure comfort of cheese and gnocchi. This recipe is easy to scale up to feed a crowd, too.

Serves 1
Preparation time: 20 minutes
Cooking time: 20 minutes

1-cal cooking spray
1 spring onion, chopped 2 cals
½ red or green pepper, chopped 15 cals
3 spears long-stemmed broccoli weighing 60g, chopped 16 cals
2 tinned artichoke hearts weighing 67g, rinsed, drained and quartered 20 cals
200g chopped tomatoes 40 cals or ½ 400g tin of chopped tomatoes 46–50 cals
100ml vegetable stock 3 cals
1 tbsp freshly chopped dill 5 cals
100g fresh gnocchi 130–160 cals
100g skinned salmon fillet, chopped 140–200 cals
40g medium-fat cream cheese, such as Philadelphia Light 58–64 cals
5g Grana Padano or Parmesan cheese, grated 19–21 cals
salt and pepper

1. Spray a cold non-stick frying pan with 1-calorie oil (or your own spray) and place over a medium heat. Add the spring onion and pepper and cook for 3–4 minutes then add the broccoli and artichoke hearts and cook for another 2 minutes.

2. Stir in the chopped tomatoes and stock, season well and simmer. After 5 minutes, stir in the dill and remove from the heat but keep warm. Preheat the oven to 200°C/400°F/Gas mark 6.

3. Spoon the gnocchi into a small ovenproof dish and arrange the salmon fillet on top. Spoon over the sauce and dot the surface with the cream cheese. Sprinkle the cheese evenly on top then bake in the oven for 20 minutes.

4. For the vegetarian option, omit the fish but add more vegetables, such as a whole pepper and twice the artichoke hearts (35 extra calories), plus 50g reduced-fat mozzarella (87 calories) along with the cream cheese.

Making sense of... when to eat

You read it here first: snacking is *so* over.

We've been told for years that eating frequently during the day raises the metabolism. In other words, we'll burn more calories (or energy) if we keep fuelling the body, so it never feels like it's running on empty. Fitness instructors and food companies like to call this grazing, rather than snacking.

So why are increasing numbers of 5:2 folks – including me – opting for a single meal at lunchtime or evening rather than the 'grazing' approach? And why did the leading researcher on intermittent fasting, Krista Varady, opt to give participants in many of her studies a single 500-calorie meal on their fasting day, rather than spreading out mini-meals during the day?

That's what I wanted to find out. And the more I've read, the more I've realised that grazing is *not* essential for good health. In fact, for many of us, eating *less often* is a more effective weapon against excess weight.

What is metabolism and what affects it?

Metabolism is the chemical processes in the body that keep us alive, including growing, renewing cells and using energy. In the media, it's often used to mean *just* the process of breaking down the food we eat to give us energy. That energy is then used in our daily activities, to help us repair or renew our cells and systems, or it can be stored as glycogen or fat (see more on this on page 276).

Our 'basal metabolic rate' (or BMR) is how much energy in calories our body needs to maintain the most critical metabolic functions: the bare necessities that carry on when we're resting or asleep, like breathing, circulating blood and maintaining our body temperature.

Our genes, age, gender, weight and height all influence our BMR, but it's only half the story. Our body composition (how much fat and muscle we have) also has an effect, and a higher percentage of muscle means we burn more energy than someone the same weight but with more fat and less muscle. We do much more than sleep or exist, so our total daily energy expenditure (TDEE) will be higher than our BMR. It depends on what we do, including how active we are at work, at home and in any leisure time.

Can you 'speed up your metabolism' by eating more?

This is one of the ideas behind grazing. The theory was that by keeping our body in a mode where we're digesting food and using the energy constantly, we'd also use more calories and therefore potentially lose more weight.

I was shocked to discover the evidence for this is thin to non-existent. And that, in fact, there are only two proven ways to increase your metabolism. You can either increase your muscle mass (something that's hard to do, especially for women) or increase your heart rate (mainly through stimulants, including caffeine or medication).

A 1997 review of studies about meal frequency found only one, out of 179 studies, suggesting that eating frequently gave better weight loss or health results than eating the same number of calories in fewer meals. The single 1989 study that showed potentially better health results in terms of cholesterol and insulin involved a 'nibbling diet' of 17 snacks each day – pretty time-consuming and difficult to maintain – and studies since haven't shown the same results. In fact, some have shown the opposite, with short-term fasting raising the heart rate and therefore the metabolic rate in some people in one 2000 study at Vienna University: perhaps as an energy boost to prompt us to go hunting, back in ancient times.

The problem with most research into meal frequency, and diets in general, is that they are self-reported (the eater tells a researcher what they ate) so they may not be accurate. And, as we've seen with breakfast research, there can be 'confounders' (those unrecorded factors, like whether people smoke, or take exercise) that can skew results.

Resisting more frequent temptation

The more meals you fit into your day, the more temptation there is to overeat. You might even tell yourself that snacking or grazing is speeding up your metabolism and use that excuse as a reason to justify having a little more. Even if you're not thinking that, the more times you're faced with a choice, the more possibilities there are to pick foods that are high in calories – or to simply underestimate how much we're eating.

Of course, it's not the same for everyone. What I am saying, again, is that you know yourself best, and you can only be guided by your *own* instincts on whether frequent meals make you eat more, or less.

What about *the time* when you eat?

One of the other things we're often told is that if we eat late, it'll affect how much fat our body will store, as we'll struggle to 'digest' the food properly once we're asleep.

Again, this *seems* to make sense, but it underestimates the body's ability to get on with the job, without any conscious instruction from us. In fact, there are no studies showing that food eaten late at night 'creates' extra fat in the body, though it *might* raise blood sugar for a longer period while we're asleep than if we'd eaten during the day while we were more active.

The bigger issue is that late-night eating can be a sign of emotional eating, or eating after a few drinks, which may mean we consume more calories than usual because we don't have the same level of willpower. And, of course, a full stomach at bedtime can make it harder to sleep. But the same meal, eaten at whatever time of day, will give the body the same amount of energy.

Time-based diets

If we limit the times we can eat, we're likely to reduce the calories we consume and find it easier to stick to than full-time dieting, as with 5:2. And it's also likely that we may find that easier to stick to than a diet that says 'eat less of this kind of food, all the time'.

In 2014, intermittent fasting pioneer Dr Krista Varady was part of a team that reviewed studies of what they called 'time-restricted feeding'. That might be limiting eating to certain times of day, or only eating during a 'window' that might last between three to twelve hours. Their conclusion was that both human and animal studies showed potential benefits in terms of reduced body weight *and* improved results in health tests. It's definitely an area where more research is needed.

5:2 is, of course, one of those approaches. By placing a strict limit of 500–600 calories twice a week, we're cutting our overall consumption, so long as we don't overdo it on the other days (which most of us find we don't).

More than a way to keep eating under control?

There may be other health advantages to fasting and time-based eating, which is what makes 5:2 so appealing, particularly the potential for the body to switch from a growth mode into a 'repair' mode, whereby cells are either repaired, tidied up or allowed to die when they stop functioning properly.

The role of insulin – which regulates blood sugar in our bodies – is also a factor. Insulin circulates after eating, to help move energy into the cells – but while it's present, the body can't burn stored fat. So leaving longer periods between eating, plus avoiding snacks, allows insulin to drop and the body to call on fat stores. More research is needed, but till we have that, we can at least be clear that 5:2 and other time-restricted diets are strategies to manage the daily food temptations that can lead to weight gain or health issues.

The dreaded starvation mode

There's one more big fear to tackle: 'starvation mode'. Dieters fear that by lowering their calorie intake for one or two days, their body will 'hoard' energy and undo all their good work.

The quick answer? It almost certainly won't happen, if you stick to one or two days' fasting at a time.

The longer answer? There is *some* evidence that in the long-term, people on reduced-calorie diets may experience lower weight loss than expected because the body works hard to combat the effects of starvation (see page 88). However, that's only after around 3–4 days of very little or no food, that potentially undesirable changes begin to take place. Even then, the human body can survive for many weeks with no food at all (though that's *not* recommended).

The good news for people trying intermittent fasting or intermittent calorie restriction is that though the body *does* try to become more efficient when it senses long-term calorie restriction, the cycle of varying fast and non-fasting days is likely to work against that. Plus, for the first two days of a fast, at least one study in 2000 has shown the metabolic rate to rise due to an increase in adrenalin: as I suggested, this may be to prime us to look for food.

Over time, as you lose weight, your basal metabolic rate *does* reduce a little, as does your overall energy requirement, because your body has to use less energy in shifting you around (try carrying a medium-size dog or weights around for ten minutes to see how much more tired it makes you). In addition, when you lose weight, part of that weight is muscle – and as we saw above, muscle helps to keep metabolism high.

Doing some resistance training during your weight-loss regime may help combat this. There are also indications that intermittent fasting may reduce the percentage of muscle mass lost, compared to conventional dieting. This evidence has come from studies of alternate-day fasting, so we don't know if this applies to 5:2, and it is certainly an area to watch.

The bad news about yo-yo dieting

If, like me, you've been a yo-yo dieter before – losing and then regaining weight several times, on any weight loss regime – then this might negatively affect your metabolism. If you've dieted several times to reach your goal weight, you may need fewer calories than someone who weighs the same but has always been the same size. This isn't specific to 5:2 or intermittent fasting, and it's another reason to try to find a weight loss method that works for you, first time.

Kate's verdict

So, when to eat? After more than two years of intermittent fasting, I know what works for me: it's eating fewer meals, snacking less often, and 'checking in' on myself mentally to ensure I am eating because I am *hungry*, rather than because someone else says it's time. It's a bit frustrating that my previous yo-yo dieting might have affected by metabolism, but that means I am even more determined to keep my weight stable now.

Limiting our eating 'windows' can be a flexible and effective strategy and I know I'm not alone in understanding that intermittent fasting is easier and more enjoyable than calorie counting 24/7.

5:2 Food Hero

FISH

Fish has played a vital role in the human diet since prehistoric times, and its nutritional benefits – plus the ease of preparation – make it as much as a winner now as it was in the Stone Age.

All about fish

There are more than 30,000 different kinds of fish, but only a small percentage tastes good. White fish, like cod, haddock and pollock, is light, fast to prepare and low in calories. Oily fish, like salmon, fresh tuna, mackerel and herring, is satisfying and intensely flavoured. It *is* higher in oil – around 10–25 per cent, and therefore calories, but a little goes a long way. Oily fish also has essential fatty acids, and fat-soluble vitamins, that help the brain and body function properly.

If you eat fish, the recommendation is to eat AT LEAST two portions each week, one of which should be oily fish.

Nutrition

White fish is lower in fat and calories. For example, a 100g portion of pollock contains around 81 calories. For that, you get a great source of protein, which helps to keep you full, and a range of minerals.

Calorie counts for oily fish vary from 140 to over 200 calories per 100g, depending on fat content and how it's been prepared. Among the many beneficial nutrients oily fish offers are Vitamin D and long-chain omega-3 fatty acids, which the body *can* make itself, but only very slowly. Consuming it has benefits for the heart and circulatory system, and can help the joints and nervous system.

Downsides

- **Allergies** Most allergies to fish are caused by seafood or shellfish, so if you have any kind of reaction, see your doctor for further tests.

- **Mercury** Some fish, including mackerel, can contain high levels of mercury and other pollutants, so it's usually advised that children, and women who are pregnant, planning to become pregnant, or breast-feeding, should eat no more than two portions of oily fish a week. The rest of us can eat up to four. Adults can eat as many portions of white fish as they like.

How to buy and store

Sustainability and freshness are the two main concerns when it comes to buying fish.

- Sustainability can be a concern because certain methods of fishing, including over-fishing, will damage the environment. See www. fishonline.org to discover more, but one of the simplest ways to help is to eat varied species, rather than one single kind of fish. If you have a fishmonger or specialist counter, ask questions about the source.

- Freshness makes sense from a flavour and nutritional point of view, as well as safety. Fish must be refrigerated, kept on ice or frozen.

- Wash your hands before and after handling raw fish, and always prepare fish on a different board or work surface.

How to cook

The best cooking methods involve preserving the flavour, and, on Fast Days, choosing methods that add as little fat as possible.

- A marinade flavours fish, but also cuts down on cooking time: juices and oil help to tenderise the flesh so it cooks more quickly.

- Both baking and grilling are fast and enable you to enhance the flavours with herbs, spices or other vegetables.

- Poaching keeps the fat content down while preserving the best texture. It works best with white fish.

- Pan-frying, rather than deep-frying, is another option, using a little coconut oil or a low-fat spray and spices.

Recipe Ideas

Vegelicious

GO GREEN FOR BETTER DINNERS

My transformation from picky vegetable avoider to vegetable lover is complete. Not only do I now prefer courgetti to traditional pasta, I am also addicted to cauliflower pizza.

I'll never lie about the things I don't like. I dismissed fishy-tasting 'zero' noodles as a step too far for me the first time I tried them. But each of these recipes has earned its place. This chapter is a celebration of the wonderful (and occasionally the weird) vegetables you can find in the produce aisle and the bean kingdom. And even if you're not a vegetarian, you could cut calories *and* bills by making one of your Fast Days meat-free.

GREAT BIG VEGGIE BURRITO BOWL

HOME-MADE PIZZA WITH CAULIFLOWER BASE
AND BLUE CHEESE TOPPING

IMAM BAYILDI

GRIDDLED RED CHICORY WITH BLUE CHEESE AND WALNUT MELT

SAVOURY SUMMER CRUMBLE WITH TOMATO AND HERBS

CHARGRILLED VEGETABLE PLATTER WITH SMOKY ROMESCO SAUCE

TWO-COLOUR COURGETTI WITH RICH TRUFFLED MUSHROOMS

KOREAN KIMCHI PICKLE WITH STIR-FRY TOFU

CHILLI CHICKPEA NUGGETS WITH MANGO DIPPING SAUCE

PLUS …

MAKING SENSE OF… BUYING GOOD FOOD

5:2 FOOD HERO: ONION, GARLIC AND FRIENDS

5:2 Lives

STANDING TALL AFTER LOSING OVER SIX STONE

'My skin glows, I look younger, I stand straighter and taller, have an intense feeling of wellbeing – and I've lost 31kg (70 lb)!'
Sharon, 53

Sharon Munsey finds it hard to know where to start when it comes to describing the revolution 5:2 has brought to her life. It's not just the obvious things – like the fact she's dropped five dress sizes and 40 kg (88 lb) in just under eight months.

It's also the difference when she goes to the supermarket. 'I feel proud of my shopping trolley nowadays and don't need to hide the cream cakes and chocolate underneath other things as I want to show off all the beautiful, healthy items I'm buying!'

And the improvement in her back pain: 'I used to have horrible sciatica but none at all for several months.' And the lack of mood swings, the energy after doing exercise, 'or the fact I now feel able to exercise at all!'

Sharon, from Bideford in North Devon, only started 5:2 in January 2014 after deciding to have 'another crack at attempting to lose weight. I've been overweight forever, certainly I was a big teenager and my weight and size has crept slowly but steadily upwards ever since, peaking at 137kg (302 lb), which shocked me. When I started 5:2 I was in the right mind to lose weight. I liked the idea that on the 5:2 nothing is banned, there are no sins, no "naughties".'

As Sharon prepared for her first Fast Day, 'I expected to feel low or headache-y on Fast Days due to low blood sugar but in reality I feel the opposite. I have loads of energy and I'm mentally sharp on Fast Days. I look forward to them, and I never thought I would hear myself saying that.'

Sharon, who works in a stressful job as a mental health day centre manager, decided that to get maximum weight loss, she'd also count calories on her non-fasting days: she's found it helpful in making better choices. 'In the run-up to Christmas 2013, before 5:2, I kept a food diary and realised that I will need to drastically drop my calorie intake in order to lose weight so I combine 5:2 with calorie counting (on Fast Days and non-fasting days).

'Whilst not strictly "pure" 5:2 I wanted to lose weight quickly over the first few months in order to keep me motivated. I don't need the sugar any more, or bread and potatoes. In fact I find bread stodgy and it makes me feel bloated.'

Instead, she loads up on vegetables. 'I laugh at those who eat 5 a day as I can top them with at least 7 a day!'

Sharon, who has been married to Jon for 33 years, is still losing as she approaches her target.

She's also had more energy to exercise. 'At first it was difficult but I had an exercise bike that was being used as a place to hang things so I dusted it off, plonked it in front of the TV and now I cycle away whilst watching *EastEnders* four times a week.'

As a veteran of other diets, why does Sharon feel *this* one is sustainable for her? 'This way of eating has changed my life and is something I will stick with even when I reach my goal (and I WILL get there!).'

Sharon's Fast Day diary

7:30 a.m. cup of red bush tea, no milk.

Various times over the morning: glasses of water to shut up my grumbling stomach.

1:30 p.m. cup of proper coffee with a little milk and a nectarine.

4 p.m. 14 picota cherries and glass of water.

I will be having dinner at around 7 p.m.: Yellow turkey curry (which contains lots of vegetables) with cauliflower rice. If I've any calories spare I will have some fresh pineapple with a little quark (a fantastic discovery since starting the 5:2; *delicious*).

I aim to eat around 500 calories on Fast Days. It's rarely much lower than this and if it goes as high as 550 I don't worry.

Sharon's non-fasting day diary

I aim to eat around 1350 calories a day on normal days but if over or under by 100 calories I don't fret too much. I'm enjoying vegetables SO MUCH MORE with this diet.

Breakfast: porridge with blueberries and wheat bran (very cheap and healthy).

Lunch: vegetable soup of some description and a piece of fruit (a peach, a nectarine or an apple).

On the drive home from work I have another small piece of fruit to keep me going till dinner. This used to be a 'danger time' for me, a chocolate-scoffing time so I've replaced this with fruit, which I enjoy very much.

Dinner: I aim to have a main meal of between 400 and 500 calories. If I have any spare calories I will have a gin with Slimline bitter lemon (which feels very grown-up and retro but I like it).

Favourite foods

Porridge! Pineapple and melon – I could eat every single day and never get bored.

I really love steak and duck and I have them both in stir-fries. Soup, especially butternut squash with fresh ginger and chilli. I didn't believe that soup could be so filling and satisfying until I started the 5:2 and made the soups from Kate's recipe book.

Thai curries. I loved going to Thailand and the food there was amazing. I love that I can still make these curries on the 5:2 with or without meat.

Best thing about 5:2?

It's working! I'm losing weight steadily AND feel so much healthier. I now look forward to every meal, Fast or non-fasting day. I enjoy each mouthful, eat more slowly, chew more and really enjoy the food mindfully.

Sharon's top tips

Choose your Fast Days for busy days so that you are distracted and focussed on something else. Mine are Tuesdays and Thursdays, my busiest days at work.

Reward yourself! I used to reward and comfort myself with chocolate and cakes. Now I treat myself to a massage every 2 weeks which relaxes me, makes me feel great and I love it when she comments that she can see and feel the difference in my body.

GREAT BIG VEGGIE BURRITO BOWL

Calories per serving: 262 plus 18–22 for optional cheese topping

Vegetarian/vegan option/gluten free

This colourful, generous dish has all the flavour punch of a Mexican burrito – without the wrap. A burrito (meaning 'little donkey') can be way too stodgy even when you're not fasting, so this recipe cuts calories but delivers on taste. We've made it even more fast-friendly by replacing the higher-carb, higher-calorie rice with cauliflower rice. It's a sociable meal, this one, great to serve to family or friends (see note for extra suggestions), but don't be put off by the list of ingredients, you can leave out one or more parts if you don't have the ingredients handy.

Makes 2 servings
Preparation time: 15 minutes
Cooking time: 5–7 minutes

Green 'rice'
Calories per serving: 50

> 250g cauliflower florets 63 cals
> 1 tbsp chopped fresh coriander 5 cals
> 1 fresh green chilli (more if you like hot food), trimmed and deseeded 5 cals
> 2 spring onions, trimmed 4 cals
> ½ tsp coconut oil 22 cals

1. Add all the ingredients except the oil to a food processor. Use the pulse button to get a texture between rice and couscous.

2. Heat the coconut oil to a high heat in a large non-stick pan, add the green 'rice' mixture and fry for 3–4 minutes, or until lightly browned.

Black beans
Calories per serving: 68–74

1 clove garlic, crushed 4 cals
½ red onion, chopped 19 cals
½ tsp ground cumin and ½ tsp smoked paprika or ground cayenne 5 cals
120g canned black beans, rinsed and drained 108–120 cals
water or vegetable stock

1. Spray a small saucepan over a low heat with 1-cal cooking spray. Add the garlic, onion and the spice of your choice and fry gently for 2–3 minutes then stir in the beans and heat through for 3 minutes. Add just enough water or stock to stop the beans drying out. Set aside.

For the sides
Calories per serving: 144

75g diced avocado flesh 120 cals
10 cherry tomatoes, halved 30 cals
2 large spring onions, sliced lengthways 4 cals
4 jalapeño peppers in brine (from a jar), sliced 1–2 cals
100g rinsed and drained canned sweetcorn kernels or thawed frozen
     sweetcorn kernels 90 cals
2 level tbsp 0% fat Greek yoghurt 17 cals or 0% fat crème fraîche 18 cals
pinch smoked paprika or cumin
1 Little Gem lettuce, leaves separated and washed 16 cals
½ lime, cut into 2 wedges 10 cals
20g low-fat cheddar cheese, grated (optional) 43 cals or reduced fat feta,
     crumble (optional) 36 cals
salt and pepper

1. Place the avocado, cherry tomatoes and spring onions into separate serving bowls. Arrange the rice, beans and vegetables in large flat bowls. Place the yoghurt or crème fraîche in a bowl, season well and sprinkle with smoked paprika or more cumin if you like. Invite guests to use the lettuce leaves to make mini vegetable rolls with their choice of ingredients. Serve the grated cheese for scattering, if using, and wedges of lime.

More ideas from the 5:2 Kitchen Use a red chilli to give a different colour to the rice, and slice red cabbage or kale in place of the lettuce. On a non-fasting day, add a few tortilla chips or use soured cream in place of yoghurt.

HOME-MADE PIZZA WITH CAULIFLOWER BASE AND BLUE CHEESE TOPPING
Calories per serving: 296–326

Vegetarian/gluten free/low carb

I keep wishing I had shares in a cauliflower farm: it's such a versatile vegetable, and is one 5:2 folks swear by. First it was cauliflower rice and cauliflower 'couscous'. Now we have cauliflower *pizza*. The Internet is alive with different versions, and this is mine. It is deeply savoury, gloriously cheesy – yet lighter than wheat, and fabulous if you're avoiding gluten. It looks fiddly, but it's not, and the blue cheese is wonderful with the cauliflower. Each pizza is a really good size, and very filling for one person. Along with the pea soup, this might just be my favourite dish in the book.

Makes 2 x 20cm pizzas
Preparation time: 15 minutes
Cooking time: 20–22 minutes

Base

400–450g cauliflower florets 100–113 cals
½ tsp dried chilli flakes or dried mixed herbs 3 cals
1 clove garlic 4 cals
20g finely grated hard cheese, such as Cheddar or Parmesan 80–84 cals
1 medium egg, beaten 78 cals
50g reduced-fat 'rubbery' cheese, such as mozzarella 87 cals or Emmental
    137 cals or 50g soft goat's cheese with herbs or other flavourings 135 cals
1-cal cooking spray

Topping

50g gorgonzola or dolcelatte cheese 155 cals
2 tbsp tomato purée 10 cals or 2 tbsp sun-dried tomato paste 28 cals
1 red onion, thinly sliced 38 cals
90g plum or cherry tomatoes, halved 18 cals
120g sprouting broccoli, (about 6 stems) steamed until tender 23 cals
2 tbsp tomato purée 10 cals or 2 tbsp sun-dried tomato paste 28 cals
handful fresh basil or rocket leaves 5 cals
black pepper

1. Process the cauliflower florets in batches in a food processor to a flour-like texture. You can grate it by hand but it'll be hard work! (Optional: microwave the 'flour' for two minutes. This seems to help the mix adhere but is not essential.)

2. Press as much moisture as possible out of the mixture using kitchen paper. Do this twice or three times before making the dough. Set the flour aside.

3. Preheat oven to 220°C/425°F/Gas mark 7. Line two baking sheets with silicone coated baking parchment and pre-heat. Place the flour in a bowl, add the chilli or herbs, garlic and grated hard cheese and combine, adding freshly ground black pepper. Make a well in the centre of the mixture, add half the egg and use your fingers to begin to mix into 'dough'. Add the 50g of mozzarella, Emmental or goat's cheese from the base ingredients and combine with your hands and add more egg if needed.

4. Divide the mixture into 2 balls and place them on the lined baking sheet. Press down on the balls with your hands to form a thin pizza base of around 20cm, pushing the mixture carefully out to the edge, keeping it as even as possible. The mixture may break up, so just re-patch it with your fingers. If you like, spray a little 1-cal cooking spray on the top to increase the crispiness.

5. Place in the oven and bake for 15–17 minutes, or until crisp. Check it after 10 minutes and if the edges are burning too much then turn the heat down to around 200°C/400°F/Gas mark 6.

6. Remove the pizzas from the oven and add the topping ingredients. Start by carefully spreading the sun-dried tomato paste or tomato purée over the base then scatter over all other ingredients, except the basil or rocket, and bake for 5 minutes or until the cheese melts.

7. To serve, trim any blackened edges (or leave them – I like those best) and add the rocket or basil leaves.

More ideas from the 5:2 Kitchen The base is a blank canvas: add a cheese, two veg and some flavourings/herbs for your favourite pizza.

IMAM BAYILDI

Calories per serving: 205–225

Vegetarian/vegan/low carb/gluten free

The origins of this fabulously flavoured, rich, stuffed-aubergine dish are Turkish. According to tradition, the name means 'the imam fainted', either in pleasure at the taste, or because he was horrified by the quantity of expensive olive oil used in making it. He'd be less shocked with our Fast Day version, because we've cut right back on the oil, but without losing the taste. I've given double quantities because it's as delicious served at room temperature the day after making!

Serves 2
Preparation time: 5 minutes
Cooking time: 45 minutes

 2 aubergines weighing 225–250g each 90–100 cals
 1 tbsp extra virgin olive oil, plus extra for brushing 135 cals
 1 red onion, sliced 38 cals
 300g ripe tomatoes, chopped 60 cals
 2 garlic cloves, finely chopped 8 cals
 1 red pepper, chopped 30 cals
 ½ tsp cumin seeds 2 cals
 ½ tsp ground cinnamon 3 cals
 ½ tsp paprika 2 cals
 1 tbsp vacuum packed sun-dried tomatoes, snipped (about 15g) 24 cals or
    1 tbsp sultanas 45 cals
 1 tbsp red wine vinegar 2 cals
 1 tbsp sun-dried tomato purée 10–20 cals
 small handful fresh parsley (ideally flat-leaf), chopped, to serve 5 cals
 salt and pepper

1. Heat oven to 200°C/400°F/Gas mark 6. Trim the stalks from the aubergines, halve them lengthways then score the flesh in a chequerboard pattern, without cutting right through the bottom. Use a pastry brush to apply oil very sparingly, season, and bake on a baking sheet for 25 minutes, or until the aubergine flesh is soft.

2. While the aubergines are roasting, add 1 teaspoon of the olive oil to a non-stick frying pan. Add the onion, tomatoes, garlic and peppers. Let them fry gently, for around 10 minutes, to soften.

3. Remove aubergines from the oven and lower temperature to 160°C/300°F/Gas mark 2. Scoop out the cooked aubergine flesh, using a spoon or melon baller, but leave the skins intact. Add aubergine flesh to the pan, along with the cumin, cinnamon, paprika, sun-dried tomatoes or sultanas, vinegar and tomato purée. Stir everything together, season and cook gently for another 10 minutes.

4. Pile the mixture into the aubergine skins. Return to the oven and bake for another 20 minutes. Check halfway through cooking and if there's any sign that the sultanas or vegetables are burning, cover with foil.

5. Drizzle the remaining oil on top of the aubergines. Sprinkle the parsley over the cooked aubergine, and serve with a green salad. If not eating immediately, leave the dish to cool then place it in the fridge in a covered container. To serve hot, reheat each half in microwave for 45–60 seconds on high. Or, you can serve these at room temperature within 24 hours.

More ideas from the 5:2 Kitchen: On a non-fasting day, double the amount of oil, and serve with crusty bread or warmed pitta.

GRIDDLED RED CHICORY WITH BLUE CHEESE AND WALNUT MELT
Calories per serving: 158

Vegetarian/gluten free

This is super-quick, tasty *and* really elegant looking. I'd happily serve it as a starter to friends. I'd always found chicory a little bitter, but griddling it transforms it into something new: bitter*sweet,* with the soft melting cheese and crunch from the nuts. Serve with something soft and creamy, like the white bean mash from page 325.

Serves 1
Preparation time: 3 minutes
Cooking time: 4–5 minutes

> 2 red chicory weighing about 140g in total 27 cals
> ½ tsp olive oil 22 cals
> 15g creamy gorgonzola or other blue cheese 50 cals
> 40g 0% fat crème fraîche 24 cals
> 5g chopped walnuts 35 cals
> salt and pepper

1. Heat a non-stick griddle or frying pan to medium-hot. Cut the two chicory heads in half lengthwise, keeping the end intact. Using a pastry brush, apply a little oil to the cut sides of the chicory then place them cut-side down on the griddle or pan. Grill for 3 minutes.

2. Meanwhile, make the sauce. Mash the cheese with a fork and beat together with the remaining oil and the crème fraîche.

3. Turn the chicory over and warm for no more than 1 minute on the other side. Place on a plate, cut-side up, and spoon over the cheese sauce. Sprinkle over the walnuts and season to serve.

More ideas from the 5:2 Kitchen This technique works well for other firm heads of lettuce, including radicchio or even romaine. Cut into wedges or quarters, and check every 60 seconds during griddling to ensure leaves brown but don't burn. Use pine nuts or pecans in place of the walnuts.

SAVOURY SUMMER CRUMBLE WITH TOMATO AND HERBS

Calories per serving: 224

Vegetarian

Crumbles don't always have to be sweet as this fantastic summery savoury bake proves. I like to make this in a retro-style tin pie dish, the red tomatoes just peeking through the crunchy topping. It's a very adaptable recipe, and incredibly fast, too. If you make extra portions of the crumble mix, freeze them individually and then simply sprinkle over prepared vegetables before baking.

Serves 1
Preparation time: 8 minutes
Cooking time: 20–25 minutes

> 5g wholewheat flour 16 cals
> 20g reduced fat Cheddar, cubed 44 cals
> 5g walnuts 35 cals
> 2 sprigs of thyme, plus extra for the vegetables
> 1 clove garlic (optional) 4 cals
> 10g rolled oats 36 cals
> 200g mixture of cherry and plum tomatoes 40 cals
> 1 red or yellow pepper 30 cals
> ½ red onion, peeled and chopped 19 cals
> few drops sriracha or Tabasco sauce (optional) 3 cals
> salt and pepper

1. Preheat oven to 200°C/400°F/Gas mark 6. For the topping, pulse the wholewheat flour, Cheddar, walnuts, 2 sprigs thyme and garlic in a food processor until well mixed. Then add the oats and pulse briefly so they're reduced in size, but not pulverised. If you don't have a processor, chop the topping ingredients finely, then combine. Season to taste and set aside.

2. Chop the tomatoes and pepper into equal-sized small chunks.

3. Spray the base and sides of a shallow ovenproof dish with 1-cal cooking spray. Place all of the vegetables into the dish (not the tomatoes) adding a few drops of the hot sauce, if using, and a few more sprigs of thyme if you like. Now layer the tomatoes on top. Season

well then sprinkle the topping evenly over to cover, but allow some of the tomatoes to peek out.

4. Bake for 20–25 minutes, or until the topping is crisp and brown. Check it near the end of cooking time. If the oats are starting to burn cover them with foil. Serve with a rocket and pea shoot salad on the side.

More ideas from the 5:2 Kitchen Swap the thyme for a good pinch of paprika, dried herbs or mustard powder in the crumble. Crumble 25g reduced-fat feta cheese (45 calories) among the vegetables before adding the tomato layer. Or, for a wintry version, use the topping over a mixture of pre-fried mushrooms and leeks. On a non-fasting day, add more topping or add a further sprinkling of Cheddar on top of the oats 10 minutes before the end of cooking time.

CHARGRILLED VEGETABLE PLATTER WITH SMOKY ROMESCO SAUCE
Calories per serving: 148–155

Vegetarian/vegan option

This is my homage to the 'calcot fiestas' of Barcelona – an entire party season devoted to the calcot. It looks like a giant spring onion, and it is barbecued until the outer leaves are black. You have to wear an apron to protect your clothes from the sweet juices. My version is less messy, but just as tasty, thanks to the red Romesco Sauce: it's smoky, nutty and absolutely delicious with more than just vegetables, so I've given the directions to make four servings, while the vegetables serve one. You can use roast peppers from a jar to skip the grilling stage. The vegan, olive-oil version is fruitier while the cream cheese version tastes smokier. Both keep for 3–5 days covered, in the fridge.

Sauce makes 4 servings
Chargrilled vegetables serve 1
Preparation time: 12 minutes
Cooking time: 15–18 minutes

Romesco sauce
Calories per serving: 76; 83 with cream cheese

75g ripe tomatoes 15 cals
2 cloves garlic 8 cals
½–1 mild fresh red or green chilli pepper 4 cals
1 red pepper, halved 30 cals
30g stale bread 66 cals
2 tbsp sherry or red wine vinegar 4–6 cals
½ tsp smoked paprika 3 cals
20g blanched almonds or hazelnuts (or a mixture) 122–138 cals
small handful fresh parsley 5 cals
1 tbsp olive oil 45 cals or 50g Philadelphia light 73 cals

Chargrilled vegetables
Calories per serving: 72

1-cal cooking spray
3 large continental spring onions or baby leeks, weighing about 70g, trimmed
    22 cals
200g mixed fresh vegetables, such as 75g baby courgettes 15 cals, 100g
    portobello mushrooms 26 cals and 25g baby carrots 9 cals
salt and pepper

1. Preheat the grill to high. Line a grill pan with foil, and add the whole tomatoes, garlic, chilli and halved pepper. Grill for around 10 minutes, turning halfway. Add the bread just before the end of grilling so it browns but does not burn.

2. Place the grilled vegetables in a bowl. When cool enough to handle, slip off the garlic, tomato and pepper skins, remove cores and seeds from the pepper and chilli.

3. In a food processor, blend the bread to crumbs, then add the vegetables, but only half the chilli pepper, the vinegar and the paprika. Process to a paste and set aside. Toast the nuts in a dry non-stick pan till they brown then add those to the processor and pulse until roughly ground. Finally add the parsley and either oil or cream, and process till it makes a sauce. Taste and add the second half of the chilli pepper if you like a hotter sauce.

4. To prepare the vegetables, slice them into even chunks or slices, but slice the spring onions in half or quarters lengthways, keeping the fresher green ends, but discarding the root end. Harder vegetables like carrots can be sliced thinly or parboiled for 2–3 minutes to soften slightly.

5. Spray 1-cal cooking spray on a griddle over a high heat. Grill the vegetables on both sides for 5–8 minutes, or until charred and softened. To serve, arrange the warm charred vegetables on a plate, season, and spoon the Romesco over.

More ideas from the 5:2 Kitchen Romesco Sauce is delicious with Chickpea Nuggets (see page 178), Quinoa Cakes (see page 50), or grilled sausages or chicken. It also makes a fantastic dip, mixed with equal amounts of crème fraîche. Or, on a non-fasting day, serve with roast or boiled baby potatoes.

TWO-COLOUR COURGETTI WITH TRUFFLED MUSHROOM CREAM SAUCE
Calories per serving: 132–171

Vegetarian/gluten free/low carb

There are so many good things about courgetti ('pasta' made with julienned or thinly sliced courgettes: see page 322 for tips). It's faster to cook than wheat pasta, is gluten free, less stodgy, more colourful and provides at least one serving of vegetables. *And,* on a Fast Day, the calorie saving means you can serve it with an indulgent sauce. If you can find them, buy one yellow and one green courgette for a lovely colour contrast. Truffle oil isn't expensive and it gives an intense flavour: you can increase the oil in this for a richer flavour if you have a few calories to play with.

Serves 2
Preparation time: 10 minutes
Cooking time: 16–18 minutes

10g dried wild mushrooms 26 cals

2 medium courgettes 68 cals

5g pine nuts 35 cals

200g mixed mushrooms such as chestnut, oyster, enoki or shiitake 26–50 cals
   depending on type

1–2 tsp truffle oil 45–90 cals

1 clove garlic, crushed 4 cals

2 tbsp 0% fat crème fraîche 18 cals or single cream 58 cals

10g finely grated Parmesan or equivalent 42 cals

few sprigs flat leaf parsley or chives, chopped 2 cals

10g truffles preserved in a jar or tin (optional) 3–5 cals

salt and pepper

1. Soak the dried mushrooms in 100ml hot water. Prepare the courgetti using a julienne peeler, a spiraliser or a sharp knife (see page 322 for tips). Gently press out any moisture using kitchen paper then allow them to dry out a little while you make the sauce.

2. Dry-fry the pine nuts in a large non-stick frying pan till lightly browned. Set aside.

3. Cut the mushrooms into equal-sized chunks. Heat half of the truffle in a frying pan over medium heat, and sauté the mushrooms for 5 minutes, stirring only occasionally, until they're browned.

4. Chop or tear the softened dried mushrooms. Add to the pan with the crushed garlic and half the soaking water. Simmer for 5 minutes, or until there's very little sauce left: add a little more soaking water if the mushrooms really dry out. Meanwhile warm some pasta dishes and a small bowl. Pour the sauce into the warmed bowl.

5. Add the remaining truffle oil to the pan then pan-fry the courgetti or courgette ribbons for 2–3 minutes, or until just browning (ribbons take a little longer). Tip the mushroom sauce back into the pan and warm through.

6. Pour pasta into the warm serving dishes, stir through the crème fraiche/cream, and top with the cheese, pine nuts, chopped herbs and shaved truffle, if using. Season and serve.

More ideas from the 5:2 Kitchen See page 322 for tips for the best 'courgetti' or courgette ribbons. Alternatively, use a 'julienne' peeler or 'spiraliser' gadget that cuts spaghetti-like strands (you can use it for carrot salad on page 203, too).

KOREAN KIMCHI PICKLE WITH TOFU STIR-FRY
Calories per serving: 154–270

Vegetarian/vegan/gluten free/nut free

Kimchi is a fermented cabbage pickle – which may not sound that appetising, but if you like chillis, pickles and intensely savoury flavours, you're likely to love this. Fermented foods like Kimchi are part of a real foodie trend right now. From yoghurt to sauerkraut, fermented foods are good for us because the process makes the nutrients more available to us, and helps promote healthy bacteria in the gut. Kimchi is very low in calories, too, and as a first experiment in fermentation, it's fun and very hands-on to make.

The only specialist ingredient needed is Korean chilli flakes, known as gochugaru, which you can buy online or in Asian stores. Sriracha sauce makes a quick and easy substitution.

One final word of warning: the longer you leave it, the stronger it gets, and kimchi can smell pretty potent. In fact, in Korea, where the average person eats 35kg (77 lb) of the stuff every year, they often have a separate fridge for it. I tend to keep mine in a jar that's kept inside a plastic bag. Anything that potent has to be good for you.

Kimchi
Makes 750g kimchi, enough for 6 servings
Calories per serving: 25–41
Preparation time: 1–5 days fermentation plus 30 minutes

    500g head Chinese cabbage 65 cals
    3–4 tsp sea salt
    200g mooli, white radish, or carrot 32 cals
    4 spring onions 8 cals
    3 cloves garlic, peeled 12 cals
    2cm-piece ginger weighing 5g, peeled 4 cals
    20g of gochugaru pepper flakes 20 cals or 2 tbsp sriracha sauce 30 cals
    1 sharp apple or pear weighing about 80g, cut into chunks 40–50 cals
    2–3 tbsp rice or cider vinegar 5–20 cals

2 tsp of sugar 30 cals or 1 tsp agave nectar or honey 15–20 cals (optional)
You will also need disposable plastic gloves or small freezer bags to protect
    your hands.

1. Slice the cabbage through the middle lengthwise, leaving the core whole. Place the halves
   in a bowl and pull the leaves apart and sprinkle each evenly with sea salt. Add filtered water
   till it just covers the leaves then place a plate on top to weigh down (I use a bag of flour to
   keep it weighed down). Leave to salt for 30–40 minutes.

2. Meanwhile prepare the vegetables and the spices. Grate the radish or carrot, slice the
   spring onions diagonally and set them aside. Peel the garlic and ginger then add to a
   food processor to mince. Add the pepper flakes or sriracha sauce, chunks of apple or pear,
   vinegar and sugar/sweetener if using. Process to a paste and set aside.

3. Wash one or several glass or ceramic pots (capacity of at least 750ml) with a flexible lid in
   hot soapy water, dry thoroughly and set aside.

4. Check the cabbage. The leaves should bend more after the brining. Rinse very well, making
   sure to get rid of all the salt. Chop through the layers of leaves, so you have pieces 1–2
   centimetres in size: discard the core. Return the rinsed cabbage to the bowl, add the
   vegetables and then the spice paste. Wearing disposable gloves, or using a plastic food
   bag to cover your hands to avoid chilli burn, mix the spice paste, prepared vegetables and
   cabbage together vigorously, squeezing and kneading so that the juices are released into
   the bowl.

5. Pile everything into the jar or pot, including the juices, and press down well to eliminate air
   bubbles. Make sure there's liquid just covering the vegetables, and seal. Leave to ferment
   either at room temperature or in the fridge: if left out, it'll ferment and sour faster, so taste
   every day till it reaches your preferred strength, then refrigerate. Remember to release the
   seal/unscrew at least twice a day to allow gases to escape.

6. Serve as a side dish or using suggestions as below. It will keep for months but gets more
   potent with age.

KIMCHI AND TOFU STIR-FRY
Calories per serving: 154–270, depending on tofu type

Vegetarian

Serves 1
Preparation time: 5 minutes
Cooking time: 3–4 minutes

  125g home-made or store-bought kimchi 25–41 cals
  100g smoked or marinated firm tofu, cubed 85–185 cals
  ¼ tsp coconut oil 22 cals
  3 spring onions, chopped 6 cals
  ½ tsp sesame seeds 16 cals

1. Remove the kimchi from the storage container. Drain off and reserve most of the moisture to add back after stir-frying. Dry any moisture off the tofu cubes with a paper towel.

2. Place the coconut oil in a small wok or non-stick frying pan placed over a high heat. When hot, add the tofu and spring onions and stir-fry for 2–3 minutes, or until the cubes begin to brown slightly.

3. Add the kimchi and sesame seeds, and stir-fry for 1 minute. Drizzle with kimchi liquid to taste and serve.

More kimchi ideas from the 5:2 Kitchen This is great served as a side dish alongside many Asian, tofu or meat dishes. It also makes a pretty mean toasted sandwich on a non-fasting day: add Cheddar or other strong cheese to one slice of bread, top with kimchi and the second slice and grill or toast in a silicon toaster bag until the cheese melts. Adapt the pickle too: try pink kimchi, made with grated, unpickled beetroot, and red onions (it'll turn everything a pretty pink).

CHILLI CHICKPEA NUGGETS WITH MANGO DIPPING SAUCE

Calories per serving: 140 with egg; 154 with oats; 170 with dip

Vegetarian/vegan option/gluten free

I wasn't intending to make these as nuggets, but my burgers kept falling apart and I realised it'd be easier to shape them into 'chicken-style' nuggets, only made with chickpeas instead. They still have a tendency to crumble, especially the vegan option without the egg, but are deliciously spicy, especially served with the tangy chutney dip. Weigh your coconut instead of using measuring spoons to get the right amount. The fried nuggets can be frozen and then reheated.

Serves 4 (4 nuggets per serving)
Preparation time: 10 minutes, plus 30 minutes chilling time
Cooking time: 5 minutes, plus 8 minutes per portion

    1-cal cooking spray
    200g mushrooms, roughly chopped 26 cals
    240g tinned chickpeas, rinsed and drained 260 cals
    2 tsp garam masala or curry powder 10 cals
    1 tsp black mustard seeds or coriander seeds (or a mixture), plus extra for
        sprinkling 5 cals
    1 red or yellow pepper, cored and finely chopped 30 cals
    4 medium spring onions, including the green tops, chopped 8 cals
    1–2 tsp sriracha or chilli sauce 5–10 cals
    2 eggs 158 cals or for vegans 60g rolled oats, 213 cals
    10g desiccated coconut 62 cals or 10g rolled oats 36 cals
    ½ tsp coconut oil 22 cals
    30g mango chutney 60 cals
    1 tbsp cider vinegar 2 cals or juice of 1 lime 10 cals
    salt and pepper

1. Spray a non-stick pan with 1-cal spray and cook the chopped mushrooms over a medium heat for 4–5 minutes.

2. Place the chickpeas in a food processor along with the garam masala or curry powder and mustard or coriander seeds, pepper, spring onions and cooked mushrooms. Process until the mixture begins to form a paste.

3. Turn into a bowl and add the sriracha and seasoning. Taste as you go, as the sauce is fiery. Then stir in the eggs or oats (for the vegan version) and refrigerate for at least 30 minutes.

4. Scatter half the desiccated coconut or rolled oats across a large plate and add a sprinkling more coriander or mustard seeds. Divide the chilled mix into 16 equal-sized 'nuggets', using a heaped tablespoon. Place your nuggets 4 at a time on the plate, and press down so the spiced coconut forms a crust, and turn them over to coat the other side.

5. Heat the coconut oil in a non-stick frying pan and place 4 nuggets at a time into the pan, flattening slightly with a spatula. Cook for 3–4 minutes, then turn and cook on the other side. If they fall apart, you can push them back together. Work through the batches, keeping the others warm in the oven.

6. For the dipping sauce, mix the mango chutney and vinegar or lime juice in a small bowl, and serve as a dipping sauce with the freshly cooked nuggets. Great served with the Sweet Potato Chips (see page 324).

To freeze the patties, once they have been fried and then cooled, place them between layers of greaseproof paper in an airtight container. When you're ready to serve them, remove as many nuggets as needed, allow to defrost in the fridge and either microwave for 30–40 seconds per serving on high, or oven bake at 180°C/350°F/Gas mark 4 for 10 minutes.

More ideas from the 5:2 Kitchen These nuggets are very adaptable. You can add ras al-hanout and whole cumin, plus a few snipped apricots, for a Moroccan flavour and you can also substitute couscous for the oats. Or for a Mexican version, make with half chickpeas and half cooked black beans, add dried chilli flakes and cumin and serve with salsa.

Making sense of... buying good food

I *love* food shopping, discovering new products and seasonal favourites, sniffing vegetables and getting ideas for new recipes.

But sometimes all the choice gets to be too much. How do we cut through the slogans, claims and special offers to find food that is good for us *and* those who produce it?

When I asked members of the 5:2 Facebook group what topics they wanted covered in the '*Making sense of...*' sections, concerns about pesticides, additives and welfare came top of the list, which is why this section is here.

What is good food?

As I've called this book *The 5:2 Good Food Kitchen,* you'd expect me to have strong views on what good food is. And I do, though they've changed over the years. I became a vegetarian in my teens. Back in the 1980s, livestock welfare standards were very mixed, and as a student, I couldn't afford the more expensive meat, so went vegetarian instead.

I certainly don't think everyone should necessarily become a vegetarian, buy organic or grow his or her own vegetables. But I do believe that once in a while we should all take stock of how we want our food to be produced – and how we can use our buying power to improve standards.

What are *your* food values?

I started writing a list of what good food meant to me, and it was getting pretty wordy. So I started again and tried to boil it *right* down. I want to eat food that is:

1. Produced with respect for the animals and people involved, and the environment where the food is grown or raised.
2. Produced with as little 'mucking about' as possible, for the sake of our health and the health of animals and people involved.
3. Sold with care and transported the minimum distance, with as little packaging or waste as is safe.

I'll take a quick tour of the issues for each priority – which is most important to you?

Kate's Good Food Priority 1: produced with respect

If you eat meat, or dairy and eggs as I do, then you must accept that animals are being 'used' to produce your food. If you're uncomfortable with that idea, then it's easier than ever to buy a good range of vegan foods and, with a little care, your diet will contain all the nutrients you need. Though, even then, you'll be concerned about the agricultural methods used.

I want to buy from producers which:

- **Have good welfare standards for animals** For example, I want to buy eggs from farms where hens have enough space to move, have access to the outdoors, and are fed an appropriate diet.

- **Pay a fair price for raw materials e.g. coffee or cocoa** This helps ensure employees and farmers are paid and looked after properly, at home and overseas.

- **Show respect for the environment** Minimising pesticides and over-farming and promoting sustainability, both on their farms and nearby land are respectful practices.

Tips for finding food produced with respect

Research welfare labels and schemes

In the UK, food packaging might include logos from schemes that do some of the work for you, by showing that certain products meet safety or welfare standards.

Logos include the Lion Mark (for British eggs, from hens vaccinated against salmonella), Freedom Food (meeting RSPCA welfare standards, which are higher than required by law) and the Soil Association (meeting organic rearing or growing standards). If you're concerned about how producers overseas are treated then Fairtrade may be a label you're looking for.

Remember that some of the schemes are businesses in their own right, or represent trade associations, rather than being consumer-led. Of course, the higher the standards, the higher the price.

Read the small print

There's a world of difference between 'free range', 'barn system' and 'enriched cages' when it comes to how laying hens live. It's hard to keep on top of all the jargon, which is why the web is so useful.

Look online

Sites like Compassion in World Farming www.ciwf.org.uk and www.freedomfood.co.uk offer advice on different products, while www.thegoodshoppingguide.com, www.ethicalconsumer.org and www.ethical.org.au offer advice, books or apps for use while you're shopping. Always look at the 'About us' sections of a site to see who is giving you the advice and how that is funded.

Ask your shopkeeper

You can't expect the cashier in your supermarket to know about every product, but most major supermarkets have information about suppliers and standards on their websites. If that doesn't answer your question, ask by email or via the local store manager: they tend to be pretty keen to appear consumer-focused.

Alternatively, buy from local specialists or wholefood stores where you can ask the sellers about suppliers. I'm very lucky that my local Infinity Wholefoods store is one of the oldest in the UK and runs as a co-operative with extensive information about the products they stock and the principles they adopt: www.infinityfoods.co.uk. When you find a store you trust, it saves you time as you know they have done a lot of the 'ethical homework' ready! If there's no wholefood store locally, many trade online or offer schemes where you can club together with neighbours to arrange deliveries. Or investigate 'veg box' schemes from nearby farmers.

Kate's Good Food Priority 2: no mucking about

My second priority is about finding 'real food', i.e. food that has been produced and processed with as little 'mucking about' as possible. Unless we personally grow everything we eat – impossible for most of us – we have to accept that it will have been processed before reaching us. But what's *your* comfort zone when it comes to what's been done to your dinner?

This can *only* be an introduction to topics that people spend their lives researching, so do follow up the links in the references section on issues that matter most to you.

Genetically Modified Organisms – mostly plants – are altered in the laboratory, with new genetic material introduced to 'improve' aspects of the crop. Early work was focused on improving pest resistance or yield for farmers, but products like purple tomatoes – created to be richer in antioxidants than red ones – are now being developed for sale to consumers.

Critics of GM foods say the knock-on effects on humans, animals and the environment are unknown, while supporters insist such crops could reduce food shortages and improve health. Currently only two GM crops are approved for cultivation in the EU, but 49 GM crops are allowed to be imported from other countries, mainly for use as animal feed. In Australia and New Zealand, crops are assessed before being allowed, and currently GM plants including soybean, potato, maize, wheat and rice have been approved there.

The rules on labelling are much stricter in Europe, Australia and New Zealand than in the US or Canada. If you prefer not to eat food from animals *fed* on GM-feed, your best bet is go for organic or grass-fed meats.

No ill-effects to human health from products currently available has been reported, but there are also concerns about insect and animal populations being affected by changes to disease resistance, for example. Campaigners are uncomfortable with the potential trademarking of the DNA of crops.

Pesticides, medication and hormones in farming

Many of us hate the idea that powerful chemicals or medicines might be used in the production of our food. Yet if you've ever discovered your carefully grown lettuces obliterated overnight by slugs (yes, that'll be me), you'll know that letting nature take its course doesn't always put salad on the table.

'Pesticide' is a general term covering substances to combat a variety of threats to crops, including chemicals to kill or deter types of fungus, insect, rodent and weed. They are regulated for their effects on humans and animals, but only a small percentage of food can be randomly tested to ensure compliance. There is also concern about knock-on effects, e.g. some believe pesticides may be the reason bee populations are falling drastically.

Medication, including antibiotics, is used to prevent or treat conditions that animals have developed or may develop during their lives: preventative treatment is more controversial, especially as some argue that this would be unnecessary if some intensive farming practices left animals, especially poultry, less prone to infection. Up to 50 per cent of antibiotics worldwide are used in farming, and there are concerns about antibiotic resistance as a result. Antibiotics can also promote rapid growth.

Hormones can be used to affect the growth and metabolism of livestock like cattle or pigs and milk yield: hormones are banned in the EU but dairy ingredients from animals given artificial hormones may be found in some processed products imported from outside the EU.

Additives or 'cuckoo' ingredients in processed food

A 'cuckoo' ingredient just has no place in a food. Unwelcome additions is not a new problem – reports of adulterated food go back to the first days of trading, when less valuable ingredients were added to bulk out food, like chalk being added to milk.

The recent horse-meat controversy in Europe – where horse meat from unknown sources was found in prepared meals labelled as containing beef – shows that illegal adulteration is still happening. Apart from relying on the authorities to track down criminal activity, as consumers, our best option seems to be to buy food that is as unprocessed as possible.

When it comes to *legal* additives, all additives, natural or artificial, must have 'e-numbers' under European regulations. For example, E300 is vitamin C, and E100 is curcumin, made from turmeric root. Companies have been under pressure to cut down on additives, especially food colourings, which were said to contribute to hyperactive behaviour in children.

Most food labels now list the name of the additive, rather than its number, which is probably no less confusing than before. Even sugar has over a dozen different 'names' (see page 302). And when one ingredient is taken away for health reasons, we need to be cautious about what is used to replace lost flavour or texture. In research by the *Daily Telegraph* in 2014, many lower-fat ready meals promoted for weight loss contained higher levels of sugar than their 'normal' equivalents, and in another study, they found mass-produced wholemeal breads with more added sugar than the white equivalents by the same bakers.

Salt is yet another concern, with a connection to high blood pressure. Most of the salt we eat isn't added by us at the table, but is present in processed foods.

Tips for finding food with the least possible 'mucking about'

- **Become label savvy** Read the small print, front and back, and learn what the symbols mean if a particular health issue is important to you. You can also look at 'traffic light' labels, which allow you to compare different foods e.g. ready meals or snacks, to see which are high in certain additives or naturally occurring sugars, salts and fats. And don't forget 'reduced fat' is not the same as low fat, or even as low calorie.

- **Watch out for serving size sorcery:** many a 5:2 dieter has been caught out by the 'salt/fat/calories per serving' label on the front of a small pack. It's easy to eat the whole pack and then realise the manufacturer counts a 'serving' as being just half the pack, so you've eaten far more salt or fat than you intended. Check nutrition per 100g on the back instead.

- **What *doesn't* the packaging say?** If a label boasts a product is free of artificial colours, then check for preservatives: they're not automatically bad things, but Google is your friend if you want to discover what packaged food contains.

- **Buy from the specialists** Buy from a farmers' market, local butcher, fishmonger's or the grower at the farm door if you want to discover how the food was made.

- **Always wash fruit and vegetables thoroughly before use** This is not just in case of pesticide residues, but also to remove insects or bacteria that can be picked up between the farm and your plate.

- **Buy organic to avoid pesticides** Some produce is more likely to contain residues than others, and if you're concerned about pesticide levels the most up-to-date information is from the US, where higher levels were found in apples, strawberries, tomatoes, grapes, spinach and peaches.

- **Consider organic meat and dairy** If antibiotics are a concern, you could think about buying organic meat and dairy. Look for the Soil Association, which has strict regulations on the use of preventative antibiotics.

Kate's Good Food Priority number 3: sold with care

My final 'respect' category is about how the food gets to us, including how it's transported, what packaging is used, and how it's marketed.

How far has your shopping travelled?

A few years ago, we were told to aim for foods with the least 'food miles', food which had travelled the least distance to our plate. This would support local growers, and help cut carbon emissions.

However, it's not just about miles. If you live in a built-up urban area you are not going to find larger-scale agriculture within a few miles. Plus, many growing methods in other countries are less intensive than ours, so they're using less energy than the journey involved. Finally, there's seasonality: are we really prepared to go back to a time when only locally grown produce is available during the winter period?

On the shelf: packaging and marketing

The packaging of food protects it but it is also used as a selling tool. New ways to package foods that nature seemed to package pretty well itself are also irritating: from 'child-friendly' pre-cut apple portions, to individually packed crackers or cheese slices. Yet portioned food is often sold to dieters: do we want smaller packs to help us control our calories, or larger packs that use fewer materials?

Finally, there's the wider issue about how food is sold and advertised: whether you're uncomfortable about the ethics of different brands, their marketing to children, honesty or omissions about contents, or their policies in developing markets overseas.

Tips for finding foods that are sold with care

- **Buy as much food as you can that's grown seasonally and/or locally** Vegetable box schemes are a great way of achieving both, and supporting local farmers.

- **Discover more about seasonal eating online** Supermarkets stock so many foods year-round that it's hard to know from the veg aisle, so instead print off a list from sites like www.eatseasonably.co.uk.

- **Be packaging aware** Look for shops where you can fill reusable containers with grains or other dry foods.

- **Speak up!** If you dislike a company's ethical or marketing plans, it's easier than ever to let them know, via social media like Facebook or Twitter. Ask questions, explain your concerns: use your consumer power to change things for the better.

Kate's verdict

I thought I was pretty savvy until I researched this section. Now I realise I want to be even more careful with my shopping, starting with buying more organic dairy and fruit. But don't try to do it at once; that's too overwhelming. Just as when you're dieting, one slip-up can lead to feelings of failure, and it's easy to feel like an irresponsible consumer. Begin with the one issue that matters most to you, or the food you eat most often.

5:2 Food Heroes

ONION, GARLIC AND FRIENDS

Bring on the garlic breath, the onion tears, the long leeks and the round shallots – these nuggets of flavour are 5:2 lifesavers, and their nutritional benefits will have you smiling through the tears.

All about onions and garlic

Onions and garlic are part of the allium family (along with shallots, leeks and chives) and originated in Asia. The compounds that give them their powerful flavour also have numerous positive effects in the body: fighting viruses and bacteria, reducing the risk of blood clotting, and providing 'prebiotics' that help prevent bowel cancer.

Nutrition

They're low in fat, and calories, but very high in micronutrients and flavour.

- **Sulphur** Both garlic and onion contain sulphurs that give them their unique taste and those stimulate the production of nitric oxide, which helps blood vessels stay elastic, lowering blood pressure and reducing the risk of heart disease and strokes. Sulphur also helps to prevent clotting. Those same sulphurous compounds, including alllicin, allin and ajoene, fight bacteria and viruses, and this is why many traditional cold remedies include garlic.

- **Cancer prevention** The benefits of eating alliums could also include cancer prevention because, as well as aiding 'friendly bacteria' in the digestive system, garlic in particular may slow down the growth of cancer cells and tumours.

Downsides

- **Tears** It's the good stuff in the onion that also makes us cry when cutting into it. Avoid cutting through the root until the last moment, as it contains most of the oils that cause our eyes to water.

- **Garlic breath** The after-effects of garlic can be pungent, but chewing fresh parsley can be effective.

- **Reactions** True allergies to garlic/onions are uncommon, but chefs may develop an allergy after handling garlic frequently. Intolerances to garlic or onions can cause stomach upsets and headaches: raw garlic may be more likely to trigger this than cooked.

- **Toxicity** Onions are toxic to many animals, including horses and dogs.

Types of onion

- **Brown or yellow** These are most commonly used for cooking, and are a great all-rounder: they caramelise beautifully when cooked (as in French onion soup, or onion marmalade). Spanish onions are larger, and generally sweeter and milder.

- **Red** The red-skinned onion looks lovely raw in salads, or grilled or roasted alongside other vegetables, though the colour can leech out onto other ingredients if left for some time. The red colour means it's high in antioxidants.

- **White** These are larger and often more pungent – good for stuffing and roasting.

- **Spring onions** have been harvested earlier, before the bulb develops fully.

How to buy and store

Buy onions and garlic without blemishes or any sign of green sprouts coming from the tips.

Garlic is mainly sold as whole, dried bulbs (you can buy it frozen or preserved, but the flavour is not as good) though you can also pick up fresh/wet garlic in the summer, with edible stems, or even wild garlic leaves and stems, which are more like a spring vegetable. Cloves of garlic should be plump, not wrinkled!

Store in a cool, dark place. You can store onions in the fridge but I never do with dried garlic. Depending on freshness and storing conditions, unpeeled onions or garlic will keep for 10 days to several months.

How to cook

As with many vegetables, eating onions or garlic raw, or with minimal cooking, allows for maximum health benefits, as cooking damages the compounds.

If cooking garlic, allow it to stand for 10 minutes after crushing or chopping, so the beneficial compounds are released.

Cut out any yellow or green roots before cooking – they taste bitter.

Burned garlic is horrible, and has spoiled many a dish. Treat it gently when frying and watch it closely.

Recipe Ideas

Kimchi page 175

Almost Instant Home-spiced Pickles page 331

Chicken Sausage Roll with Leek, Mushrooms and Thyme page 228

Spice World

FLAVOURFUL FAST DAYS

Sometimes all it takes is one exciting new flavour to transform your Fast Day – and this chapter celebrates the amazing range of spices and herbs that can make a meal something extra-special. The smoky mussels might bring back memories of sunset meals on the beautiful Spanish coast while the Korean rice pot offers the promise of exciting flavours and cuisines you'd still love to explore.

All the dishes in this chapter have one thing in common: they definitely earn their place on *your* dinner table, whichever corner of the globe you call home.

STAR ANISE DUCK WITH CORIANDER SLAW

SRI LANKAN TRIPLE COCONUT CURRY

CURED SALMON FISHCAKES

LAMB LOLLIES WITH POPPED-SPICE CARROT SALAD

SWEET AND SOUR FIVE-SPICE TOFU

SMOKY SPANISH MUSSELS

LEMONGRASS AND GINGER PORK WITH NOODLES

'BIBIMBAP' KOREAN RICE WITH FRESH PICKLES

PLUS ...

MAKING SENSE OF... ALLERGIES

5:2 FOOD HEROES: HERBS AND SPICES

5:2 Lives

FASTING YOUR WAY TO FEWER PILLS AND A SIZE 12

'Having lost my mother too young from diabetes complications, I didn't want to follow in her footsteps - and now I don't need hospital treatment anymore.' Susan, 52

For Susan Vedhera, losing weight was about so much more than how her clothes fit.

'I weighed over 78kg (172 lb) and had a BMI of over 32, in the obese category; I was finding it difficult to find size 20 clothes to fit me. I had tried lots of other diets without success and being treated for diabetes. Having lost my mother to diabetes-related complications when she was only 67, I did not want to follow in her footsteps, yet the diabetes consultant wasn't happy with my blood test results, even though they kept increasing my medication. They wanted me to try to get my BMI under 30 within six months or have to face insulin injections sooner rather than later.'

Susan, from Newcastle-upon-Tyne, knew she had to do something – and urgently because people of Indian and Asian origin have a higher risk of developing diabetes and complications. And then she heard about 5:2 from a close family friend who had successfully reduced his blood sugars and weight purely by fasting.

She started on 22 April 2013 with her specialist's permission and fourteen months on, she's lost 15kg (31 lb), and has ditched the size 20s for size 12s. She's at her lowest weight for 25 years, and the losses continue.

Critically, her BP and cholesterol readings have improved, and she's actually been discharged from the hospital diabetes department. 'The consultant who approved of me doing 5:2 was so pleased she reduced my medication and I've been discharged from hospital care.'

It's a huge relief to Susan, her husband of 30 years and her three adult children. Intermittent fasting has affected her diet on non-fasting days too. 'I have always enjoyed plenty of fruit and vegetables but 5:2 has helped reduce my sugar cravings and I am no longer a chocoholic, and don't binge eat anymore. I eat butter instead of margarine and raw nuts instead of crisps.'

This greater awareness of what she eats has been revolutionary for Susan. 'For the first four or five months I calorie counted and logged everything I ate. This was an eye opener for me and I was shocked at what a normal portion size actually was.

Susan, who works as an insurance broker, relies on the 5:2 Facebook group for support: 'With the help of the members, I found Fast Days relatively easy right from the beginning.'

Susan's Fast Day diary

On a typical Fast Day I have one cup of tea with a splash of milk at around 7 a.m. (15 calories). I then wait till around 2 p.m. and have home-made vegetable soup or, if it's really warm weather, salad and cottage cheese (around 100 calories). I have lots of hot water with lemon or fennel seeds or sparkling water with lime, and black tea.

Usually for dinner (7– 8 p.m.) I'll have eggs (my favourite is a spicy scrambled eggs made with onions, spices and coriander). Or fish or chicken with lots of green vegetables. *Protein and plants* is my mantra.

Susan's non-fasting day diary

For breakfast I normally have Greek yoghurt with berries and seeds. For lunch I'll have either soup or salad or sometimes a sandwich. I always enjoy my evening meal, which could be homemade chicken curry with chapattis or roast chicken with vegetables and gravy.

Favourite foods

I love all Indian food and tend to cook this at home: chicken curry, vegetable curries including bhindi and cauliflower, dal and kidney bean curry.

Best thing about 5:2?

It actually works for me, and for my family and friends who have tried it after seeing my success. It's flexible and it's easy to do and I can have a social life without feeling guilty that I've spoilt my diet.

Susan's top tip

Try fasting two days a week for four to six weeks and you'll notice the amazing difference it makes to your life. And on your Fast Days, remember, 'Tomorrow, tomorrow – you can eat it tomorrow – it's only a day away!'

STAR ANISE DUCK WITH CORIANDER SLAW

Calories per serving: 316

Gluten free/low carb/nut free

Star anise 'petals' aren't just a pretty face, as this exotic-tasting duck dish proves. They are so powerful you only need two petals. The anise-flavoured duck fillets top a zingy salad that bursts with flavour.

Serves 1
Preparation time: 10 minutes
Cooking time: 5 minutes

½ red pepper, thinly sliced 15 cals
1 carrot, thinly sliced 34 cals
¼ white cabbage, thinly sliced 17 cals
handful beansprouts 17 cals
10g coriander, leaves and stalks separated 5 cals
juice of ½ lime 10 cals
½ tsp sesame oil 22 cals
2 individual petals (pods and seeds) from a star anise 2 cals
100g duck mini fillets or 100g thinly sliced duck breast
    194 cals
1-cal cooking spray
salt and pepper

1. Make the slaw first by putting the pepper, carrot, cabbage and beansprouts into a bowl. Finely slice the coriander stalks and add them to the vegetables. Whisk together the lime juice and sesame oil with 1 teaspoon cold water. Season then stir the mixture into the slaw.

2. Grind the star anise in a pestle and mortar or finely chop it on a board. Season the duck and toss it with the star anise.

3. Spray a cold, non-stick frying pan with 1-calorie cooking spray (or your own spray) and place over a medium heat. Add the duck to the pan and stir-fry until golden all over. Spoon the slaw into a bowl, top with the duck and serve with the coriander leaves on top.

More ideas from the 5:2 Kitchen The slaw is delicious with any grilled or stir-fried meat, or grilled tofu.

SRI LANKAN TRIPLE COCONUT VEGETABLE CURRY

Calories per serving: 241–269

Vegetarian/vegan/gluten free

My first ever trip to Asia was to Sri Lanka, after I won a holiday. Winning helped me overcome two fears: coconut and flying. I now love the subtle sweetness and flavour coconut gives curries (still not a huge fan of flying, but I will do it) and this one is rich, satisfying and spicy. Don't be put off by the long ingredients list. You can use garam masala in place of individual spices and leave out the desiccated coconut if you wish; but the coconut milk *is* pretty essential for this delicious dish. Choose a rainbow of vegetable colours and textures.

Makes 2 servings
Preparation time: 10 minutes
Cooking time: 13 minutes

1 tsp coconut oil 45 cals

1 tsp black mustard seeds 5 cals

1 red onion, chopped 38 cals

½–1 small, hot red chilli, seeded, finely chopped 2–4 cals

2 cloves garlic, finely chopped 8 cals

1–2cm-piece ginger, peeled and grated, to taste 3–4 cals

1 tsp turmeric 5 cals

few black peppercorns

400g mixed vegetables, diced or chopped into equal size pieces, including 80g baby aubergines 16 cals, 150g mixed butternut squash and sweet potato 92 cals, 1 medium courgette 34 cals, 1 red pepper 30 cals (150–200 cals in total)

10g desiccated coconut, plus a little extra for serving 62 cals

1 tsp curry leaves 5 cals

1 tsp tamarind paste 7 cals or juice of ½ lime 10 cals

80ml coconut milk made up to 200ml with cold water 140 cals

100g Chinese cabbage, pak choi, or other greens 17 cals

few fresh coriander leaves, chopped to garnish (optional) 2 cals

1. Heat the coconut oil in a large non-stick saucepan over a medium heat. Add the mustard seeds and cook for 1 minute till they pop slightly. Reduce the heat and add the onion, chilli, garlic, ginger, turmeric, peppercorns and fry gently for 2 minutes.

2. Add the chopped vegetables and desiccated coconut and fry for 2 more minutes. Add the curry leaves, tamarind paste and coconut milk and water mixture and, bring to a simmer. Let it cook for 6 minutes.

3. Add the Chinese cabbage or greens and cook for a further 2 minutes.

4. Serve sprinkled with the reserved coconut and chopped coriander. Delicious served with cauliflower rice page 320 to soak up every drop of sauce, or 50g basmati or jasmine rice per person (166–175 calories per serving).

To freeze, simply allow the second portion to cool before freezing in an airtight plastic container. Defrost the curry before reheating in a pan or the microwave.

More ideas from the 5:2 Kitchen For more protein, add tofu, cooked prawns or cooked chicken at the same stage as the coconut milk.

CURED SALMON FISHCAKES
Calories per serving: 199

Gluten free

These are fishcakes with a twist – they haven't actually been cooked. Instead, the fish cures in the intensely fragrant lime and sesame mix, before being formed into a 'cake' with fresh courgette, and served with salad. The pinks and greens make a really pretty dish, and it feels both rich and healthy.

Serves 1
Preparation time: 15 minutes, plus marinating

½ small courgette, diced 16 cals
100g raw salmon, finely chopped 140 cals
1 spring onion, finely chopped 1 cal
zest and juice of ½ lime 10 cals
½ tsp sesame oil 22 cals
handful of cress 5 cals
4 leaves Little Gem lettuce 5 cals
salt and pepper

1. Place the courgette, salmon and spring onion in a bowl. Add the lime zest, lime juice and sesame oil and stir together. Season, cover with cling film and leave to marinate in the fridge for up to 3 hours.

2. When ready to serve, put a large scone cutter on a serving plate and pack it with the cured salmon mixture. Lift up the cutter then top the salmon cake with the cress. Place the Little Gem leaves on the side and use them to scoop up the cured salmon mixture. Serve immediately.

More ideas from the 5:2 Kitchen On a non-fasting day, serve this with sourdough bread and half a sliced avocado – pour the other half of the lime over the avocado to keep it from going brown.

LAMB LOLLIES WITH POPPED-SPICE CARROT SALAD

Calories per serving: 180

Gluten free/nut free

I love this quick, cute way of serving lamb. These 'lollies' are actually cutlets, coated in coriander, then grilled. The sweetness of the carrots is a great contrast with the popped whole spices in the salad. The lamb calorie count looks low because of the bone in the cutlets.

Serves 1
Preparation time: 15 minutes
Cooking time: 8 minutes

¼ tsp each whole cumin seeds and mustard seeds 5 cals
¼ tsp ground coriander 2 cals
3 lamb cutlets (130g) cut from a rack of lamb and trimmed of any fat 116 cals
1 carrot, cut into matchsticks 34 cals
50g white cabbage, shredded 13 cals
2 tbsp fresh coriander, chopped 5 cals
1 tbsp lemon juice 5 cals
salt and pepper

1. Toast the cumin and mustard seeds in a dry frying pan over a medium heat until the seeds start to pop. Remove from the heat and add to a salad bowl.

2. Rub the ground coriander into each side of the lamb cutlets. Preheat the grill to high. When hot, grill the lamb for 3–4 minutes each side, depending on their thickness. Set aside to rest.

3. Add the carrot, white cabbage, coriander and lemon juice to the salad bowl, season well and toss everything together.

4. Spoon the salad onto a plate, top with the lamb cutlets and serve.

More ideas from the 5:2 Kitchen Try smoked paprika instead of coriander on the 'lollies' and serve with a simple, sweet salad of grated carrot, red onions and a few sultanas.

SWEET AND SOUR FIVE-SPICE TOFU

Calories per serving: 154

Vegetarian/vegan/gluten free/nut free

Tofu needs a firm hand – strong spicing and high temperatures bring out its strengths, as in this quick, low-calorie version of the Chinese takeaway favourite. The small amount of oil here is important because it helps the tofu to brown well before we add the sweet and sour sauce: you could also use coconut oil.

Serves 1
Preparation time: 10 minutes
Cooking time: 10 minutes

½ tsp sunflower or olive oil 22 cals
75g tofu, cut into cubes 64 cals
½ each red and yellow pepper, thinly sliced 30 cals
¼ tsp Chinese five spice powder
juice of ½ orange 35 cals
1 tsp white wine vinegar 1 cal
1 tsp chopped fresh parsley 2 cals
salt and pepper

1. Heat the oil in a saucepan over high heat until hot. Add the tofu and season well. Cook for 3–5 minutes, tossing the pan every now and then until the tofu is browned on all sides.

2. Add the peppers and the Chinese five spice powder, and cook for another 2–3 minutes.

3. Stir in the orange juice and vinegar, cover with a lid, and bring to the boil. Reduce the heat and simmer for about a minute until the sauce is syrupy.

4. Scatter over the chopped parsley, spoon into a bowl and serve straight away.

More ideas from the 5:2 Kitchen For a more substantial meal, serve with brown basmati or cauliflower rice, or some broccoli stir-fried with sliced red chilli. For a chicken version, use 75g thinly sliced chicken breast instead of the tofu – the dish will still only add up to 218 calories.

SMOKY SPANISH MUSSELS
Calories per serving: 287

Gluten free/nut free

This dish looks, smells and tastes knock-out. It's a fiesta in a pan, with all the smoky savouriness of Spanish late summer nights. My advice: serve it to seafood-loving friends, soak up the praise and refuse to give them the recipe.

Serves 1
Preparation time: 5 minutes
Cooking time: 10 minutes

    1 shallot, thinly sliced 7 cals
    30g cooking chorizo, chopped 149 cals (check for gluten-free if needed)
    ½ each red pepper and yellow pepper, sliced 30 cals
    1 tsp smoked paprika 5 cals
    250g mussels, checked and picked over 96 cals
    salt and pepper

1. Put the shallot and chorizo in a saucepan and fry over a medium heat for 3–4 minutes, or until the chorizo starts to release its oil and turn golden.

2. Stir in the peppers and paprika and cook for 1–2 minutes. Add the mussels and 100ml water and season well. Cover the pan securely with a lid and allow the mussels to steam open for about 3–5 minutes. It is important that you discard any mussels that have not opened after the cooking time. These are dead and eating them will make you ill.

3. Spoon into a bowl and serve.

More ideas from the 5:2 Kitchen On a non-fasting day, this is delicious served with a good dollop of aïoli (buy ready-made or add fresh crushed garlic to good-quality or home-made mayonnaise). Serve with potato wedges for an easy '*patatas bravas*'.

LEMONGRASS AND GINGER PORK WITH NOODLES

Calories per serving: 356

Gluten free/nut free

The Eastern flavours in this dish go so well with the pork – and it's a really satisfying supper dish that would also work very well, doubled up, for a casual meal with friends. Rice noodles are a good option if you're avoiding gluten, though do check the soy sauce if you're very sensitive, as traces of wheat gluten can remain in the finished sauce.

Serves 1
Preparation time: 20 minutes, plus marinating time (optional)
Cooking time: 15 minutes

   100g pork escalope 182 cals
   ½ lemongrass stalk, finely chopped 5 cals
   2cm-piece fresh root ginger, peeled and finely chopped 4 cals
   ½ shallot, finely chopped 3 cals
   1-cal cooking spray
   25g rice noodles 93 cals
   50g mixture of baby corn and sugar snap peas 17 cals
   50g broccoli florets 16 cals
   zest and juice of ½ lime 10 cals
   ½ tsp sesame oil 22 cals
   1 tsp soy sauce 2 cals (use gluten-free if required)
   ½ red chilli, sliced 2–5 cals

1. Put the pork escalope in a dish with the lemongrass, ginger and shallot. Toss the meat to coat. If you have time, place the dish in the fridge to allow the pork to marinate for up to an hour.

2. Spray a cold, non-stick frying pan with 1-calorie cooking spray (or your own spray) and place over a medium heat. Add the pork and fry it for 3–4 minutes on one side. Turn over, adding more spray to the pan, if needed. Continue to cook the pork on the other side until golden and cooked through in the middle. Set aside to rest.

3. Bring a small pan of water to the boil. Add the noodles and cook for 5 minutes or following the instruction on the pack. Add the baby corn and sugar snap pea mixture as well as the broccoli florets, then turn off the heat and allow to cook in the hot water for 1–2 minutes.

4. Drain the noodles and vegetables, toss well to mix then return them to the pan. Stir in the lime zest and juice, sesame oil, soy sauce and chilli then spoon onto a plate. Slice the pork and arrange on top, then drizzle round any of the rested juices.

More ideas from the 5:2 Kitchen For a lighter dish, serve without the rice noodles, on a bed of finely shredded cabbage. Or on a non-fasting day, a lovely extra is a quick satay sauce: just combine equal qualities of peanut butter and sweet chilli sauce, and a squeeze of lime.

'BIBIMBAP' KOREAN RICE WITH FRESH PICKLES

Calories per serving: 423

Vegetarian/ gluten free

The interest in Korean cuisine is one of the foodie trends I can get behind – from spicy fermented Kimchi (see page 175 to make your own) to the warming properties of huge bowl of 'Bibimbap,' which I first fell in love with at a local café, Namul, here in Brighton. It's a super filling rice dish with lots of seasoned vegetables, chilli sauce and an egg, or sliced meat. This is our – admittedly simplified – version, which omits the hard-to-find ingredients (but you can use home-made kimchi in place of the pickles). This dish is high in calories, but it's enough to keep you full all day!

Serves 1
Preparation time: 10 minutes
Cooking time: 20 minutes plus resting time for rice

    50g sushi rice 175 cals
    1 tsp tomato purée 2 cals
    1 tbsp rice or white wine vinegar 2 cals
    good pinch hot chilli powder or gochugaru pepper flakes from Asian grocers
    3 radishes 3 cals
    1 small slice ginger, thinly sliced 2 cals
    1 tbsp rice or white wine vinegar 2 cals
    1-cal cooking spray
    1 medium egg 78 cals
    25g beansprouts 7 cals
    ½ small carrot, cut into matchsticks 17 cals
    ¼ red pepper, cut into matchsticks 7 cals
    ¼ courgette, cut into matchsticks 9 cals
    3 baby chestnut mushrooms, sliced 2 cals
    25g soya beans 112 cals
    salt and pepper

1. Rinse the rice several times then put in a small non-stick casserole with 70ml cold water. Cover, bring to the boil then turn the heat down low and simmer for 10 minutes. Turn the heat off, leaving the lid on the pan, and set aside while you prepare the sides.

2. Make the chilli sauce by putting the tomato purée, rice or white wine vinegar and chilli powder or gochugaru pepper into a small bowl, mix together and set aside. Then make the pickle pot in a separate bowl by mixing together the radishes, ginger and rice vinegar or white wine vinegar with a pinch of salt. Set this aside as well.

3. Spray a cold non-stick frying pan with 1-cal cooking spray (or your own spray), heat over a medium heat and carefully crack the egg into the middle, cover the pan with a lid and cook until set and the yolk is just runny.

4. Meanwhile put the covered rice back on the hob over a high heat. Allow it to heat until very hot, to make the rice deliciously crispy on the bottom, then uncover and place on a dish. Arrange the beansprouts, carrots, red pepper, courgette, baby chestnut mushrooms and soya beans in sections all around the rice in the dish. Place the egg in the middle and serve with the chilli sauce and pickle pot on the side.

More ideas from the 5:2 Kitchen For a meat version, replace the egg with 50g shredded lean roast pork, without any fat. The dish will then contain 419 calories.

Making sense of... allergies

Have you ever given up gluten? Ditched the dairy? Or simply bought one of the many thousands of 'free-from' products now available in shops?

If you answered yes, then you're part of a growing market in these foods, which is worth £360m in the UK alone. Studies say at least 6 per cent of Britons are avoiding dairy and 5 per cent avoiding gluten for general health reasons, and 4 per cent because they believe they have an allergy.

The free-from boom is great news for people with allergies, as gluten- and dairy-free options are now much tastier and more widely available. But do most of us really need to be buying these products – or cutting entire food groups out of our diets? The jury is out.

Allergies and intolerances – what's the difference?

There's a *big* difference, even though people often use the terms interchangeably.

An allergy is a rare reaction (around 1–4 per cent of adults in the UK are affected, for example) to the proteins in food. In the most common type, the immune system interprets even the tiniest amount as a threat and releases a chemical fight-back within seconds or minutes. Allergies can cause:

- A rash/hives

- Itchy sensation in the mouth, throat or ears

- Wheezing

- Swelling of the face including lips and tongue

- Vomiting

- In serious cases, anaphylaxis – where someone is struggling to breathe or losing consciousness – can be life-threatening and needs emergency care.

Food-related reactions cause around 10 deaths in England and Wales each year.

Diagnosing an allergy

- Allergy testing is usually carried out in a specialist clinic where common allergens are applied to the skin, which is then 'pricked'. Reddening or a bump suggests an allergy to that substance.

- Exclusion and elimination diets are also used.

- The most common causes in adults are milk and eggs, nuts (including peanuts) and seeds like sesame, shellfish, fish, wheat, soya and some fruits such as citrus and kiwi.

- For children, cow's milk, eggs, soy and wheat are also common allergens but many young people will outgrow these as they mature: nuts are the exception.

Intolerances or sensitivities

These are much more common, and the symptoms, which usually affect the digestive system, come on more slowly. It often takes quite a lot of the food to cause the reaction, and you may not feel the symptoms for several hours. You might actually crave the food(s) that causes the problems. Reactions include:

- Bloating/wind

- Stomach cramps and diarrhoea

- Migraines can also be triggered by certain foods but this is a different type of reaction.

Diagnosing an intolerance

It's a lot harder to diagnose a sensitivity or intolerance.

- The only reliable way to diagnose is through food diaries and elimination diets, ideally under the supervision of a registered dietician.

- Various tests available from pharmacies, health food shops and online are expensive and mostly unproven and unreliable. Sometimes they suggest eliminating so many foods that you may have an improvement in symptoms without knowing which one caused the original problem.

- Many different food types are associated with intolerances, including dairy, wheat, yeast, alcohol and histamines (found in alcohol, fermented and pickled vegetables, and a variety of other foods).

Specific conditions

Lactose intolerance is when the body lacks the enzymes needed to digest lactose – the sugar found in milk and dairy products.

- This may affect up to one in five of us to some extent, and ethnic background is significant. Fewer than 1 in 50 people of northern European heritage are affected, while most people of Chinese origin may suffer to some extent. This could be because populations exposed to dairy over centuries have developed the ability to digest it.

- The main symptoms are stomach pain, bloating and diarrhoea, and people affected either avoid lactose, or can sometimes benefit from substitutes for lactase, the enzyme needed to break down the milk sugars. Some sufferers can tolerate small quantities of milk, in hot drinks for example, but have problems with higher amounts.

Coeliac disease is not an allergy or intolerance, but a serious medical condition.

- The immune system mistakenly sees a protein in gluten as a threat. The immune response causes inflammation and damage in the small intestine, leading to bloating, diarrhoea, weight loss and, if left untreated, malnutrition.

- Gluten is found in wheat, rye and barley and it's estimated 1 in 100 people in the UK have coeliac disease, but only a quarter have been diagnosed, which could mean up to half a million people are untreated. The condition is diagnosed by a blood test or biopsy.

Oral allergy syndrome is a specific syndrome which can be triggered either by pollens, or certain raw fruit, vegetables or nuts and, most rarely, latex.

- It causes painful reactions in the mouth and throat, including itching and swelling.

- It usually settles down after an hour, but it's important to have full medical allergy testing to ensure you understand the cause and severity.

I think I have an allergy or intolerance: what should I do?

If your systems are painful, persistent or getting worse – or if there's blood in your bowel motions or you're losing weight – then you should see your GP to rule out a true allergy, or coeliac disease.

But for many of us, that won't lead to a diagnosis. So, what next? The answer is to try to identify what's causing the problems through keeping a food diary.

Keeping a food and symptoms diary

- If you've ever had a *SEVERE* reaction, as under allergies above, then it is absolutely essential to see your GP first in case eliminating and then reintroducing a foodstuff causes a serious allergic reaction.

- For best results with food diaries and elimination diets, work with a registered dietician (see the British Dietetic Association website to understand the difference between legally regulated dieticians, and others who offer nutrition advice, www.bda.uk.com).

- Start by keeping a diary of everything you eat and drink for two weeks, and note symptoms: when they happen; how severe they are; and how long they last.

Eliminating common causes

- After two weeks of recording normal eating, begin to eliminate common causes of intolerance, like dairy or wheat (gluten). It's easier to do this with professional help, to make sure you really are excluding all sources *and* still getting adequate nutrition from other sources.

- This elimination period should last from two to six weeks: keep the diary going to note if and when you feel better.

Reintroducing foods

- After two to six weeks, reintroduce types of food *one at a time,* and monitor your response in your food diary. By eliminating those foods, you've increased the chances of your body reacting quite strongly when they're re-introduced, which will help diagnose what may be causing the problems.

- If you have a severe response, seek medical attention.

Specialist diets

- A FODMAP diet is a specific diet which is low in 'fermentable oligosaccharides, disaccharides, monosaccharides and polyols' – foods which are harder to digest and ferment in the gut, causing painful bloating or diarrhoea. (If you think of how fermenting beer produces bubbles, imagine something similar happening in the gut!) Difficulty digesting and absorbing nutrients from these foods can be a cause of Irritable Bowel Syndrome (IBS) and other digestive conditions. However, as so many foods may be involved, it's recommended that you do this under the supervision of a registered dietician.

Spotted the trigger – now what?

Even if you are intolerant of certain foods, the level of reaction can vary a lot. Some of us are able to tolerate a small amount of wheat or dairy, but the best way to discover this is to experiment. You can also explore different types of dairy or wheat, which may be lower in allergens.

- **Wheat intolerance?** Breads or types of wheat may cause less of a response. Most mass-produced bread uses the 'Chorleywood' method, which speeds up the process by missing out a traditional second rising stage. Bread baked using traditional methods may be easier to digest, as may bread containing 'wild' sourdough yeasts, so both are worth seeking out.

- **Read the labels:** dairy and wheat derivatives can turn up in the most unexpected places – for example, some flavours of crisps contain milk powder – so keep a close eye on processed foods.

- Ancient grains like spelt are also worth trying: spelt still contains gluten, but has a different structure to modern wheat, and may also be easier to digest.

- A simple option is to try toasting your bread – cooked wheat may also be gentler on the stomach.

- **Dairy intolerance?** Fermented dairy products, like yoghurt or the more liquid Turkish kefir, may be easier on the stomach as much of the lactose is fermented. The same is true of hard cheeses like Cheddar and Parmesan.

Kate's verdict

This is close to home for me: I suffered from mild IBS for years (though it didn't feel mild when stomach pain woke me up every day). I've never had the patience to follow a complete elimination diet, but I do know that if I overdo wheat, my symptoms seem worse. And as I admit on page 240, I do crave toast at times, which can be another sign of intolerance.

My problem is, I like bread and baked goods, and I don't want to eliminate wheat from my diet. I deliberately never had an intolerance test, as they're expensive and unreliable, but I manage symptoms by eating less bread overall, and certainly less mass-produced supermarket bread. I might choose some gluten-free cakes as treats (e.g. brownies made with almond flour) and if I overdo it, I accept there may be some symptoms.

I really recommend the www.allergyuk.org website for lots of detail, advice and information on allergies and intolerances.

5:2 Food Heroes

HERBS AND SPICES

Whether it's freshly ground black pepper, a few fresh basil leaves or a blend of whole spices to create the perfect curry, herbs and spices are rich in flavour *and* health benefits.

All about herbs and spices

We group the two together, but a herb is generally the fresh or dried leaves from a plant while a spice tends to be the dried seed, root or fruit instead. Both are used to add flavour, and many have powerful medicinal properties. Many also help fight the insects or microbes which make food go 'off', which is why the hotter the country, the more powerful the spices used in their cuisine.

Nutrition

Oil and fats Many spices are actually rich in oil or fat and protein and seem quite calorific per gram, but we're using small amounts.

Concentrated micronutrients They also contain vitamins, minerals and antioxidant compounds. These concentrated micronutrients help preserve food *and* protect the health of your cells.

Downsides

Side effects More powerful herbal remedies can cause effects for people with particular medical conditions or who are taking certain medications.

Contamination There have been some cases of contamination or adulteration (mixing the herbs with less expensive ingredients). So always get your spices from a reliable source (see How to buy and store).

Four Superheroes

To write about every heroic herb and spice would fill several books, but here are four top picks.

Turmeric Recognisable for its intense orange colour, turmeric has a warm, peppery flavour. It is mostly used ground, and is an essential ingredient in many curries. You can sometimes find the fresh root, which can be grated and used in small quantities, like ginger. The compounds it contains, including curcumin, are subject to medical research to see if they can prevent or treat a host of diseases, including cancer, diabetes and digestive conditions.

Ginger This is another root, from the same family as turmeric, and it's most commonly used ground, or grated from the mature root. Both ground and fresh ginger have a hot, intense flavour, though ground ginger is more commonly used in sweet or baked dishes. It's used in many Asian cuisines, from Chinese stir-fries, to Indian masala chai or Japanese pickled ginger. It's often used to fight nausea, and may slow cancer growth and protect the digestive system from infections.

Mint This familiar herb comes in many varieties, but peppermint leaves have anti-spasmodic effects that can help with digestive problems like Irritable Bowel Syndrome as they help the muscles relax. In many cultures, mint leaves are steeped in hot water and the resulting drink is taken after eating to aid digestion. The oils contained in mint are being researched for their potential effect on tumours, anti-microbial action, and allergies.

Cumin This is a seed, and it is frequently used in Asian and South American cuisines, and even Dutch cheese. It is used in herbal medicine to calm the digestion, and is being tested for possible positive effects on epilepsy, diabetes and the immune system.

How to buy and store herbs and spices

- You can buy fresh herbs from supermarkets or markets, either bunched or 'growing' in pots.

- Growing your own is also an option – either from seed or small plants. Some, like rosemary, thyme or mint, will regrow year after year, while others like coriander or chervil may not last longer than a season.

- You can also freeze leftover herbs in small bundles, or dry them, though the texture and colour will change.

- When buying spices, find a reliable source, whether it is a large supermarket, or a small shop specialising in ethnic ingredients. You want to find somewhere with a rapid turnover, otherwise your jar or bag of spices might have been on the shelf for months, even years, before you bought it.

- Dried herbs and spices lose their flavour over time, so it's wise to buy smaller quantities and replace them as the colour changes or the smell becomes less powerful.

- Exposure to light or heat speeds up the 'ageing' process, so I buy bags of spices and decant small quantities into a metal spice tin. I then keep the larger bags in an airtight tin out of the sun to help them last longer.

- You can also buy frozen or puréed spice or herb mixes, useful if you are in a hurry.

How to cook with herbs and spices

- Fresh leafy herbs like basil, mint and dill are best used as a garnish, either chopped or torn, to preserve their delicate texture and oils.

- Woodier fresh herbs like rosemary and thyme can be added at the beginning of the cooking time to impart deeper flavours. Remove the stems before serving.

- Whole spices like coriander, mustard seeds or cumin can be added as they are to a dish, or ground or gently crushed before using. You can also toast them in a dry, hot pan.

- Ground spices like cinnamon, ginger, chilli powder or turmeric are best added with liquid or fat, and it's best to add a little at a time, then taste, because there's not much you can do once you've added too much ground spice.

Recipe Ideas

Coconut and Chicken Thai Broth page 76

Many of the dishes in the Spice World chapter page 194

Herb Infusions page 293

Comfort and Joy

Food can be exciting and full of challenging new ingredients but it can also be reassuring, wholesome and a weapon against the wind and the rain. So here is a selection of dishes that give you a virtual hug, and make you feel ready to face the world again. Sometimes it's about twisting the familiar, as with the fresh take on 'fish and chips', or it's about rediscovering an ingredient, as with the pearl barley risotto. It can even be about transforming the humble omelette into something to put a *very* cheesy grin on your face.

PEARL BARLEY RISOTTO WITH SHERRIED MUSHROOMS, CAVALO NERO AND SAGE

CHICKEN SAUSAGE ROLL WITH LEEK, MUSHROOM AND THYME

PLAICE, LEMON AND CAPERS WITH COURGETTE FRITES

CHILLI-SPICED CHICKEN BURGER ON A MUSHROOM 'BUN'

JAMBALAYA WITH PRAWNS

SPRING FISH PIE

TWO-CHEESE SOUFFLÉ OMELETTE WITH ROCKET AND ONION SALAD

GRILLED PEPPER STUFFED WITH MILLET AND CHICKEN

ONE-PAN PORK WITH SAGE AND ROAST VEGETABLES

PLUS …

MAKING SENSE OF… EMOTIONAL EATING

5:2 FOOD HEROES: WHOLE GRAINS

5:2 Lives

ESCAPING FROM 27 YEARS IN 'DIET PRISON'

'It really suits my "all or nothing" approach to dieting, and IT WORKS! I've inspired at least five more people to do 5:2.' Trudie, 52

For Trudie McCallum from Tauranga in New Zealand, dieting felt like a 27-year prison sentence.

And when the 52-year-old retail manager embarked on 5:2 in October 2013, she felt like she'd finally found the key to escape.

'I wanted to achieve weight loss, of course, plus gain body confidence and to enjoy shopping for clothes. I also wanted to break free from 27 years of yo-yo dieting. I calculated I'd spent over NZ$1000 on diet clubs and lost and gained over 100kg over those years.'

It's a familiar feeling for so many dieters – and for Trudie, 5:2 lived up to expectations. She broke free in a big way: losing 13kg (28½ lb) and seeing her BMI drop from the obese level to close to the healthy range. More importantly to her, 'my waist measurement is now less than half my height so I'm happy with that' (see page 14 for why your waist measurement matters).

Her doctor is impressed, too, as Trudie's blood pressure, cholesterol and glucose levels have all improved. 'I feel I have finally found a way of eating that I can stick to forever. I don't ever want to restrict myself to low-calorie diets ever again.

It wasn't always a completely steady loss, with a few hitches along the way. But Trudie kept the faith: 'If you hit a plateau don't get disheartened. I stayed the same weight for a couple of months, but kept going and just changed things slightly and away it went again.'

I have only ever "failed" two Fast Days, which has really surprised me. And I don't count calories on feast days. Whenever I see other diet plans and shakes, bars, etc being promoted I just want to shout, "Try 5:2! It works!" '

She also finds herself taking more notice of her body's signals. I am quite happy to go four to five hours without food, whereas before I'd be raiding the fridge or nipping to the supermarket for a wee treat (working in a shopping mall means food is very accessible). But now I know it's OK to be hungry sometimes!'

But there is one downside: 'I've found that my sensitivity to alcohol has changed and have suffered a few severe hangovers!'

Trudie is now spreading the word, starting with her own husband, Kenny, who is also doing 5:2, but also showing others what can be done.

Trudie's Fast Day diary

Breakfast: 7 a.m. Two Weetabix with trim milk (a type of low-fat milk) and artificial sweetener. Cup of tea with trim milk.

11 a.m. Small Trim Flat White coffee.

Lunch: 2 p.m. 1 boiled egg, 1 apple, 1 carrot, cut into sticks (and I usually have some mid-morning as well).

Dinner: 6:30 p.m. Shakshouka (made with half tin Mexican tomatoes and 1 egg), or soup or salad with tuna or chicken.

I always fast on a work day so that temptation isn't close. Sometimes I might go over 500 with a mandarin or kiwi fruit) but I figure 30–40 calories won't kill me.

I drink coffee or tea with allocated trim milk, herbal tea and about 2 litres of water.

Trudie's non-fasting day diary

I don't count but try to eat sensibly and find that I get full quicker than before. I always eat breakfast. I tried going without on a Fast Day, but it didn't make much difference so went back to having it. I eat plenty of fruit and vegetables, eggs and have meat on most feast days. I enjoy bread, nuts, muffins, scones, cheese and crackers all in moderation, and have the odd takeaway or meal out (probably once every six to eight weeks). I also enjoy a few glasses of wine at the weekend.

Favourite foods

Roast dinner (just love tasty beef or chicken and roasted vegetables with gravy), chocolate (no explanation needed), garlic bread (tasty and crunchy), and a glass of Chardonnay or Sauvignon Blanc (we have some of the best wine in New Zealand after all).

Best thing about 5:2?

You have a 'diet holiday' every week, and it fits perfectly into my lifestyle. It really suits my 'all or nothing' approach to dieting, and IT WORKS!!

Trudie's top tip

Plan, plan, plan, and know that breakfast is only a sleep away!

PEARL BARLEY RISOTTO WITH SHERRIED MUSHROOMS, CAVOLO NERO AND SAGE

Calories per serving: 328; 348 with truffle oil

Vegetarian/vegan/nut free

This dish is our cover star – and no wonder. It's a hearty, warming, autumnal meal that uses pearl barley, an ingredient that deserves a renaissance (see more about unusual grains on page 359). Apart from anything else, it's much less effort than traditional risotto because you don't have to stand by the pan stirring constantly. This will reheat well the next day in the microwave so the recipe makes two portions.

Serves 2
Preparation time: 10 minutes
Cooking time: 35–40 minutes

1-cal cooking spray or ½ tsp butter 1–19 cals
50ml sherry 58 cals or white wine 33 cals
150g fresh chestnut mushrooms 20 cals
5g porcini mushrooms 13 cals
3 cloves garlic, chopped 12 cals
1 medium leek, chopped 40 cals
125g pearl barley 440 cals
5 fresh or dried sage leaves 2 cals
550ml fresh vegetable stock 14 cals or made with 1 tsp Marigold bouillon 12 cals
60g cavolo nero, leaves roughly chopped 23 cals
15g reduced fat cheddar cheese, to serve 32 cals
½ tsp truffle oil (optional) 22 cals

1. Spray a medium non-stick saucepan with 1-cal cooking spray, or use ½ teaspoon butter, add a teaspoon of the sherry, and gently cook the mushrooms over a low heat, moving them as little as possible so the edges caramelise. Meanwhile, soak the porcini mushrooms in 2 tablespoons of hot water.

2. Remove the fried mushrooms from the pan with a slotted spoon and set them aside. Add the garlic and leek to the same pan and gently fry for 5 minutes (add a little stock if they stick).

Add the barley, remaining sherry, sage, dried mushrooms with soaking water, plus three-quarters of the stock. Bring to the boil then reduce to a simmer and cook for 20 minutes, or until the water has been absorbed. Stir every few minutes and add more stock if it sticks.

3. Return the cooked mushrooms to the pan and add the cavolo nero. Cook for 10 minutes, adding more stock or water if the mixture is drying out.

4. Serve in a bowl topped with the cheese sprinkled over, and drizzle with truffle oil if using.

More ideas from the 5:2 Kitchen To add even more body to the dish, add ½ drained tin cooked white beans, such as cannellini (105–120 calories). Or try cubed squash, peas or borlotti beans and a little bacon, and use thyme instead of sage.

On a non-fasting day, be more generous with the cheese, and add a nice dollop of mascarpone or sour cream, stirred through at the last moment, to make it deliciously creamy.

CHICKEN SAUSAGE ROLL WITH LEEK, MUSHROOMS AND THYME
Calories per serving: 289

Nut free

Mmm, sausage rolls: the ultimate comfort food. And this is *better* than a normal sausage roll because there's no processed meat involved, and you know *exactly* what went into it. The leeks, garlic and thyme give it such a fresh flavour *and* you eat it fresh and golden, straight from the oven. To make it worth buying the filo pastry, make four and freeze them for future Fast Days.

Makes 4 large rolls
Preparation time: 30 minutes
Cooking time: 30 minutes

2 tsp olive oil 90 cals
250g leeks, chopped 55 cals
1 garlic clove, sliced 4 cals
4 thyme sprigs 3 cals

100g baby chestnut mushrooms, quartered 13 cals
300g skinless chicken breast, chopped 360 cals
25g wholewheat breadcrumbs 55 cals
4 sheets of filo pastry 576 cals
salt and pepper

1. Heat 1 teaspoon of the oil in a non-stick frying pan over a low heat. Add the leek and 1 tablespoon water. Fry gently for 1 minute, or until the leek is just starting to soften. Stir in the garlic, thyme and mushrooms and cook for 5 minutes, or until just golden.

2. Spoon into a bowl, pull out and discard any stalky bits of thyme and leave the mixture to cool. Preheat the oven to 200°C/400°F/Gas mark 6. Line a baking sheet with non-stick baking paper.

3. Add the chicken and breadcrumbs to a bowl, stir them together and season well.

4. Lay one filo sheet out on a board and fold it in half. Spoon one-quarter of the mixture onto the pastry, leaving a 2cm border at the side and at the bottom. Roll up the pastry starting from the bottom, tucking in the ends as you go to make a long sausage. Brush the end with the remaining teaspoon of oil, roll and tuck in and brush the top again. Place on the prepared baking sheet.

5. Do the same with the rest of the filo and filling. Bake for 30 minutes until golden, or freeze following the tip below. Serve immediately.

Freeze once all the sausages are shaped and wrap each one individually in cling film. Well wrapped, these will freeze for up to a month. To use, remove from the freezer, unwrap and bake from frozen at 200°C/400°F/Gas mark 6 for around 40 minutes, or until golden on the outside and hot all the way through.

More ideas from the 5:2 Kitchen These are great served with roast vine tomatoes (17 calories per serving). Take 75g of tomatoes on the vine per person, place in an ovenproof dish, season with salt and pepper and sprinkle over either dried chilli flakes, a teaspoon of balsamic vinegar or a few torn basil leaves. Roast alongside the sausage roll for the last 20 minutes.

PLAICE, LEMON AND CAPERS WITH COURGETTE FRITES
Calories per serving: 216

Gluten free/nut free

Instead of being tempted by the chippy on your way home, cook this yummy fish dish, which incorporates the ingredients from tartare sauce, rolled *into* the fillet, keeping it moist and infusing flavour through cooking. And dismiss those heavy, soggy chips in favour of these fantastically savoury courgette frites, plus a juicy baked tomato.

Serves 1
Preparation time: 15 minutes
Cooking time: 20–30 minutes

¼ tsp olive oil 11 cals
1 tbsp white wine vinegar 2–3 cals
good pinch smoked paprika
1 courgette, trimmed and sliced into discs 34 cals
1 plaice fillet, weighing about 125g, skinned and halved into long pieces
    106 cals
½ shallot, finely chopped 4 cals
1 tbsp capers 4 cals
1 tbsp chopped fresh parsley 5 cals
zest of ¼ lemon 1 cal
75g plum tomato, halved 15 cals
sea salt and black pepper

1. First make the frites. Preheat the oven to 200°C/400°F/Gas mark 6 and line a baking sheet with non-stick baking paper. Mix together the oil, vinegar and smoked paprika and brush the mixture over each side of the courgette discs. Lay them on the baking sheet and roast for 15 minutes.

2. Lay the plaice fillets on a board and sprinkle over the shallot, capers, parsley and lemon zest. Roll up, from the shortest end and put in a shallow baking tin. Season the fish with a little black pepper.

3. When the courgette frites have roasted for 15 minutes, turn them over to cook the other side. Put the plaice rolls and the halved plum tomato (cut-side up) alongside, sprinkling the

tomato with a little seasoning as you go. Leave everything to roast for 10–15 minutes, or until the courgettes are golden and the plaice is cooked through.

More ideas from the 5:2 Kitchen As an alternative to the tomato, try using minted peas: boil or microwave 50g of frozen *petit pois* (25 calories) following the instructions on the pack, then season well. Add a few finely chopped mint leaves before squashing lightly with a fork.

CHILLI-SPICED CHICKEN BURGER ON A MUSHROOM 'BUN'
Calories per serving: 150

Gluten free/nut free/low carb

This could be the 'surely too good to be true' burger: low carb, gluten free, nut free – *and* it tastes brilliant. The only downside is that it has a tendency to disappear within seconds of being made, as happened at our photo shoot (you have been warned). But with such a low calorie count, you could always make two!

Serves 1
Preparation time: 10 minutes
Cooking time: 15 minutes

> ½ red pepper, halved and deseeded 15 cals
> ¼ red onion, sliced 10 cals
> 1 tsp red wine vinegar 1 cal
> 1 skinless, boneless chicken thigh, roughly chopped 95 cals
> 1 shallot, finely chopped 7 cals
> ½ red chilli, finely chopped 2 cals
> leaves picked from 2 sprigs of thyme 2 cals
> 1 portobello mushroom 18 cals
> handful rocket 2 cals
> salt and pepper

1. Preheat the grill to hot. Put the pepper on a baking sheet, skin-side up, and grill until the skin has blackened and blistered. Meanwhile, place the red onion slices into another bowl with a pinch of salt, pour over the vinegar and set aside to marinate. When the pepper

is done, remove it from the heat and place it in a bowl. Cover, and set aside to allow the steam to loosen the skins. Peel away and discard the skin and stalk, then slice thinly and put in a bowl with the juices.

2. Put the chicken, shallot, chilli and thyme into a food processor. Season well, then pulse until the chicken is finely minced. Scoop out the mixture and shape it into a burger. Make sure it's not too thick or it won't cook all the way through.

3. Place a non-stick frying pan over a medium heat and spray with the 1-cal cooking spray. Cook the burger for 5 minutes on each side, or until cooked through. To test, pierce the middle with a skewer. When the juices that run out are clear and not pink, the chicken is done. Set aside on a plate.

4. Put the portobello mushroom into the pan and cook for 1–2 minutes, or until heated through. Transfer to a plate, spoon on the marinated red onion and put the burger on top, followed by the pepper, rocket and any juices from the burger and pepper.

More ideas from the 5:2 Kitchen The mushroom 'bun' is a great alternative to bread if you want to avoid carbohydrates. You could even try it with normal beef burgers on a Fast or non-fasting day. Or for vegetarians, place a 50g slice of reduced-fat halloumi (128 calories) on top of the mushroom and serve with red onion slices and chilli sauce.

PRAWN JAMBALAYA
Calories per portion: 358

Nut free

Rice, especially brown rice, is such a comforting food and this Creole-style jambalaya is vibrant *and* soothing, with so many colours and herby flavours. The calorie count is on the high side for a Fast Day (have a soup or a couple of cheese and apple muffins with salad for lunch), but it's *so* worth it.

Serves 1
Preparation time: 20 minutes
Cooking time: 25 minutes

½ tsp olive oil 22 cals
1 spring onion, chopped 1–2 cals
1 celery stick, chopped 6 cals
50g green beans, chopped 14 cals
50g runner beans, chopped 12 cals
½ yellow pepper, chopped 15 cals
4 cherry tomatoes, halved 12–20 cals
1 garlic clove, sliced 4 cals
2 tsp tomato purée 7–25 cals
¼ tsp each paprika, cayenne, dried oregano and dried thyme 5 cals
50g long-grain brown rice 177 cals
300ml hot vegetable stock 8 cals
100g cooked prawns 65 cals
1 tbsp fresh parsley, chopped 5 cals
¼ lemon 5 cals
salt and pepper

1. Heat the oil in a small saucepan over a low heat and add the spring onion, celery, the beans, pepper and cherry tomatoes. Stir in 1 tablespoon of water, cover with a lid and let the mixture cook for 10 minutes, or until softened.

2. Stir in the garlic, tomato purée, spices and dried herbs, season well and cook for a further 3 minutes.

3. Stir in the rice, cook for a minute then pour over the stock. Cover the pan with a lid, bring to the boil and then turn the heat right down low and simmer for 25 minutes, or until the rice is cooked.

4. Stir in the prawns and parsley and set aside for 5 minutes to allow all the flavours to come together, then serve with the wedge of lemon on the side.

More ideas from the 5:2 Kitchen Jambalaya, which means 'mix up', originated as a New World version of paella. So, why not add chorizo? Fry 10g finely chopped chorizo (49 calories) in a non-stick pan until golden. Use 50g of prawns, and stir them in along with the chorizo in step 4. This version is 353 calories.

SPRING FISH PIE

Calories per serving: 310

Nut free

This is easy to make, though takes a little extra time. The combination of a buttery dill sauce, spring vegetables, cod, salmon *and* a crunchy filo topping works so well, and makes for a great sharing dish, too.

Serves 4
Preparation time: 20 minutes
Cooking time: 20–25 minutes

> 15g butter 111 cals
> 25g plain flour 84 cals
> 300ml skimmed milk 105 cals
> 1 tbsp fresh dill, chopped 5 cals
> 200g white fish, such as cod, cut into large chunks 192 cals
> 200g salmon fillets, cut into large chunks 280–400 cals
> 50g kale, chopped 18 cals
> 50g frozen peas, thawed 35 cals
> 8 asparagus spears, weighing about 100g 27 cals
> 2 sheets filo pastry 288 cals
> 25g Grana Padano cheese, finely grated 96 cals
> salt and pepper

1. Preheat the oven to 200°C/400°F/Gas mark 6. Melt the butter in a small pan, stir in the flour and cook for 1 minute. Take the pan off the heat and slowly stir in the milk. Return the pan to the heat and slowly bring to the boil, stirring, for 3–5 minutes, or until thickened. Stir in the dill and season well.

2. Put the fish into a large ovenproof dish. Scatter over the kale, frozen peas, asparagus and sauce.

3. Loosely scrunch up each piece of filo and put on top of the pie. Scatter over the cheese and bake for 20–25 minutes. Serve immediately.

More ideas from the 5:2 Kitchen Steamed long-stemmed broccoli with a little lemon rind grated over this would make a lovely side dish.

TWO-CHEESE SOUFFLÉ OMELETTE WITH ROCKET AND ONION SALAD

Calories per serving: 230–270, plus salad 23

Vegetarian/nut free/gluten free

This is a 'cheat's' soufflé, made quick as a flash in a frying pan. And it definitely qualifies as comfort food, despite the lightness of the dish, because it's so decadently cheesy. I also like to think that beating the egg whites by hand burns a couple more calories on a Fast Day. You can serve it folded over in the traditional way, but I like it pizza-style with salad on the side.

Omelette
Serves 1
Preparation time: 5 minutes
Cooking time: 6–7 minutes

2 eggs, separated 158 cals
small handful fresh herbs, such as chives and parsley 5 cals
1-cal cooking spray or ½ tsp olive oil 22 cals
10g grated reduced-fat mature cheddar 22 cals or Emmental cheese 40 cals
15g soft goat's cheese with garlic and herbs 45 cals

Rocket and onion salad
To serve: 23 cals

30g rocket 8 cals
¼ of a red onion, thinly sliced 10 cals
1 tbsp balsamic vinegar, to taste 5–20
salt and pepper

1. Place the yolks in a bowl, season and stir in the chopped herbs. Whisk the whites in a clean, dry bowl until stiff, then very gently fold the whites into the yolk mixture, taking care not to lose too much air from the whites.

2. Preheat the grill to high. Spray a small frying pan that can go under the grill with 1-cal cooking spray or add the oil. Place over a medium heat and tip in the egg mixture. Cook for 3–4 minutes (check the underside is lightly browned by lifting with a spatula) then crumble over the goat's cheese and grated cheese.

3. Place the pan under the grill for 2–3 minutes. It should puff up so leave room under the grill for that to happen.

4. Once the omelette is brown on top, slide it onto a plate. Either serve open, or score a line down the middle with a knife, and fold over. Serve without delay while still puffed up, with the rocket and onion salad, dressed with the vinegar, on the side.

More ideas from the 5:2 Kitchen You could add dried Provençal herbs or finely shredded baby spinach to the yolks. For fillings, try cooking thinly sliced mushrooms until soft, season and add to the centre of the freshly cooked omelette before you fold it. Smoked salmon or avocado would also be tasty as fillings, added just before serving.

GRILLED RED PEPPER STUFFED WITH MILLET AND CHICKEN
Calories per serving: 214

Nut free/dairy free

Millet has had a raw deal from the folks who describe it as birdseed. In fact, it's an ancient grain with a slightly nutty taste, plus an impressive nutritional cv, (see page 248), and you can use it anywhere you'd use rice. This dish makes the most of its versatility to create a satisfying bake for two (or eat one, and freeze the other portion for the next Fast Day).

Makes 2 portions
Preparation time: 15 minutes
Cooking time: around 25 minutes

½ tsp olive oil 22 cals
½ onion, chopped 19 cals
75g chicken breast, chopped 90 cals
50g millet 189 cals
175g butternut squash, peeled, deseeded and chopped
    70 cals
200ml hot chicken stock 8 cals
good pinch dried mixed herbs
1 red pepper, halved, cored and deseeded 30 cals
salt and pepper

1. Heat the oil in a saucepan and add the onion. Cook over a low heat for
   5 minutes to start to soften the onion.

2. Stir in the chicken, millet and squash and continue to cook for 2–3 minutes. Season well.

3. Pour in the stock and herbs, cover and bring to the boil. Turn the heat down low and leave to
   simmer for 15 minutes. Preheat the grill to high.

4. Put the pepper halves on a baking sheet, skin-side up, and grill for 15 minutes, or until
   slightly softened.

5. Spoon the hot millet mixture into the pepper halves to serve.

To freeze, leave the stuffed peppers to cool then put them into an airtight container. These will keep for up to a month in the freezer. To serve, thaw overnight at a cool room temperature then microwave on low until heated right through.

More ideas from the 5:2 Kitchen Add mushrooms and leeks in place of the chicken for a vegetarian version, and sprinkle a little reduced-fat cheddar or pumpkin seeds over the pepper halves before grilling.

ONE-PAN PORK WITH SAGE AND ROASTED VEGETABLES

Calories per serving: 329 calories

Gluten free/nut free

Sage smells of Sundays to me; it's the scent of roasts and steamy autumnal lunches. This dish is definitely one to warm the cockles of your heart when there's a nip in the air. The sage fragrances the kitchen, and the lovely mixture of pork and colourful vegetables will fill your belly *very* nicely – for just over 300 calories! It's a one-pan wonder.

ServesPreparation time: 25 minutes
Cooking time: 40 minutes

200g sweet potato, cut into wedges 172 cals
½ red pepper, halved and deseeded 15 cals
1 medium courgette, halved then halved again through the middle 34 cals
1 large plum tomato, halved 16 cals
½ red onion, halved 19 cals
1 tsp olive oil 45 cals
200g pork tenderloin, cut into two 100g pieces 280 cals
4 sage leaves, chopped 2 cals
2 slices Parma ham 62 cals
300ml hot chicken stock 12 cals
salt and pepper

1. Preheat the oven to 200°C/400°F/Gas mark 6. Line a large roasting tin with non-stick baking paper.

2. Put the sweet potato, pepper, courgettes, tomato and onion into the tin. Whisk the oil together with 2 tablespoons water and drizzle all over the vegetables. Season well and roast for 20 minutes.

3. Season the pork, then rub the chopped sage all over and wrap each piece of pork in a slice of Parma ham. Add the pork to the tin and pour over the hot stock. Roast for a further 20 minutes until everything is cooked through and golden.

4. Serve half the vegetables per portion, alongside a piece of the pork, drizzled with any stock left behind in the pan.

More ideas from the 5:2 Kitchen You can vary both the herbs and the vegetables in this. At 40 calories per 100g, autumnal butternut squash would be even lower in calories than the sweet potato. And for a different flavour, replace the sage with rosemary.

Making sense of... emotional eating

Do you have a food you crave when you're fed up?

Mine is buttered toast with, or without, peanut butter, honey or avocado. I tell myself I can have just one slice, and sometimes I can. But if I am feeling really tired, stressed or down in the dumps, it's *very* hard to stop.

It doesn't matter what your foodie Achilles Heel is: chocolate, ice cream, chips or cheese. When I asked people in the 5:2 group, savoury food came top, with chocolate next: more unusual options included tinned tomato soup, chips with gravy, and wine gums. If you recognise those cravings, then you probably don't need to be told how emotional eating can sabotage your weight loss, *and* make you feel like a failure.

So why do we eat emotionally? Which foods are most likely to trigger it? And most important of all, what can we do to control it?

Why do emotions sometimes trigger eating?

Emotional eating is when we eat, not because we're hungry, but because we're craving food for other reasons, which might be boredom, frustration or any kind of emotional upset.

As I explained in *Making sense of… appetite* (see page 86), hunger is never a purely 'physical' response because the brain has such a central role in how we experience appetite. And for many of us, there are definitely times when the urge to eat has nothing to do with rumbles in the tummy.

Many of the factors from the 'appetite' chapter have a bearing on emotional eating, ranging from which foods were offered as a reward or comfort to us when we were children, to the environment we're in. Stress is also a big factor: the hormone cortisol is released when we feel stressed, and this can make us hungry.

How common is emotional eating – and is it an eating disorder?

Eating chocolate occasionally to cheer you up is very different to binge-ing every few days. The NHS use the 'SCOFF' questionnaire to screen people for eating disorders see (Resources for links, page 378) but the questions do seem weighted towards anorexia. The National Institute for Clinical Excellence estimates 1.6 million people in the UK have a disorder, though another study in 2007 suggests the true incidence is 6.4 per cent, of the population, and one-quarter of those may be male.

So do see your GP or contact the BEAT helpline below if you feel that food is dominating your life. There are a number of treatments – including talking therapies and medication – that can help.

For most of us, comfort eating is more frustrating than traumatic. I asked members of our 5:2 group about the problem, and of almost 300 who answered, only 1 per cent had sought help, but more than two-thirds said they did comfort eat, and they didn't like how it made them feel. Though stress or upset can have the opposite effect: 12 per cent said they couldn't face eating at all during emotional or difficult times.

How does emotional eating feel?

We all know how it feels to sit down for a long leisurely meal, maybe outdoors, savouring every bite. Emotional eating isn't like that. It can feel:

- **Urgent** The need to eat is more important than anything else, and only certain foods, often those high in sugar or fat, will satisfy the craving.

- **Addictive** You try to stop, but fail.

- **Like a way of burying the negative emotions you're feeling** You may feel you're literally 'pushing them down' by eating to fill yourself up.

- **Unsatisfying** You don't actually taste the food at all, but you want more of it.

- **Hurried** You're already planning the next piece of chocolate or slice of toast as you eat the current one.

- **Punishing** Even as you're eating, you don't like what you're doing but can't seem to stop. And when you're finished, especially if this problem is leading to weight gain, you feel even worse about yourself.

- **Out of control** You can't stop until the food is finished.

- **Shameful** You do it alone, and you hide any evidence, like empty packaging.

Controlling it

To gain control over emotional eating, you need first, to understand and recognise what's happening and why. Second, you need to find strategies to avoid or limit the damage.

Understanding what makes YOU eat emotionally

The simplest way to begin to understand is to keep a food and emotions diary. It might even be enough to help you control your cravings.

- In a notebook, write down whenever you eat and how you feel at that moment in time. Include normal meals as well as any emotional episodes.

- Remember, no one has to see what you're writing, so you can be honest. Find a safe place for your notebook.

- Go into as much detail as you can when the eating is emotionally driven. Ask yourself:

  - When did I last eat? Is there an element of physical hunger? How am I experiencing this? Is it a feeling in the brain, the body or a mixture?

  - What has happened that might trigger this need?

    - Boredom or frustration

    - General stress

    - Low mood or depression

    - A specific issue e.g. family, financial or work problems.

- Once you've been keeping your diary for a week or two, review what you've written.

  - Look for patterns – times of day, specific days, or places when the urge to overeat happens.

  - Look for the foods you eat – are there particular foods or groups of food that you always crave?

  - Look for causes – does it happen in response to a range of emotions or situations, or can you identify one or two?

Strategies

If this is happening more than a couple of times a week, think about asking for outside help.

Otherwise, make a list of strategies you can use at the time of a craving, and to prevent yourself acting on it. For example:

1. **Postpone eating** Set a timer for just 10 minutes and do something else before you let yourself eat. Even writing how you feel in your diary could help.

2. **Find alternatives** Keep a list of activities, especially if eating is triggered by boredom. Walk round the block, go online or play a game on your phone, read a book, put on some music and dance, call a friend, clean the loo, watch a comedy sketch online, make a hot drink with no calories or sip a pint of water.

3. **Seek support** Is there a friend or family member you can call for help when you're having a craving? Enlist their support and call, text or email as soon as you feel a craving so they can remind you what to do. Shame adds to our feelings of isolation, so sharing your feelings with the right person can be very helpful.

4. **Learn relaxation techniques** Simple deep breathing or mindfulness can help take the focus off food. Try www.headspace.com for a 10-minute-a-day course.

5. **Tackle the issues head on** If you're stressed, work out what the cause is and try to divert your energy from food and into dealing with the problems. This may not work during a craving, but you could use your notebook to list what needs to be done, whether that's calling your bank to discuss your overdraft, or sitting down to talk to your partner.

6. **Clear the larder** This is a very practical step. If you don't have your trigger foods nearby at home or work, you'll have to make a special trip, by which time the urge may be controllable. It's not nearly as satisfying to eat vegetables compulsively, and if you do, you're unlikely to feel as guilty afterwards. If your partner or family members like the foods that trigger you, ask them to keep them somewhere you can't find them.

Kate's verdict

If you're an occasional emotional eater, then I hope
some of these strategies help: I find slowing my eating
down definitely works, nine times out of ten. But don't
forget, professional help is available, from your GP or
via www.b-eat.co.uk and www.nhs.uk/conditions/
Binge-eating.

Food is a pleasure, and a comfort. Sometimes you will
reward yourself for hard work, or deal with tricky times by
enjoying a good moan with friends over food, perhaps
with wine. And if you do slip up, remember tomorrow is
another day.

5:2 Food Heroes

WHOLE GRAINS

Grains seem to be Public Enemy Number 1 for some dieters. But *whole* grains, which have undergone the minimum processing possible, are high in nutrients and can nourish us, without making us feel bloated or hungry again straight afterwards.

All about grains

We're talking about cereal grains here, which are the 'fruit' of grass-like crops. But don't get confused: breakfast cereals in brightly coloured packets tend to be heavily processed, and contain added sugars, so many are not good choices.

First grown by humans around 12,000 years ago, grains have been an essential part of our diet ever since. For maximum benefit, grains should be consumed whole because it is the outer parts that contain the nutrients and these are lost in processing. As a VERY general rule, processed cereals are likely to be white or pale, while whole grains are brown and the grains themselves may be larger.

Nutrition

Processing (turning wholemeal wheat flour into white, for example) doesn't just remove nutrients. It also reduces the fibre content, which would normally slow down digestion. Processed grain foods, like white bread or white pasta, are digested quickly, causing rapid rises in blood sugar, which is followed by that familiar 'slump' after a carbohydrate- or starch-heavy meal. To minimise, eat protein and a little fat with carbs at meal times.

Calorie content of grains depends on how they've been processed, and/or cooked. But they are typically around 350–400 calories per 100g of flour or whole grain.

Overall, the following grains, minimally processed, can have benefits for your heart and circulatory systems, encourage, 'friendly' bacteria in the digestive system, and also contain minerals and amino acids that support the cells, nervous system, eye health, bone and skin growth and repair, and enhance your immunity.

- **Wheat** The most common cereal in Western nations, wheat is made into bread, breakfast cereals and pasta, and used in many other foods, from soy sauce to sausages. There are many types of wheat, including more ancient forms like spelt, which can be tolerated by some people who have reactions to wheat, though spelt is not gluten-free. You may find that switching to bread made on a smaller scale by local bakers, or to sourdough bread, which uses the yeasts or 'ferments' in the air to develop the dough, may be easier for you to tolerate.

- **Rice** This forms a large part of the diet in Asia and, overall, provides more than one-fifth of the calories consumed worldwide by humans. Brown rice is higher in fibre, and slightly higher in other nutrients including B vitamins, vitamin E and a range of minerals, along with 'lignans', which may protect against cancer and heart disease. Basmati rice, especially the brown version, is a lighter, fragrant rice, with a lower Glycaemic Index (see page 305) than white rice.

- **Maize** Also referred to as sweet corn, maize is a staple part of the diet in the Americas and Africa and, in a related form, is also a very important crop for livestock. It can be eaten as a meal or flour, or as hulls as in popcorn. Polenta is a type of porridge made from cornmeal that is very popular in Italy.

- **Oats** These hardy grains are roasted as part of their processing, but still retain many benefits. They contain a type of fibre, beta-glucan, which can stabilise blood pressure in Type 2 diabetics, boost immunity, lower cholesterol levels, and reduce the risk of stroke or heart disease.

- **Barley** A nutty, fibre-rich grain, barley is possibly best known for its use as malt in beer, and it is often also used as animal feed. However, it is enjoying a revival as a human food, too. Barley's large grains can be used in soups, stews and as a side dish. Like oats, it includes beta-glucan, which has a positive effect on blood cholesterol. Pearl barley is the most processed, so the nutritional benefits are reduced, but it can be difficult to find the less processed versions. It *does* contain gluten.

- **Ancient grains** Millet and amaranth offer different textures and tastes. Millet is milder while amaranth is bitterer; both cook fairly quickly. Millet comes in different colours, and has a range of minerals, including phosphorous and magnesium. Amaranth is an Aztec grain, and as well as being simmered, it can be 'popped' like popcorn in a dry pan, to add flavour and nutrients to a dish.

Downsides

- **Gluten allergy and intolerances** These are a big talking point and you can read more about the discussion on page 213.

- **Carbohydrates** The carbohydrate content of grains is also a source of debate because of the effect on blood sugar. See page 276 for more information on this topic.

Pseudograins

You may be surprised to read that quinoa and buckwheat are not cereals at all. They're 'pseudograins', but I have included them in this chapter because they're used in similar ways to whole grains, and are great alternatives to more conventional cereals. Quinoa is a tiny 'grain-like' seed, grown originally by the Incas. It is a complete protein, contains no gluten, but is high in fibre and minerals. Buckwheat isn't wheat at all. It's actually distantly related to the rhubarb family. It is another gluten-free ingredient, with high levels of nutrients and has a more balanced effect on blood sugar than other true grains.

How to buy and store

Buy grains from stores with a quick turnover. So, for the more unusual grains, you probably want to visit a health food store that offers customers a range of grains, and the choice is likely to be wider, too.

Store at home in airtight containers or jars, in a cool place, ideally out of sunlight. Whole grains will keep for six to twelve months, flour for a little less time.

Increasingly, you can buy sealed microwavable pouches of rice or other mixed whole grains. They're very convenient, especially for grains with a longer cooking time, and are good for trying flavours new to you.

How to cook

Cooking instructions vary hugely according to the recipe, so follow the pack instructions or the specific recipes in this book. Generally, most whole grains need cooking or sprouting to make them digestible.

Recipe Ideas

Grilled Red Pepper with Millet and Chicken page 236

Buckwheat Pancakes with Breton Toppings page 259

Pearl Barley Risotto page 227

Brilliant Batch Cooking

We all lead busy lives, and it's hard to resist grabbing the first ready-meal you see in the supermarket after a long day at work or looking after the kids. Not all ready-meals are bad news, of course, but there's something a bit soulless about food that might have been prepared and packed in a distant factory weeks, even months, ago.

But what if your fridge and freezer were full of delicious, fast-friendly dishes you'd made yourself? That's what this chapter is all about. These aren't the only dishes that freeze well, or can be kept in the fridge (see the individual chapters for tips on which other recipes work well). However, we've picked these because they really lend themselves to batch cooking, saving you money, and time, while making you feel – deservedly – a teeny bit smug about cooking your own.

CHICKEN CHILLI WITH CREAMY AVOCADO TOPPING

POLENTA TRIANGLES WITH RICH SAUSAGE RAGÙ

BUCKWHEAT PANCAKES WITH BRETON TOPPINGS

PIZZA OMELETTE POPOVERS

COUNTRY-STYLE RABBIT STEW WITH BEANS, BARLEY AND GREMOLATA

MEATLOAF MUFFINS WITH SUPER-GREENS ON THE SIDE

BLACK BEAN STEW WITH CREAMY CHEESE TOPPING

RICH PORK LASAGNE WITH LUCKY-SEVEN VEGETABLES

BEST-EVER BEEF AND BAY CASSEROLE WITH CHESTNUTS

PLUS …

MAKING SENSE OF… CARBOHYDRATES, FATS, PROTEINS

5:2 FOOD HEROES: BEANS

5:2 Lives

TWIN SISTERS ARE DOING IT FOR THEMSELVES; 40KG (87 LB) DOWN!

'When you get up the next day, it's amazing how good you will feel. And we don't crave fast food anymore.' Pam, 58

For twin sisters Pam and Pat Lejman, losing weight was a family affair.

Pam explains. 'We knew we were out of control in our eating and drinking habits and needed to make a change. We have a history of heart problems on our mother's side and diabetes on our father's side of the family. We physically felt bad and knew if we didn't make changes that we were going to have health issues sooner than later.'

Pam and Pat, who are 58, share a house together in Wake Forest, North Carolina: both are 185 centimetres tall. 'As we're so tall, it is easier to hide the extra weight than with a shorter person. But I needed to lose 16–18kg (35–40 lb) and Pat needed to lose 23kg (50 lb).

'In May 2013, a close friend of ours told us about seeing a show on the PBS (Public Broadcasting Service) channel about the 5:2 way of eating. She knew we were at our wit's end trying to decide what path to take. We got the 5:2 book and read about the fasting and it made sense to us. We started 5:2 the next week and haven't looked back.'

It took some getting used to at first. 'This way of eating is simple but sometimes not easy, especially when you first get started. But once you get rolling you will look forward to your

Fast Days, because when you get up the next day, it's amazing how good you will feel. Lighter.'

And they don't just *feel* lighter, they *are* lighter. Pam, who works as a logistics expert, reached her goal just before Christmas in 2013, losing 15kg (32½ lb), and has lost another 2.25kg (5lb) since, reaching a BMI of 21. Pat has lost 23kg (50 lb) *and* an amazing 26 centimetres (10.5 in) from her waist, with a healthy BMI of 22.4.

Pam recently had a full physical check-up. 'My BP was 120/60. My doctor was impressed with this new way of eating and encouraged me to continue it. I have more energy and I feel like I can do so much more now than a year ago.

Before, we were eating fast food multiple times a week, now it's maybe once every other week. We have always tried to make good choices but the biggest difference now is portion control. Since we have been doing this way of eating we haven't been able to eat as much as we used to. We don't crave the bad foods anymore.'

Pat and Pam's Fast Day diary

Breakfast 5 a.m.: cup black coffee, ½ grapefruit, 2–3 slices deli meat.

Lunch 11 a.m.: miso soup or small amount of carrot or piece of fruit.

Dinner 7 p.m.: usually a salad with light dressing and a protein (grilled chicken, fish or beef).

Drinks: water.

Non-fasting day diary

Breakfast: fruit smoothie.

Lunch: If we make our own we make a sandwich or if we eat out we make healthy choices on the menu and only eat half of the portion and take the other half home.

Dinner: Basically anything we want, only smaller portions. We do not count calories on Feast days; it's enough to do it on Fast Days!

Pat and Pam's favourite foods

We both love any pasta dish, but now we chose a lighter pasta, like orzo. We love anything cooked on the grill including grilled vegetables. Pan-seared trout is also a favourite. As far as drinks, our preferred drink is red wine. We used to drink martinis every Friday night, but now with the weight loss we cannot tolerate hard liquor like we used to!

Best thing about 5:2

We love the flexibility of this way of eating. Moving the days to suit our schedules, fasting two days and being able to eat anything we want, within reason, for five days. It is the main reason we have been able to stick with this for over a year and a half. This is something we know we can do the rest of our lives!

Pam and Pat's top tip

Drink lots of water! It really does help flush out your system and fills you up at the same time. The days we didn't drink enough water we found we didn't drop any or only a little weight. When we did drink enough water, we lost weight.

CHICKEN CHILLI WITH CREAMY AVOCADO TOPPING

Calories per serving: 205; plus topping 239

Nut free/gluten free

How about a big bowl of chilli to spice up your evening? You'll get more for your Fast Day with this dish, and it freezes like a dream. Here the usual beef has been replaced with lower-fat chicken, which makes an equally delicious dish but a bigger portion! It freezes like a dream and the avocado topping is a fab creamy contrast to the spices.

Serves 4
Preparation time: 20 minutes
Cooking time: 25–30 minutes

    1 tsp olive oil 45 cals
    1 onion, finely chopped 38 cals
    1 carrot, finely chopped 34 cals
    1 celery stick, finely chopped 6 cals
    1 garlic clove, crushed 4 cals
    400g chicken breast, finely chopped or minced 480 cals
    ½ tsp each ground cumin and coriander 5 cals
    good pinch dried chilli flakes 1 cal
    100g canned kidney beans, rinsed and drained 111 cals
    400g tin chopped tomatoes 72–100 cals
    1 tbsp tomato purée 10–20 cals
    250ml chicken stock 10 cals
    1 baby avocado, around 75g flesh, chopped 120 cals
    small handful coriander leaves, chopped 5 cals
    4 tsp fat-free Greek yoghurt 12 cals
    salt and pepper

1. Place the oil in a saucepan over a medium heat and add the onion, carrot and celery. Cook for 5–10 minutes, adding 1 tablespoon of water if the mixture looks as if it might stick.

2. Stir in the garlic, chicken and spices and continue to cook for 5 minutes to brown the chicken.

3. Stir in the kidney beans, tomatoes, tomato purée and chicken stock. Season well and simmer for 15 minutes, or until the chicken is cooked.

4. Meanwhile, stir the chopped avocado and coriander leaves into the yoghurt. To serve, place a good spoonful of the yoghurt mixture onto each portion of chili.

To freeze, spoon the sauce into a freezer-proof container. When it has cooled, seal the container, then freeze for up to three months. To cook, thaw overnight in the fridge, then transfer to a pan and reheat gently until hot right through.

More ideas from the 5:2 Kitchen You can either mince the chicken in this recipe, or finely chop it to give it more texture. For a dairy-free option, simply leave out the yoghurt, or use soy yoghurt. This dish is great served with cauliflower rice (see page 320) or plain 'courgetti' (see page 322), or serve it in crispy taco shells on a non-fasting day.

POLENTA TRIANGLES WITH RICH SAUSAGE RAGÙ
Calories per serving: 209–273

Gluten free/nut free/vegetarian and vegan option

Think of this as a bit like Italian sausage and mash, with chunky cornmeal polenta baked until crispy, and a rich sausage sauce with Mediterranean flavours. It's perfect to have in the freezer, ready for when you need some hearty nosh. Polenta is gluten free and good to have in the cupboard.

Makes 4 servings
Preparation time: 15 minutes
Cooking time: 35 minutes

> ½ tsp salt
> 1 tsp freshly ground black pepper 5 cals
> 125g quick-cook polenta 452 cals
> 2 tbsp fresh parsley 10 cals

3 good-quality Italian 90% pork sausages 482 cals or 3 vegetarian sausages
240 cals
2 shallots, finely chopped 14 cals
1 tsp olive oil 45 cals
½ small aubergine, finely chopped 20 cals
½ red pepper, finely chopped 15 cals
200g chopped tinned tomatoes 36–50cals
good pinch dried thyme 2 cals

1. Line a 17cm-square tin with non-stick baking paper. Pour 650ml water into a saucepan over a high heat. Add the salt, then cover with a lid and bring to the boil. Pour in the polenta then cook for 5–8 minutes, stirring until thick and creamy. Add a splash more water if it looks very thick (it should still be quite loose). Stir in the parsley, then pour into the prepared tin and put to one side to cool and set.

2. Skin the sausages and put them in a pan with the shallots, oil, aubergine and 1–2 tablespoons water. Place over a medium heat and cook for 10 minutes, breaking down the sausages into little bite-size nuggets with the edge of the spoon, until the sausage starts to cook and the shallots and aubergine soften.

3. Stir in the pepper and continue to cook for 5 minutes more, or until the vegetables have begun to wilt. Add the tomatoes, herbs and 100ml water. Season well and bring to a simmer. Leave it to cook over a low to medium heat for 15 minutes, or until the sauce has thickened.

4. Take the polenta out of the tin and divide it into quarters. Cut each polenta quarter on the diagonal to make two triangles per serving. Spoon over the sauce and serve.

To freeze, after you have sliced the polenta into the portions, wrap each one well in cling film and freeze for up to a month. Spoon the sauce into individual single-portion containers, cover and freeze for up to a month. Leave to defrost overnight at a very cool temperature. Reheat the sauce in a pan with a splash of water then spoon over the polenta to serve. If you prefer the polenta warmed up, you can reheat it very gently in the microwave.

More ideas from the 5:2 Kitchen Top the polenta with anything you like. I love it with creamed mushrooms, with a sprinkling of cheese on top.

BUCKWHEAT PANCAKES WITH BRETON TOPPINGS

Calories per pancake: 67, plus topping

Gluten free/nut free/vegetarian option

Pancake day doesn't have to come just once a year. With these easy-to-freeze and gluten-free pancakes, you can whip one up any time. Buckwheat (see more about this ingredient on page 249) is a good alternative to wheat flour if you can't tolerate gluten. These are a little smaller and denser than the ones you'd be served in Brittany because they're lower in fat, but they still have that nutty taste. Once you've made and frozen these, they make a quick supper or lunch for Fast – or non-fast – days. Serve one or two with your choice of topping.

Makes 6 servings
Preparation time: 10 minutes, plus resting
Cooking time: around 15 minutes

> 75g buckwheat flour 251 cals
> pinch salt
> 1 medium egg 78 cals
> 75ml skimmed milk 26 cals
> 1 tsp olive oil 45 cals

1. Make the galettes by sifting the flour into a bowl. Stir in the salt. Make a well in the middle and add the egg and milk. Whisk together briefly until smooth. Cover and set aside for 30 minutes.

2. Heat half the oil in a frying pan over a medium heat and, once hot, pour in 2 tablespoons of the mixture. Allow it to spread into a pancake of about 15cm round. Cook for 1–2 minutes, or until bubbles appear on the surface of the pancake. Flip the pancake over and cook the other side. When the other side is golden, remove from the heat and keep warm in the oven in a plate while you continue to cook the pancakes until you've made 6 and all the batter has been used up.

Ham and egg filling
Calories per serving: 95

    1-cal cooking spray
    1 medium egg 78 cals
    20g thinly sliced ham 17cals

1. Spray a non-stick frying pan with 1-cal cooking spray. Add the egg and fry over a medium heat until the white is set and the yolk is just the way you like it.

2. Place the ham on a pancake and set the egg on top to serve.

Scrambled egg and spinach filling
Calories per serving: 185

    ½ tsp of butter 19
    2 medium eggs 156 cals
    1–2 tbsp of skimmed milk 5–10 cals
    small handful baby spinach leaves or chives, chopped 5

1. Melt the butter in a small saucepan over a medium heat.

2. Whisk the eggs and milk together then pour them into the pan. Cook gently until it begins to scramble, spoon over pancake and pile the chopped spinach or herbs on top to serve.

Goat's cheese filling
Calories per serving: 68–83

    25g plain goat's cheese 68 cals or goat's cheese with garlic and herbs 83 cals

1. Simply crumble the cheese over the top of the pancake and serve.

To freeze, just wrap them individually in cling film and seal them in an airtight container. Remove as many as you need at a time, unwrap and allow to thaw for an hour or so. Microwave until warm, for around 10–20 seconds per pancake.

PIZZA OMELETTE POPOVERS

Calories per serving: 105

Vegetarian/gluten free

Quick, easy, veggie, and freezer-friendly: you'll find lots of different names for the basic recipe for this on the Internet, such as 'crustless' quiches, omelette muffins, mini frittatas. The 'pizza' flavours in this one are cheese, onion, sun-dried tomato, olive and oregano, but use any combination of strongly flavoured ingredients (this isn't the time for subtlety). I find a silicon muffin 'tin' works best to allow you to gently squeeze the cooked muffins out without sticking.

Makes 6
Preparation time: 7 minutes
Cooking time: 15–18 minutes

> 30g mature reduced-fat Cheddar cheese, finely grated 65–82 cals
> 3 medium salad onions, finely chopped 6 cals
> 6 medium eggs 468
> 7–8 vacuum packed sun-dried tomatoes, weighing 30g in total,
>   snipped or chopped 48 cals
> 40ml skimmed milk 15 cals
> 5 olives, stoned, finely chopped 25 cals
> leaves from 2 sprigs fresh oregano, snipped into small pieces
> plenty of salt and pepper

1. Preheat the oven to 200°C/400°F/Gas mark 6 and lightly grease a 6-hole muffin tin with 1 cal-spray cooking spray.

2. Put half of the cheese aside and mix the remaining half with all the other ingredients in a large bowl. Season well then divide the mixture evenly between the muffin holes and sprinkle the reserved cheese over the top.

3. Bake the popovers for 15–18 minutes, or until they are puffed up and golden. Serve immediately.

To freeze, allow the popovers to cool and then place 1 or 2 in separate re-sealable plastic bags and store them in an airtight container (or keep them in a sealed plastic box in the fridge for up to four days). To use from frozen, let them thaw and then reheat in the microwave for 35–45 seconds each.

More ideas from the 5:2 Kitchen Try an English breakfast muffin by adding cooked sausage and mushrooms to the mixture with a little swirl of tomato purée, and serve with baked beans on the side.

COUNTRY-STYLE RABBIT STEW WITH BEANS, BARLEY AND GREMOLATA
Calories per serving: 252

Gluten free/nut free

Rabbit is the perfect meat for Fast Day – lean, tasty and protein-packed – and in this recipe, it benefits from the long, slow cooking with comforting beans and barley. The twist is a gremolata topping of herbs and olives, which really lifts the earthy flavours. This is a great dish to cook on a Sunday. Eat it for dinner, and then freeze the extra portions for a rainy day.

Makes 6 servings
Preparation time: 30 minutes
Cooking time: 1½ hours

    1 tsp olive oil 45 cals
    2 shallots, chopped 14 cals
    1 carrot, chopped 34 cals
    1 stick of celery, chopped 6 cals
    150g piece butternut squash, peeled and cut into small chunks 60 cals
    1 pepper, halved, deseeded and cut into small chunks 30 cals
    750g rabbit, jointed into six pieces 855 cals
    6 garlic cloves, left whole 24 cals
    4 sprigs rosemary 3 cals
    50g pearl barley or farro 66 cals

good pinch dried chilli flakes

600ml hot chicken stock 24 cals

400g tin cannellini beans, rinsed and drained 240–260 cals (depending on brand)

200g green beans, halved 56 cals

8 Queen green olives, finely chopped 40 cals

handful chopped fresh parsley 5 cals

zest and juice of ½ lemon 10 cals

salt and pepper

1. Preheat the oven to 170°C/325°F/Gas mark 3. Heat ½ tsp of the oil in a large casserole with 1 tablespoon of water over a low heat. Add the shallots, carrot and celery and fry for 5 minutes, or until just starting to turn golden. Add the squash and pepper along with another tablespoon of water. Cover then cook for a further 5 minutes, checking every now and then to make sure the vegetables aren't sticking.

2. Scoop the vegetables out of the pan and add the remaining ½ tsp of oil to the casserole. Increase the heat and brown the pieces of rabbit until golden.

3. Return the vegetables to the casserole and season well. Tuck the garlic cloves around the rabbit pieces, along with the rosemary sprigs. Sprinkle over the pearl barley or farro, add the chilli flakes, then pour in the stock. Bring everything up to the boil then transfer to the oven for 1 hour.

4. Stir in the cannellini beans, green beans and 200ml boiling water and return the dish to the oven for a further 30 minutes, or until the meat is tender.

5. For the gremolata, stir together the olives, parsley and lemon zest and juice, and season well. Serve the stew with the gremolata sprinkled evenly over the top.

To freeze, allow the stew to cool completely then divide it into portions. Place each portion in an airtight container. Put a spoonful of the gremolata topping on top of each, then seal and freeze for up to three months. To serve, take out of the freezer and defrost overnight at a cool room temperature or in the fridge. Reheat in a pan with a splash of cold water if all the sauce has been absorbed through freezing.

More ideas from the 5:2 Kitchen On a non-fasting day, soak up the delicious stew.

MEATLOAF 'MUFFINS' WITH SUPER-GREENS
Calories per serving: 173; 177 including salad

Nut free

These mini-meatloaves are excellent for Fast Days with this vitamin-rich and crunchy raw vegetable side dish. Great for family meals, too, when you don't feel like sharing your portion.

Makes 6
Preparation time: 20 minutes, plus cooling
Cooking time: 25–30 minutes

1 tsp olive oil 45 cals
2 shallots, finely chopped 14 cals
1 pepper, finely chopped 30 cals
1 carrot, finely chopped 34 cals
1 celery stick, finely chopped 6 cals
100g butternut squash, finely chopped 40 cals
1 garlic clove, crushed 4 cals
1 tbsp freshly chopped sage or oregano or marjoram 5 cals
200g 5% fat pork mince 204 cals
200g 5% fat beef mince 336 cals
100g reduced-fat feta, crumbled 180 cals
2 cocktail gherkins, finely chopped 5 cals
1 medium egg, beaten 78 cals
25g wholewheat breadcrumbs 55–70 cals
1 spring onion, thinly sliced 1–2 cals
50g baby spinach 13 cals
50g long-stemmed broccoli, thinly sliced 13 cals
squeeze fresh lemon juice
salt and pepper

1. Put 6 muffin cases into a muffin tin. Heat the oil in a large saucepan over a low to medium heat. Add the shallots, pepper, carrot, celery and squash and stir in 2 tablespoons water. Cover and reduce the heat to low. Cook for 10 minutes, or until the vegetables are tender, shaking the pan every now and then to stop the vegetables from sticking.

2. Stir in the garlic and herbs and season well. Leave it to cook for 1–2 minutes then tip the mixture into a large bowl to cool completely.

3. Preheat the oven to 190°C/375°F/Gas mark 5. Set aside a couple of tablespoons of the vegetable mixture. Add the pork and beef mince, the feta, gherkins, egg and breadcrumbs to the rest of the vegetables and stir everything together really well to mix.

4. Divide the mixture evenly into the prepared muffin tin then place a spoonful of the remaining vegetable mixture evenly on top of each. Bake for 25 minutes, or until the muffins are hot all the way through.

5. Toss the spring onion, spinach and broccoli in a bowl with the lemon juice and season with a little black pepper.

6. Serve the meatloaf muffin with the salad on the side.

To freeze, allow to cool then wrap each one tightly in cling film. Freeze for up to three months. To serve, take a muffin out of the freezer and thaw overnight at cool room temperature. Reheat, loosely covered, in the microwave.

BLACK BEAN STEW WITH CREAMY CHEESE TOPPING
Calories per serving: 141; 155 including topping

Vegetarian/nut free/gluten free

This is the dish black beans were made for, with intense smoky flavours and – if you use cacao or cocoa – a rich bittersweet undertone. It's great served as it is, with a little crunch from tortilla chips and creamy sourness from the cheese.

Makes 6 servings
Preparation time: 10 minutes plus soaking if using dried beans
Cooking time: 90–135 minutes (25 minutes for tinned beans)

200g dried black beans 692 cals or 2 x 400g tins cooked black beans, rinsed and drained 624 cals
1-cal cooking spray or ½ tsp coconut oil 22 cals

1 small onion, chopped 38 cals

4 cloves garlic, thinly sliced 16 cals

2 tsp ground cumin 10 cals

1 tsp whole coriander seeds 5 cals

1 tsp smoked paprika 5 cals

1 dried chipotle pepper rehydrated in hot water 20 cals or use 1 tsp chipotle paste 2–8 cals (depending on brand)

400g tin chopped tomatoes 72 cals

1 tbsp unsweetened cocoa powder 54 cals or raw cacao powder 57 cals (optional)

10g Cheshire or Lancashire cheese 40 cals or 20g reduced-fat feta cheese 36 cals

10g tortilla chips 48 cals (check label to confirm)

small handful chopped fresh coriander leaves (optional)

salt and pepper

1. Rinse dry beans, then soak overnight in fresh, cold water, so they will cook more easily the next day.

2. Spray a non-stick saucepan with 1-cal cooking spray or use coconut oil, and place the pan over a medium heat. Add the onion, garlic and spices, including the chipotle pepper and fry for 1–2 minutes.

3. If you are using beans that have been soaked overnight, add them to the saucepan and cover with fresh water (do not add salt yet). Bring to the boil, reduce to a simmer and cook for 1–2 hours, or until the beans can be easily pierced with the prong of a fork. Add ½ tablespoon salt now, and cook for another 20 minutes or so. If using tinned beans simply add them to the saucepan with a little water and mix with the onion, garlic and spices until combined.

4. Add the tomatoes and cacao/cocoa powder, if using. Heat until piping hot again. To serve, crumble over the cheese and tortilla chips, and sprinkle over the coriander, if using.

To freeze, allow the stew to cool completely then divide it into portions. Place each portion in an airtight container to freeze. To serve, allow to defrost and then microwave for 45–60 seconds per portion, or reheat in a saucepan with a little extra water.

RICH PORK LASAGNE WITH LUCKY-SEVEN VEGETABLES
Calories per serving: 289

Nut free

This is a perfect batch-cooking dish, with the surprising extra benefit of seven different types of vegetable and pulses to create a lovely big portion. The lentils give richness and extra body to the meat layer, while the pepper, aubergine and slices of squash become extra 'lasagne' layers with different tastes and textures. It's slightly fiddly to make, but a great investment of time when you'll have six portions to show for it!

Makes 6 portions
Preparation time: 1 hour
Cooking time: 30 minutes

Neck end of a 300g butternut squash 120 cals
1 red or yellow pepper, halved 30 cals
1 medium aubergine, sliced 30–35 cals
1-cal cooking spray
1 tsp olive oil 45 cals
1 onion, chopped 38 cals
1 small fennel bulb, chopped 62 cals
250g lean pork mince 435 cals
100g uncooked green or brown lentils 331 cals
400g tin chopped plum tomatoes 72–100 cals
1 tbsp tomato purée 10–20 cals
good pinch dried thyme 2 cals
500ml hot chicken or vegetable stock 25 cals
6 spinach lasagne sheets 367 cals
40g Grana Padano cheese, roughly grated 154 cals
salt and pepper

1. Preheat the oven to 200°C/400°F/Gas mark 6. Put the squash, uncut and unpeeled, on a baking sheet with the pepper halves.

2. Put the aubergine slices on another baking sheet lined with non-stick baking paper. Spritz the aubergine with the 1-cal cooking spray. Place both baking sheets in the oven to roast for 30–40 minutes, or until the aubergine has cooked and the squash is tender. Remove all the vegetables from the oven. Once cool, peel the squash and slice it into rounds.

3. Place the oil in a saucepan over a medium heat and add the onion and fennel, along with 2 tablespoons water. Cover, reduce the heat to low and cook for about 5 minutes, shaking the saucepan every now and then so that the vegetables don't stick.

4. Transfer the vegetables to a plate and add the mince to the saucepan. Flatten it out on the bottom using the back of a wooden spoon and cook until browned on one side. Flip over the mince and cook the other side. Add the lentils to the saucepan along with the tomatoes, tomato purée, thyme and stock. Season, then cover and simmer for 40 minutes, or until the lentils are tender. Towards the end of the cooking time, preheat the oven to 200°C/400°F/Gas mark 6.

5. Spread one-third of the mince mixture over the bottom of a 2-litre ovenproof dish. Top with half the aubergines and one-third of the squash slices. Cover with half the lasagne sheets and repeat the layer again.

6. Discard the stalk and seeds from the pepper and cut each half in half again. Cover the last layer of lasagne with the remaining mince then top with the squash slices and pepper quarters. Sprinkle over the cheese and bake in the oven for 30 minutes before serving.

Kate's tip If the idea of cutting into a squash makes you nervous (I have had a few near misses), the easiest way to prepare a big chunk of squash for this recipe is to roast it whole. The skin then peels off like magic, and you can slice it easily into rounds.

BEST-EVER BEEF AND BAY CASSEROLE WITH CHESTNUTS

Calories per serving: 264

Gluten free/nut free/dairy free

There's something about the combination of flavours in this casserole that makes it pure magic. It's so warming you'd never guess it was low in calories. The bay and chestnuts go beautifully with beef, and the winter vegetables melt in the mouth after the slow cooking, and all for less than 270 calories. No wonder we're calling it the best ever.

Makes 4 servings
Preparation time: 20 minutes
Cooking time: 1 hour–1 hour 10 minutes

    1 tsp sunflower or olive oil 45 cals
    250g lean braising beef, cubed 443 cals
    1 red onion, chopped 38 cals
    2 carrots, roughly chopped 68 cals
    300g roughly chopped parsnip 225 cals
    300g roughly chopped swede 114 cals
    2 bay leaves
    500ml hot beef stock 25 cals
    1 tbsp tomato purée 10–20 cals
    50g cooked chestnuts, halved 82 cals
    1 tbsp freshly chopped parsley 5 cals
    salt and pepper

1. Heat the oil in a large non-stick casserole over a medium heat and add the cubed beef. Cook for around 5 minutes until seared on all sides.

2. Transfer the beef to a plate and add the onion, carrots, parsnips and swede. Cook for 5–8 minutes, tossing the vegetables every now and then, until golden on all sides.

3. Add the bay leaves to the saucepan, followed by the beef cubes. Pour in the stock then stir in the tomato purée. Season well, cover and bring to the boil. Then turn the heat down low and simmer for 30 minutes.

4. Towards the end of the cooking time, boil 250ml water in a kettle. Add the chestnuts to the saucepan along with the boiling water. Cover again and continue to simmer for 30–40 minutes, or until the beef is tender.

5. Lift out and discard the bay leaves, then sprinkle with the parsley and serve.

To freeze, spoon the stew into a freezer-proof container and leave it to cool. Seal and freeze for up to three months. Thaw overnight in the fridge, then to cook, spoon into a saucepan with a splash of water and heat gently, stirring occasionally, until thoroughly hot.

More ideas from the 5:2 Kitchen This is satisfying on its own but it's also great with cauliflower rice on a Fast Day, and for extra indulgence on a non-fasting day, serve with crusty garlic bread or Dauphinoise potatoes.

Making sense of... carbohydrates, fats, proteins

We used to think of food as, well, food.

But increasingly, we talk about our diet in a different way. People say they're 'avoiding carbohydrates because they make you fat' or insist, 'I can't even get up in the mornings without a protein shake'. Meanwhile, your doctor is telling you to cut down on saturated fat because your 'bad' cholesterol is high, yet there's a guy at the gym who swears by heavily saturated coconut oil to keep slim.

In some ways, it's a great thing that more of us are aware of the basic building blocks of nutrition. But there's now huge potential for over-simplification *and* extreme diets cutting out entire food groups.

So what's the truth about carbohydrates, fats and proteins? And what's the perfect ratio for health and longevity?

The truth is... no one knows for sure

Hundreds of diets, thousands of books, tens of thousands of research studies, and millions of web posts and articles have been published on this topic – and as a consumer, it's almost impossible to know which to believe.

I won't tell you what to eat. That's a personal decision, and one of the beauties of 5:2 is that you have freedom to eat whichever foods you believe are the healthiest. But I will explain what the main issues are, and tell you where I stand.

Fat, protein and carbohydrates: the big three

Fat, protein and carbohydrate are known as '*macro*nutrients', and they are the main sources of fuel our body uses when we eat. Foods also contain '*micro*nutrients', including vitamins and minerals, which help support the many processes the body performs.

1: Fat facts

Fat is found *in* the human body, and we also consume it in our body, via animal and plant sources. And that double meaning for the word is one of the issues that gets in the way of understanding its role: many people assume that eating fat, makes us fat.

It's certainly higher in calories than either carbohydrates or protein: fat contains 9 calories per gram, while carbohydrates and protein contain only 4. But that's because of the way it's used by living things, as a concentrated way to store lots of energy for leaner times, when it can provide fuel.

But fat *inside* our bodies doesn't just provide a reserve for leaner times: it also helps protect and cushion the organs from damage; insulate us from the cold; and allows the body to absorb certain vitamins that are only 'fat soluble' (vitamins A, D, E and K).

There are also some fats – essential fatty acids – that the body can't make itself, so we need to take those from our diet. Those help the brain, the immune system and your heart and circulation.

In addition, the fat we eat provides energy to be used immediately. In fact, the body prefers using carbohydrate and fat for energy, so it can use the protein we eat to repair and build our cells.

The $64-million question

So if fat has so many important functions, what's the problem? Well, we know that too much fat stored in your body is *not* a good thing, as obesity is associated with a range of serious health issues, from type 2 diabetes, to coronary artery disease.

The question is which food groups do the most damage in terms of obesity. Should saturated fat (the kind found in meat and dairy products) take the blame? That's what several influential scientists decided in the 1960s and 70s. Their view was that saturated fat intake was directly linked to high levels of blood cholesterol and that in turn led to cardiovascular/heart disease.

It's what led to many governments worldwide advising their

populations to cut down on those, and eat more starches (the carbohydrates found in grains, bread, pasta and vegetables). The fats people *did* take in should mainly come from unsaturated – i.e. plant – sources.

Yet some critical scientists say that the most influential research, the Seven Countries Study, was based on inaccurate assumptions and left out other results that didn't support the argument. They say if the missing data is added back in, the links between fat, cholesterol and heart disease are much less clear-cut. There is even growing evidence that low-carbohydrate diets may offer better protection against cardiovascular disease than low-fat: one recent study from three US universities followed 148 men and women, who followed either a low-fat or low-carb diet. After a year, those following a low-carb diet had lost more weight *and* showed improvements in risk factors for disease than those following a low-fat plan.

I've read countless books and articles on this, and though I'm not a scientist, I do know that demonising fat hasn't helped us get any slimmer. In fact, since that advice became widespread, obesity has increased, along with the health issues that go with it. We've simply swapped high-fat foods for calories from other sources, often those with less nutritional benefit. At best, the advice on fat was an over-simplification; at worst, it has completely skewed our view of what 'real food' is.

So which fats are good for me, and which should I avoid?

Much government health advice is still very firmly advising us not to eat saturated fats, while other research has found that saturated fats are *no more* associated with higher rates of heart disease than vegetable oils. There's also evidence that one of the most criticised saturated fats – coconut oil – may be good for us after all, because it contains anti-microbial lauric acid, which is rich in medium-chain triglycerides, a form of fat that our bodies and brains find easier to use as fuel.

Cooking is another area of confusion. For example, olive oil is delicious and has health benefits, but is not 'stable' at high temperatures, which damage the beneficial compounds. So it is better to fry or roast with small amounts of butter or coconut oil.

Much more consistent is the advice to steer clear of trans fats, found in some margarines and highly processed foods: these are associated with higher rates of heart disease. I definitely avoid food with 'hydrogenated' or 'partially hydrogenated' oil on the label, which is another way to recognise trans fats.

Too much fat of *any* kind in the diet can lead to weight gain because it's calorie-dense. But eating a varied diet including whole foods which naturally contain fat, like seeds, nuts, avocados, and oily fish, will help you get the nutrients you need.

As always, if you want to follow up on fat or the other topics in this chapter, see the references, starting on page 375.

2: Protein facts

The second macronutrient, protein, is made up of combinations of amino acids, which perform different roles in repair and growth in the body. There are 20 kinds of amino acids; the body can manufacture 11 of them (though some, only very slowly) while nine need to be obtained from food sources, and they're known as the 'essential amino acids'.

Animal and plant foods both provide proteins. Animal foods including meat, dairy and eggs, offer complete proteins in a single 'package', along with a limited number of plant foods, including quinoa and soya. Vegans can also consume more complete proteins via many staple food combinations, for example, rice and beans or peas, or hummus (containing chickpeas and sesame seeds). It used to be thought that vegans *had* to eat these at the same meal, but now it's clear that so long as the complementary proteins are eaten within the same day or two, the body can still use both to ensure good nutrition.

Too much of a good thing?

Protein seems like the simplest of the macronutrients to deal with, because if our bodies use proteins to grow and repair, then surely eating lots of them is a good thing?

It's not quite that simple. As the original BBC *Horizon* programme on fasting highlighted, raised levels of a hormone called Insulin-like Growth Factor-1 (IGF-1) have been associated with early death in mice, due to cancer, diabetes and other cardiovascular diseases. Yet when the scientist behind the research, Valter Longo, studied a group of people with a genetic disorder that stopped them producing IGF-1, he found that they never developed any of those diseases, though those people also never grew to a normal height.

Higher protein diets are associated with higher levels of IGF-1, and Longo's most recent work has linked the two to risk of death, attracting dramatic headlines. The research, published in 2014, showed that in middle-aged humans (50–65), a high protein diet is associated with a 74 per cent higher risk of premature death from any cause, and four times the risk of dying of cancer as people eating a lower-protein diet.

But, after the age of 65, that situation is *reversed*, and people with a higher protein diet show a *lower* risk of death. In each case, low-protein means under 10 per cent of daily calories are coming from protein, and high-protein would be over 30 per cent.

The theory is that high levels of protein, and therefore IGF-1, encourage the body's cellular activity to 'race', which might help faulty or cancerous cells to grow. Whereas lower levels of IGF-1, due to lower protein intake or intermittent fasting, may encourage the body to 'put itself in for repairs', by either repairing cells or allowing them to die once they've outlived their usefulness, but before they damage the body.

And the sudden switch over the age of 65? Longo points to a natural fall in IGF-1 levels over that age. Eating plenty of protein after that age may encourage more repairs in ageing bodies.

Critics of the study have highlighted that many other factors may have influenced the results (as always, do your own research if you wish to know more). But it does highlight why you can potentially have too much of a good thing. One other interesting point from this research is that it was *animal* proteins – dairy and meat – that seemed to have the greatest negative effect. Plant proteins, like those in pulses like lentils and beans, did not show the same risks.

3: Carbohydrate facts

Our third macronutrient, carbohydrate, is the hot potato (and hot toast, hot crossed bun and hot fried rice) in the nutrition world right now. So much so, that I've awarded sugar (a refined or 'simple' carbohydrate) its own chapter, starting on page 302.

Starches are the main way plants store energy – it's built up from sugars. In the human body, carbohydrates/starches are used for energy, producing glucose for immediate use, and also glycogen, which is stored in the liver and muscles to be used when the body needs extra energy rapidly – like a reserve tank of petrol.

Simple carbohydrates are sugars, which are digested and used very rapidly. Complex carbohydrates, found in vegetables and grains, are linked chains of sugars and take longer to break down. Starchy vegetables and fruits contain vitamins and minerals that help our bodies run well, and all grains or sugars can provide energy for intense activity.

The concern about carbohydrates is around how our body deals with them in the short and medium term, which leaves us prone to blood sugar issues and weight gain. There's more on both effects in *Making sense of... sugars and sweeteners,* page 302.

The perfect human diet?

We know we're getting it wrong right now – the rise in obesity rates worldwide is proof of that. As the World Health Organisation states on its website:

> *In 2008, more than 1.4 billion adults were overweight and more than half a billion were obese. At least 2.8 million people each year die as a result of being overweight or obese. The prevalence of obesity has nearly doubled between 1980 and 2008. Once associated with high-income countries, obesity is now also prevalent in low- and middle-income countries. 65 per cent of the world's population live in a country where overweight and obesity kills more people than underweight.*

Something has to happen, but are we any closer to finding the 'perfect diet' for human health and longevity?

My own view now is that there may be no such thing as a single perfect diet, because genetic and environmental differences mean we all have different requirements, tolerances and digestive capabilities. I am also much more wary of vested interests trying to persuade us to choose this food over that on the basis of incomplete evidence.

In the meantime, what on earth should we have for dinner?

Kate's verdict

I personally don't believe carbohydrates, grains, fats or proteins will ever be isolated as the single cause of the obesity epidemic. I think we're here because of a toxic mix of environmental, psychological, physical and commercial factors including:

- the survival instinct making us want to eat whenever the opportunity arises, at a time of unparalleled food choice and availability

- a food industry that produces food that satisfies our cravings, without paying nearly enough attention to longer-term effects on health

- flawed advice on meal *frequency* that has led us to snack and eat constantly and lose touch with what our bodies need

- a reduction in knowledge about how to shop and cook unprocessed foods

- our own personal responses, emotional and physical, to food.

It adds up to what researchers call an 'obesogenic' environment. Here's how I cope with that:

- **I don't cut out an entire food group.** Banning entire food groups – whether that's carbohydrates, grains or saturated fats – is very hard for most of us to sustain. We are likely to become *more* aware of those foods, and that makes us more likely to succumb. Plus, vegetables are carbs: banning these is a bad idea!

- **I am carb-aware, not carb-phobic. I try to keep sugars down in most foods, but enjoy cakes and bread as a treat, without guilt.**

- **I eat fats, and cook with them.** Advice does keep changing but at the moment I use coconut oil, sesame oil, butter or reduced fat sprays for frying at high temperatures. I use olive and nut oils for dressings and for drizzling over hot food. And I use butter for bread, baking and sauces. I haven't had margarine in my fridge since the early 1990s.

- **I buy more unprocessed foods and try to experiment with new ingredients because balance and variety keep me on the straight and narrow.**

Over to you. What would you like *your* rules to be?

5:2 Food Heroes

BEANS

There's a lot more to beans than Heinz. Where would we be without garlicky hummus, Mexican black beans, comforting lentil dal and the many soy products? Beans are multi-coloured, nutrient-rich, protein powerhouses that cost, well, no more than beans.

All about beans

Dried beans and lentils are collectively known as legumes or pulses, and they range from tiny lentils to hearty butter beans and even groundnuts (also known as peanuts). Lentils were among the first cultivated plants to be grown, and traces have been found on archaeological sites dating back 8000 years.

Pulses are low in fat, high in protein (especially for a plant-based food), rich in nutrients, and slow to digest so they keep you feeling fuller for a longer time and avoid spikes in blood sugars. People who consume several servings of beans each week can cut their risk of cancer, heart disease and blood sugar problems, such as diabetes.

Nutrition

- **Calories** A serving of around 100g of cooked pulses will be 100–130, depending on the type.

- **Fibre** The fibre content of beans – with lentils and kidney beans at the top – is a key factor in reducing blood pressure and harmful cholesterol. There are also benefits in terms of helping 'friendly bacteria' in the digestive system, which help keep your bowels working properly (and potentially reducing the risk of cancer).

- **Vitamins and minerals** Legumes also contain vitamins and minerals including folate and magnesium, which are associated with heart health.

- **Protein** Beans are a great source of vegetable protein, so have a particularly important role to play in vegan diets.

- **Phytonutrients** We often associate phytonutrients with fruit and vegetables, but the skin of beans like black beans also offers these beneficial 'flavonoids', which act as antioxidants, reducing the stress placed on the body's cells by daily life.

- **Discovering potential benefits** Research is ongoing about other potential benefits of different beans, including bone health, gum disease and weight management. A discussion about the benefits of soya beans is also underway, as there are differences between how these products are digested by people in different countries.

Downsides

- **Flatulence** When we talk about the digestibility of beans, we generally mean one thing – flatulence. The problem comes because our bodies lack enough of the enzymes needed to digest the starches (known as oligosaccharides) found in beans and other vegetables, like broccoli or cabbage. The difficulty digesting them is actually one of the reasons they're good for our guts. But you can lessen the issue by soaking the beans before cooking them thoroughly, chewing well and also by gradually introducing more beans to your diet so that enzyme production steps up. Adding the sea vegetable Kombu to the cooking liquid may also help.

- **Toxicity if uncooked** Certain beans – including red and kidney beans – need to be boiled for at least 10 minutes due to a toxin they contain that can be dangerous. Canned kidney beans are safe to eat as they come.

- **Allergies** Soy allergies are more often found in children than adults, and most commonly in children with eczema so be aware of this if you are looking for dairy-free alternatives.

How to buy and store

- Dried beans that you then cook yourself are the cheapest. Buy them from a store with a quick turnover, such as a busy health food store, and keep dry for up to one year.

- Canned beans are a fast, convenient option, and pulses processed this way retain most of their nutrients. Avoid pulses stored in brine or saltwater or rinse well before use.

- Lentils come in a wonderful array of colours and types, from 'gourmet' puy lentils with their 'Farrow and Ball' grey colour, to easily digested red lentils.

How to cook

- After rinsing, tinned beans can simply be heated in the saucepan or used cold in salads.

- Cooking dried beans can be intimidating if you haven't done it before but it's actually easy (if time-consuming).

  - Wash beans well under running water and do a quick check for any grit.

- Soaking the pulses in fresh, unsalted water overnight, or longer, will improve digestibility and make them faster to cook. Drain then cook in fresh water.

- Follow pack instructions for how long to cook. For example, black beans take much longer then delicate lentils. Some beans, such as red and kidney beans, do need to be boiled rapidly at first for safety reasons.

- A small amount of bicarbonate of soda added to the liquid – half a teaspoon for two portions – can cut your cooking time, but don't add salt until the beans are almost cooked as it can make the skins tougher.

- You can keep the beans in a covered container in the fridge for 2–3 days. Or freeze for up to three months, either with a little of the cooking water, or drained.

- For soya beans and products, avoid the over-processed powders and drinks used by body builders: they don't give the full benefits of using 'whole' products like tofu, edamame beans or canned soy. Consider fermented products too, like miso, tempeh or fermented tofu, which may contribute to the health benefits of soy in the Japanese and other Asian diets.

Recipe Ideas

Chickpeas: Sunshine Mezze page 133

Lentils: Creamy Chicken and Tomato Soup page 77

Black Beans: Black Bean Stew page 265

Thirst Quenchers and Sweet Treats

We all know we should drink water and avoid sweet things, but there are some days when we need a pick-me-up – and that's what this chapter is all about.

Of course, one of the joys of 5:2 is that nothing is banned on non-fasting days, so if you're a keen cake-maker like me, then that's the day to indulge your 'Bake-off' hobby. But with a bit of care, you can still enjoy desserts, or even a truffle or two on a Fast Day, without any guilt.

Drinks are important for us. While there may be disagreement about the old 'drink 2 litres of water a day' advice (see page 21), staying hydrated helps the body function at its best. In hot weather, a cooling drink will refresh and distract from any hunger pangs, and on colder days, a hot drink can be just what you need to heat your body from the inside out. I look at the issues around diet drinks in *Making sense of…* later in the chapter, but this chapter has plenty of natural home-made drink ideas. Cheers!

Thirst Quenchers

BERRY MINT SMOOTHIE

BLACK FOREST YOGHURT DRINK

BEETROOT AND GINGER BOOSTER

MANGO SMOOTHIE

INFUSIONS: HOT AND COLD DRINKS FROM THE GARDEN

FLOWER POWER/FRUITFUL/WILD THING/SAVOURY

Sweet Treats

AFFOGATO: INSTANT ESPRESSO SUNDAE

SPICED RASPBERRY AND APPLE YOGHURT ICE

WHIPPED VANILLA MOUSSE WITH RED FRUIT RIPPLE

PRUNE AND NUT CHOCOLATE TRUFFLES

PLUS ...

MAKING SENSE OF... SUGAR AND SWEETENERS

5:2 FOOD HERO: THE BERRY

5:2 Lives

FORGET LIPOSUCTION – TRY FASTING INSTEAD!

'I often used to joke about having liposuction and this diet is the non-surgical equivalent!'
Louise, 42

For many dieters, having 5.5kg (12 lb) to lose would be the end of their weight loss journey, not the beginning, but Louise Woodward from Guildford in Surrey still felt uncomfortable and out of condition after giving birth to her fourth child.

'I wanted to be my pre-pregnancy weight and to stay that way. I was having to squeeze into my old size 10s and refused to buy new clothes in a size larger, so needed the muffin top to go.'

Louise, who runs an online business alongside looking after her children, decided 5:2 was the way to go in 2013. And she lost steadily, reaching her goal within six months. 'I have gone from feeling a bit overweight after having my fourth child to feeling slim, healthy and younger again. I often used to joke about having liposuction and I feel that this diet is the non-surgical equivalent. The muffin top has been literally sucked out of me. Now I'm a size 8–10.'

Calorie awareness that holds the key for her: 'On Fast Days, food feels like fuel to keep me going. I don't deviate from the 500 calories and on normal, non-fasting week days I try to eat very healthily but do have wine and treats. And at the weekend I eat exactly what I want, which does include Kettle chips and ice cream and drinking alcohol.'

Like many 5:2 fans, she has come to enjoy her Fast Days. 'I actually look forward to my Monday Fast as it feels a very healthy start to the week, eradicating the excess of the weekend. If I ate what I thought I wanted the whole time, I estimate I would be a size 14.'

Louise's Fast Day diary

No breakfast. Lunch is Little Gem lettuce and dry-fried onion and dry-fried chicken with teriyaki sauce. For dinner, fish and vegetables and one individual square of dark chocolate.

Sometimes I can't be bothered to cook and have a small portion of cracked black pepper Ryvita with my favourite St Agur blue cheese and a few red grapes.

I have a huge glass of ice with diet tonic and lime slices, which is the closest thing to alcohol I can find. I also drink water, coffee and Diet Coke. The only negative is that I do sometimes lack energy on a Fast Day, though that might have something to do with my 2-year-old and only getting an average six hours sleep per night!

Louise's non-fasting day diary

Fruit for breakfast; lunch Ryvita with St Agur blue cheese and red grapes, dark chocolate. In the afternoon, a nectarine or apple or Frappuccino. For dinner, grilled chicken or fish with vegetables or salad. Frozen yoghurt and maybe a glass of red wine or some more dark chocolate.

I do try to be healthy Monday to Friday and I have created some Fast Day meals that I will now often choose on a normal day, as I like them so much. For example, I love lettuce chicken teriyaki wraps, which are filling, tasty and very low calorie. I add a tablespoon of sesame seeds on a feast day. I do still have the odd day where I eat too much chocolate but do an extra fast to compensate.

Favourite foods

Steak and salad. Strawberries, dark chocolate, red wine, coffee, tonic water. And those teriyaki wraps.

Best thing about 5:2?

It works! It's so easy to stick to you can lead a totally normal life but only diet when you choose to. That is the key to its success.

Louise's top tip

Be very busy on Fast Days. I find it best to go out and shop or meet friends as the day goes faster and I nearly always go to bed early so the next feast day comes round quicker.

5:2 Thirst Quenchers

I gave up pure fruit juice years ago, but smoothies made with whole fruit and vegetables can still make a convenient 'meal' if you're on the go. Just drink slowly, as it's very easy to consume calories in a glass without really noticing!

The drinks here require no specialist equipment except a stick blender – the kind used for soup. If you really enjoy juicing, then it may be worth investing in a centrifugal juicer. There are lots of good Facebook groups with juicing tips, while www.juicemaster.com and www.rebootwithjoe.com/juicing are by existing juicing authors, but contain lots of free resources.

To dip your toe in the juice and find out if it's for you, give these a try. Drink them on the day you make them.

BERRY MINT SMOOTHIE
Calories per serving: 31 (without honey)

Dairy free/vegan

The mint gives this smoothie a welcome freshness, and you can adapt your blend to what's in season, or use a frozen berry mix. However, if the mix includes tart fruit like red currants, you might want to add a little honey or agave nectar to sweeten the drink. The mint gives it a lift and with this one, the mint flavour does develop over a few hours. You can also use soy/dairy milk (or even water) but remember to allow for the extra calories.

Makes 600ml (Serves 2)
Preparation time: 2 minutes

> 90g fresh or frozen berries 40–60 cals
> small handful fresh mint leaves 2 cals
> 150ml unsweetened almond milk 20 cals
> 1 tsp agave nectar (optional) 15 cals or honey (optional) 20 cals

1. Place the ingredients in a beaker and blend. Test for sweetness before adding honey or agave nectar.

More ideas from the 5:2 Kitchen Try a different culinary herb for a change. For example, basil and strawberry might sound unusual, but is very good.

BLACK FOREST YOGHURT DRINK

Calories per serving: 92

Vegetarian/nut free

The classic Black Forest Gâteau was the inspiration for this creamy drink. The cocoa or cacao is unsweetened but gives a chocolate undertone, and the cherry skins help give it an extra-thick milkshake texture. It tends to settle, so give it a good shake or stir before drinking if it's been kept in the fridge. Frozen cherries are good value and work well in this drink.

Makes 150ml (Serves 1)
Preparation time: 2 minutes

    80g fresh or frozen black cherries, pitted 48 cals
    80g 0% fat Greek yoghurt 44 cals
    ½ tsp unsweetened cocoa or raw cacao powder 9 cals

1. Blend all the ingredients together with a stick blender. If the texture is too thick for you, add a little almond or skimmed milk. Drink immediately.

More ideas from the 5:2 Kitchen This is good with frozen raspberries, too. You can also try it with 0% fat crème fraîche for a slightly more tangy drink.

BEETROOT AND GINGER BOOSTER
Calories per serving: 60

Vegan/nut and dairy free

This juice looks the same as the Berry Mint Smoothie, but you'd never confuse them once tasted! It's a grown-up drink that'll wake you up instantly with a strong lemon and ginger tang. Adjust to suit *your* taste by adding a little of each at a time. *Please don't use cooked beetroot in vinegar* because a glass of vinegary juice is not the best way to start the day.

Makes 225ml (Serves 1)
Preparation time: 5 minutes

  100g beetroot, cut into chunks 43 cals
  ½ small celery stick weighing about 20g, chopped 2 cals
  juice of ½ lemon 10 cals
  150ml filtered water
  1cm-square piece of ginger, roughly grated 2 cals
  10g mild green leaves, such as baby spinach or outer leaves of lettuce 3 cals

1. Add all of the ingredients to a blender beaker and blend. Taste and add more ginger or lemon if you like.

More ideas from the 5:2 Kitchen If it's too tangy for you, add sweetness with half an apple or a pear, cut into chunks, or use half apple juice/half water. Instead of celery, you can add cucumber or, if your blender can handle it, raw carrot.

MANGO SMOOTHIE

Calories per serving: 171; 207 calories with the oats

Vegetarian/gluten free

If you've ever had a lassi drink in an Indian restaurant, you will recognise the same intense creamy fruitiness in this drink. How sweet it is will depend on how sweet the fruit is: I love the slightly sweet-sour flavour but you can add a little honey if required. A tablespoon of oats also adds extra body and makes it more filling if you're having this as a breakfast drink.

Serves 1
Preparation time: 10 minutes

    150g ripe medium-size mango 100–110 cals
    1 tsp desiccated coconut 16 cals
    100ml 0% fat Greek yoghurt 55 cals
    10g oats (optional) 36 cals
    1 tsp agave nectar (optional) 15 cals or honey (optional) 20 cals
    pinch ground cinnamon

1. Put the mango on a board and slice down one side of the stone to cut off the cheek. Scoop out the flesh and put into a mini blender.

2. Add the coconut and yoghurt, along with the oats and agave nectar or honey, if using. Whiz until smooth. Stir in 75–100ml cold water, depending on how thick you would like the drink to be, and then pour it into a glass and serve dusted with a little cinnamon.

Infusions: hot and cold drinks from the garden

One of my favourite hot drinks is fresh mint tea – just leaves from the garden steeped in boiling water. Fresh mint tea is refreshing *and* also great for digestion after a meal.

But why stop with mint? A window box, the herb section of your supermarket or even the wild flowers and plants from your local park can offer a whole range flavours and nutrients. **And they're virtually calorie-free!** Choose one of the herbs, flowers or fruits below and brew up. Here are a few tips:

Brewing a herb infusion

- Start with a small handful of fresh herbs, or a little less for dried herbs, which have a more intense flavour. A 'base' leaf like dandelion, nettle, raspberry or blackberry leaves or mint will give you your first hit of aroma, and then you can add different flavours to create your own unique blend.

- Place the leaves in a teapot, a heatproof glass or a glass infusing pot. Add boiling water and then allow the herbs or flowers to steep for several minutes. Taste and, if you like, add honey to sweeten, but don't forget to keep track of the calories!

- Remember you can serve a herb infusion hot *or* cold. For the cold infusions, try mixing with sparkling water.

Warning

Pregnant women and nursing mothers need to be careful with many herbs and leaves, including raspberry leaves and sage, so it's best to avoid making infusions unless under the supervision of a herbalist.

Flower power

Chamomile is probably the best known of the 'flower' teas, but why not try some of these? Remember to ensure the flowers have not come into contact with pesticides. If they weren't grown for culinary purposes, it's best to avoid them.

- **Lavender tea** The scent is known to be relaxing, so this can be a nice bedtime drink. You can use both the flowers and the leaves in a tea. Use around 1 tablespoon per cup, and add mint or lemon balm leaves to counter the floral flavour if it's a bit too intense.

- **Rose petal tea** If you can't find flowers from a trusted source, use pure distilled rosewater labelled as organic, for a hot or chilled drink with sedative and anti-bacterial properties.

- **Rosehip tea** Rosehips – the berry-like round fruits at the centre of the flower – are full of vitamin C and have sedative and anti-inflammatory effects. They're at their best picked after the first frost: use slice four or five through the centre, remove the hairy seeds from the middle and then leave to steep in boiling water for at least 10 minutes. Discard the hips before drinking. You may need to sweeten this tea a little.

- **Elderflower tea** The cordial is well known, but use two to four fresh flower heads (again, from a trusted source or your garden) for a tea traditionally used to fight colds or fevers.

Fruitful

Commercial fruit teas are a standby for many of us on a Fast Day, so why not experiment with your own recipes? You can achieve delicious fruit flavours *without* the calories of the whole fruit.

- **Citrus infusions** A slice or quarter of an unwaxed lemon steeped in boiling water is very refreshing. But try adding herbs with citrusy flavours as well, such as lemon verbena and lemon balm leaves.

- **From the orchard** You can use a fresh apple or pear twice, once in the infusion and then next day with yoghurt and oats or blended into a smoothie for breakfast or brunch. Slice the fruit into a jug, add boiling water and herbs or spices: mint or cinnamon with apple, ginger or cardamom with pear.

- **Apple cider vinegar soda** ½ teaspoon of raw cider vinegar (with the 'mother', the strings of enzymes that form in the bottle) to sparkling water. Result: a lovely, tangy but dry drink that reminds me of cider. It's a little sour for some, but cider vinegar may help control blood sugar and help weight loss, so it's worth a try.

- **Berry, berry good** Strawberry water is a delicious cool drink and great for using the tops cut off of hulled strawberries. Simply add seven or eight tops to a pint of water and refrigerate. The taste gets stronger with time and the strawberries 'fade' in colour as they release their aromas.

Wild things

If you're collecting wild plants, do make sure you are 100 per cent certain you know which plant it is *before* consuming, as some can have unpleasant or dangerous effects.

- **Nettles** Their iron content is high and they offer other potential benefits, including kidney-stone prevention, allergy reduction and blood-sugar balancing. Wearing gloves and long sleeves, choose nettles from sites where pesticides won't have been used, and steep a small handful of nettle tops per cup of just-boiled water for 10–15 minutes.

- **Dandelion leaves and flowers** These are rich in antioxidants and compounds that may aid immunity. Try them on their own, in nettle tea, or mixed with just a little fresh cranberry juice (maybe 50ml of the unsweetened kind) for a cool, refreshing drink.

Savoury flavours

We tend to expect teas to have an underlying sweetness, like mint or chamomile, but the more savoury herbs are also beneficial. You may wish to combine with sweeter herbs or a little juice. Try:

- **Sage** Anti-bacterial and anti-viral with particular benefits to the mouth and gums; anti-spasmodic so it can reduce pains in the stomach or cramps; and calming and soothing for hormonal issues in women. It may even improve memory. Steep the fresh or dried leaves, and try combining with other 'savoury' herbs for complementary benefits.

- **Thyme** This herb is good for mouth, gum or throat infections, as well as coughs and colds; **rosemary** is anti-inflammatory; **dill** is good for digestion and may help blood sugar regulation; **oregano** is recommended for colds and for menstrual cramps; **basil** has eugenol in the oil in the leaf, which can reduce inflammation in the digestive tract and joints; **parsley** supports the kidneys and bladder.

AFFOGATO: INSTANT ESPRESSO SUNDAE

Calories per serving: 24–40 with coffee; 44–60 for hot chocolate

Vegetarian/nut free

This sits halfway between drinks and sweet treats. *Affogato* in Italian simply means drowned, and ice cream 'drowned' in strong coffee makes for the simplest but most delicious quick pudding ever. I had an amazing hot chocolate affogato in a chocolatier in Melbourne, and realised it'd work a treat with lower-calorie hot chocolate, too. Portion control is important to keep calories low, so measure your ice cream first time to get an idea of how much 30ml is. But the fun of this *is* the ritual: serve it in a cute, tiny bowl and serve the coffee or chocolate in an espresso cup.

Serves 1
Preparation time: 2 minutes

  1 espresso coffee 0 cals or ½ sachet reduced-calorie chocolate drink, such as Options 20 cals
  1 heaped tbsp vanilla ice cream or about 30ml frozen yoghurt 24–40 cals

1. Make the espresso using a machine or powder, or make the hot chocolate using half a sachet of lower-calorie chocolate drink: use around 2 tablespoons of boiling water and mix thoroughly so chocolate is thick and well blended. Pour into a small jug or espresso cup.

2. Scoop the ice cream into a small bowl. Simply pour the hot liquid over the drink at the table, so the ice cream melts.

More ideas from the 5:2 Kitchen On a non-fasting day, you can add a measure of a favourite liqueur to your ice cream (amaretto is delicious) and then top with a crumbled Amaretti biscuit, flaked almonds or grated chocolate.

Kate's tip Choose a lower-calorie, creamy ice cream or frozen yoghurt. Two of my favourite are Lick Fat-Free Straight Up Creamy Frozen Yoghurt (just 79 calories per 100ml) and Yeo Valley Organic Greek-Style Yoghurt and Honey Dairy Ice Cream (117 calories per 100ml).

SPICED RASPBERRY AND APPLE YOGHURT ICE

Calories per serving: 63

Gluten free/vegetarian

I used to have a thing for 'slushies' when I was a teenager – those ice-drinks made in unlikely colours. This has all the fun of a slushie, with none of the out-there colours.

Makes 4 servings
Preparation time: 10 minutes, plus freezing time

200g fresh raspberries 104 cals
100ml apple juice 36–49 cals
200g fat-free yoghurt 110 cals
½ tsp cinnamon 3 cals

1. Whiz the raspberries in a food processor until puréed. Spoon the mixture into a resealable container then stir in the apple juice, yoghurt and cinnamon.

2. Cover and freeze for 2 hours. Give the mixture a good stir again, making sure that you stir any of the frozen bits on the side right into the mixture then freeze again for another 2 hours.

3. Repeat this process once more until the mixture is almost frozen, then freeze for another hour.

4. Scoop into balls to serve (dipping the ice-cream scoop into a jug of boiling water first helps shape the sorbet when scooping it out of the container).

More ideas from the 5:2 Kitchen This recipe is a great way to use up a glut of berries. For a darker, more intense ice, try making it with blackberries.

WHIPPED VANILLA MOUSSE WITH RED FRUIT RIPPLE

Calories per serving: 52; 62 with honey

Nut free/vegetarian option (see more ideas)

This is light as air, with a delicious fruity flavour and it looks so pretty in martini or liqueur glasses. I actually prefer it without the honey, but it's lovely either way. See under main recipe for a vegetarian version without gelatine.

Serves 4
Preparation time: 15 minutes
Chilling time: 2 hours

> 200g strawberries 64 cals
> zest and juice of ½ medium orange 20 cals
> 60ml hot water
> ½ sachet of gelatine 5–10 cals
> 125ml light reduced-fat evaporated milk 135 cals
> ½ tsp vanilla extract 2–5 cals
> 2 tsp honey (optional) 40 cals

1. Purée half the strawberries with the juice of the orange in a food processor or blender. Slice the remaining half of the strawberries, reserving 4 perfect berries. Mix the sliced and puréed strawberries with half the orange zest. Add to the bottom of four glasses or serving dishes.

2. Measure out 60ml of freshly boiled water into a bowl. Whisk in the gelatine powder and set aside. Stir together the milk, vanilla extract and 1 teaspoon honey, if using, in a bowl. Taste and add second teaspoon if required (or you can drizzle the honey over before serving). Add the gelatine and water, then whisk together till light and airy and roughly double the volume (this takes around 2 minutes with an electric whisk).

3. Spoon the mousse on top of the fruit and carefully 'ripple' the fruit through the mix by stirring through the mousse with a spoon. Chill for at least 2 hours.

4. Before serving, slice the reserved strawberries without cutting through the hulls, and 'fan' out one on top of each serving.

Vegetarian version Vegetarian setting/gelling agents like agar-agar aren't suitable for this recipe, because most require a mixture to be brought to boiling point. Instead, you can simply make the fruit mix as suggested, and place in the bottom of serving dishes. Then, just before serving, whisk the milk, vanilla and honey (if using) together: you don't need the water. Spoon gently over the top of the fruit: it won't set firm but has a fab frothy texture that is just as delicious.

More ideas from the 5:2 Kitchen If you can't find the light evaporated milk, try using 70ml normal evaporated milk plus water to make it up to 125ml. This recipe is a great base for other flavours, like coffee or chocolate.

PRUNE AND CHOCOLATE NUT TRUFFLES
Calories per truffle: 27

Gluten free/dairy free

I've saved the most indulgent till last. Even though the ingredients in these rich, dark truffles all have benefits, thanks to the powerful anti-oxidants in the chocolate, the minerals and weight-stabilising qualities of the almonds and the fibre in the prunes, they certainly shouldn't be your main source of calories on a Fast Day. Keep them in the freezer and take a single truffle out at a time to have with your coffee or tea to celebrate the end of a great Fast Day.

Makes 18
Preparation time: 15 minutes, plus soaking
Cooking time: 5 minutes

    25g prunes 40 cals
    25g flaked almonds 158 cals
    50g dark chocolate (90% cocoa solids), broken into pieces 280 cals

1. Put the prunes into a small bowl and cover with 25ml boiling water. Set aside to soak for 30 minutes.

2. Toast the almonds carefully in a non-stick frying pan over a high heat or under a hot grill, watching closely so they don't burn. Whiz them in a small food processor until finely ground, then tip into a bowl. Put the prunes into the processor with any liquid left and purée.

3. Melt the chocolate in a bowl resting over a saucepan of boiling water (make sure the base of the saucepan doesn't touch the water). Once the chocolate has melted, take the bowl off the heat and stir in the prunes and almonds. Cool and chill to allow the mixture to set overnight.

4. The next day, scoop up about ½ teaspoon, roll it into a ball in your hands and put it on a plate. Do the same until you've made 18 balls. Store in a resealable container in the fridge for up to a week or freeze for up to 3 months.

More ideas from the 5:2 Kitchen I'd never get tired of these, but to vary the flavour, try adding spices, like a good pinch of cinnamon, ground ginger or chilli powder.

Making sense of... sugar and sweeteners

Orange juice was my watershed.

As a kid, I thought juice was an essential part of a healthy breakfast – even if it sometimes came powdered in a packet or from a frozen concentrate.

But then I tried low-carbing ten years ago (I lasted only a few months, but that's another story). As part of my avid mission to track down carbohydrates in all their forms, I discovered that there was very little difference, sugar-wise, between cola and orange juice. A large glass contained up to eight teaspoons of sugar. As someone who has never added sugar to drinks, I was shocked. I'd rather consume those calories in a tastier – and more nutritious – way.

I felt the same way about bananas and smoothies, too, even though everyone was necking them to get one or two of that 5-a-day. I went back to eating carbohydrates after low-carbing proved unsustainable, but my ban on fruit juice and smoothies stayed. When I said no to OJ, people would look surprised. 'But it's so *healthy*,' they'd insist. 'It's fruit sugar.'

I hate to say I told them so, but OJ sales are now down, and smoothie firms are trying to rebrand products that many argue are little better for us than a chocolate bar.

Sweet nothings

What most of us know as sugar – table sugar crystals in a bowl – is a mixture of two kinds of simple (i.e. refined) carbohydrates: glucose and fructose (the two together are technically known as sucrose).

But there are dozens more ways to describe sweeteners with similar make-up, and many manufacturers use these different names in ingredients labels. This can make it difficult to work out how sugary a product is. It could be described as: sucrose, dextrose, fructose, lactose, malt extract, malt, honey, caramel, agave, treacle, palm sugar, molasses, high-fructose corn syrup, maple syrup, golden syrup… the list goes on.

You might be surprised to see that list including 'natural' sugars like honey or agave. Aren't they different? Well, there are slight differences, with some containing small quantities of nutrients, but simple sugars all have similar effects on the body however they've been produced or sourced.

Sugar in the body

When we eat, the sugar (glucose) in our blood rises causing specialist cells in the pancreas to release insulin, a hormone that tells cells to use the glucose as energy to perform their different roles.

Our cells only need a certain level of energy, so the key to body weight and health is what happens to excess energy from food. We do have a 'reserve tank' of fuel, known as glycogen, stored in the liver and muscles, for when we're not eating or digesting. And when there's excess sugar in the blood, it'll be used to refill the glycogen stores.

But what happens when the reserve tank is full and when we don't *need* the sugar we've just consumed? That's when the body begins to store fat in the fat cells (it will do the same with protein if we have too much of that). Through adulthood, the number of fat cells we have remains constant, though they become, well, fatter, the more we eat. The body stores fat most easily from the fat content of foods, but can do it with carbohydrates and protein, too.

Reading that, you'd think that fat was, therefore, more likely to make you fat: it certainly has higher calories than both carbohydrates and protein, and eating too much of it *will* lead to weight gain.

But… the big but is about how *fast* we digest foods. A meal with plenty of fat or protein, and less refined sugar, will be digested more slowly and that means the level of glucose in the blood stream stays constant for longer – it's like the difference between a trickle of water, or a flood. So while a mixed meal offers energy that can be used over time without being converted to fat, refined sugary foods flood the body with glucose energy that has to be converted immediately because it has the potential to damage the body. That flooding overwhelms the normal systems, forcing the body to convert glucose to fat.

It's one of the reasons why many nutritional scientists see sweet, fizzy drinks (as well as fruit juice and smoothies) as public enemy number 1. Any type of sugary drink floods straight into the bloodstream, with minimal digestion needed, hitting the body with an excess of glucose that needs immediate action. And, as soon as that excess has been dealt with, the sudden low sends many of us back to the fridge or biscuit tin. And it's hard to resist sweet temptation: we're primed to love that taste from birth.

Habit, genetics, childhood experiences and even gender all influence how susceptible we are to the effects of, and the craving for, sugar. If you feel you have a sweet tooth, you'll know that very well.

The insulin problem

But sugar crashes and calories are only part of the picture.

One of the biggest health threats from obesity globally is type 2 diabetes, when the body either stops secreting as much insulin, or stops reacting to it as strongly, or both. Glucose then builds up in the body, causing serious damage that can include heart disease, blindness, nerve damage and lead to amputations, especially of the lower limbs. It is scary stuff: not just for individuals but for health services, which are facing rising bills and patient numbers.

So if we want to avoid diabetes, do we need to avoid all food with sugars in it? Or even all carbohydrates?

A question of balance

Luckily, we rarely consume products where the sole ingredient is sugar (except those fizzy drinks I mentioned earlier). As you've read, a meal containing protein, fat and/or *complex* carbohydrates will take longer to be broken down by our digestive system.

It's why I feel concerned about people avoiding all carbohydrates. They assume that all carbohydrates have the same potential for damage as sugars. But it's just not the case: vegetables contain carbohydrates, so if we took the fear of carbohydrates to extreme, we'd ban them completely from our diet, with obvious health consequences.

Similarly, whole grains are rich in fibre and nutrients. Increasing research is focusing on the role of 'resistant starches', which are types of fibre that have beneficial effects on the digestive system, on satiety or fullness and on other functions including eye and brain health, and insulin sensitivity.

Even high-fructose fruits are much better for you served whole. An orange has micronutrients and fibre, which slows down the digestion and rise in blood sugar. It's also highly unlikely that we'd want to eat six oranges in a row, which is roughly how many it takes to make a large glass of juice. And if we did, it'd take us much longer than it does to drink the juice.

The food speedometer

The speed at which we digest foods is measured in numbers known as the glycaemic index – though the related glycaemic load calculation may be more useful as it takes into account the portions we normally eat of different foods and the overall carbohydrate content. There is more information in the resources section on page 379.

Processing and cooking both affect how quickly foods are digested: most fruit and vegetables are at their best when they've undergone the minimum of processing, though the resistant starches in whole grains are a little more complex as most do need cooking.

However, there's a difference between cooking at home, and industrial processing to isolate the qualities of certain 'wholesome foods', as the fructose story illustrates.

The fructose story: from goodie to baddie?

So, whole fruit is better than juiced fruit. But what about the specific sugar found inside fruit? If we could isolate that, surely it'd be better for us than the sugar made from sugar beet or cane?

It sounds logical, but in fact, that particular sugar – fructose – is a concern to some doctors. You can buy 'fruit sugar' in health food shops, and it's used as a sweetener commercially, partly because it's much sweeter than glucose. But our bodies actually treat fructose differently when it's digested: in the liver, it's converted to fat and is implicated in fatty liver disease, while glucose is converted first to glycogen (that reserve fuel we've talked about).

Our ancestors – and wild animals – would have benefited from storing fructose from autumnal fruit as fat: it would sustain life through cold winters when food was scarcer. But the story is different today, when there's simply too much food available for many human populations. That's led influential doctors, including author of *Fat Chance* Dr Robert Lustig, to identify a higher fructose intake as a significant factor in the increase in obesity and metabolic diseases, including diabetes. They point particularly to the use of high-fructose corn syrup, which is produced from maize and used extensively in the US, though not so much in Europe.

Other researchers are less convinced that it's fructose specifically that is causing damage. There is concern that focusing on a single sugar is missing the point: it's our overall diet that's the issue.

The sweetest things

Whenever sweeteners are mentioned on the 5:2 Facebook group, things tend to get a bit confrontational. People regularly post links alleging all kinds of highly toxic effects, while others say they couldn't get through Fast Days without diet colas.

Here's *my* take on sweeteners.

'Natural' syrupy sweeteners: sugars by another name

Honey, molasses, maple syrup and agave nectar are all delicious and sweet, but are they really much better for you than sugar?

Most of them *do* contain traces of micronutrients including minerals and B vitamins, but you'd have to eat vast amounts to consume beneficial levels. They have more complex flavours than white sugar, and in the case of agave, they are sweeter due to high levels of fructose, which means you should theoretically be able to use less.

A new kid on the block – or at least, one being promoted heavily at the moment – is rice malt or brown rice syrup, which is popular with some sugar avoiders because it's free from fructose. But its high glucose content means it has a very high glycaemic index.

What's the bottom line? In all these syrups, there is still processing involved getting them to your table – and they are typically more expensive than table sugar. I'd say that if you enjoy them, and can limit your consumption, then they're fine. But don't kid yourself that they are a 'health food'.

Other sweeteners

Sweeteners can have natural *or* artificial origins, though all involve processing to put them into a form we can use. For example, stevia comes from a South American plant and its leaves can be processed to form a sweetener that is hundreds of times sweeter than sugar, and contains very few calories. In many ways, it appears the perfect sweetener. It may even increase insulin sensitivity and lower blood pressure.

But (there's always a but) stevia leaves a bitter aftertaste that some people really dislike. Stevia also needs processing, and there are reported side effects, including stomach upsets. And as for long-term use, we don't yet know.

Xylitol is also found in fruits and vegetables, though in reality, it's mostly extracted from hardwoods or corn cobs. It's a 'sugar alcohol' and while it has been shown to protect young children's teeth from decay, it can cause stomach upsets if you eat too much of it.

Artificial sweeteners have been developed or produced in the lab, often as a result of other research on food or drugs. They include aspartame, sucralose, saccharin and acesulfame K.

The two big questions about artificial sweeteners

There are two main areas of concerns about artificial sweeteners, such as aspartame, sucralose, saccharin and acesulfame K, whose names may be familiar from food packaging. The first concern is the safety of the individual sweeteners themselves, and second, the effect on the body of eating or drinking very sweet foods.

Concerns about direct health risks of different sweeteners include worries about bone loss, kidney problems or cancer. There isn't space to consider every single sweetener here when it comes to safety, but even though I am pretty sceptical about many food issues, and about government regulation, I do believe that if there were clear evidence of toxicity for any of these, official approval for their use would be removed.

Of course, if you notice ill effects like migraines after eating or drinking certain things, check the labels. If artificial sweeteners appear, then see if cutting them out helps. Or if you have specific worries, like bone loss, for example, read around it online. You may decide to avoid all sweeteners, or just fizzy drinks with phosphorous or caffeine.

The second question is whether consuming foods containing low-calorie sweeteners may be damaging. It may be behavioural: there are studies that suggest those who drink a lot of diet drinks, for example, might then feel they can 'eat' the calories they've saved, leading to weight gain. Or it may be physical: if we can become accustomed to very sweet food or drink, then we may crave more, including from higher calorie sources. There is also ongoing research about whether the sweetness still makes the pancreas secrete insulin to deal with the sugar that isn't actually present in the blood. The evidence so far is not consistent.

Certainly, drinking diet versions of fizzy drinks doesn't automatically make us slim. But I admit I still have the odd Diet Coke or diet lemonade, perhaps two or three cans a week. I think it's the better choice for me than drinks with sugar, as I simply prefer not to drink my calories.

I don't tend to use many sweeteners in cooking, not out of any particular safety concerns, but because I prefer to cut down on processed foods. However, it's not a total ban: I've made home-made jellies with different sweeteners, and very low-calorie shop-bought jellies definitely helped me through the odd sweet craving in my early fasting days, though I never have one now.

One thing is certain: with the concern about sugar, the market for alternative sweeteners is set to grow and grow. I would always advise you to research any wonder sweeteners, and keep up to date – and an open mind – when it comes to the latest science.

Kate's verdict

You've seen what *I* do: I try to achieve a balance, read labels more carefully, and prefer to avoid foods with what I consider inappropriate sweetness. But at the same time, I love chutneys and savoury dishes with a hint of sweetness, like a vegetable korma, for example. I don't see carbohydrates as the enemy, and I'm certainly not going to 'ban' the baked goodies I enjoy making and eating. I have cut down on carbs, to avoid too many calories, but really savour a gooey brownie or freshly baked slice of cake.

My number one rule is *I never drink my calories*. With three exceptions: booze, jetlag and hangovers. You've read my views on alcohol on page 19: I enjoy it and keep an eye on the calories. But soft drinks aren't a regular part of my diet. I have self-prescribed a fruit smoothie three times in the last five years for an instant energy boost: twice after a long-haul flight, and once the morning after a party. But mostly, I prefer *my* sweet moments to involve melted chocolate.

5:2 Food Hero

THE BERRY

Juicy, colourful and sweet but not *too* sweet, berries are full of flavour and nutrients, and you can enjoy them without adding too many calories on Fast Days.

All about berries

Strawberries, raspberries, blueberries, blackcurrants and blackberries are all delicious, though only one – the blueberry – is a 'true' botanical berry. Never mind. We're including every one of these luscious jewels of juiciness, because their flavour and potential health benefits make them heroes in *our* book.

Nutrition

Berries are a better choice than many fruits if you're trying to lose weight or cut down on sugar. It's partly because they're small, so you can add a few to your dishes more conveniently than, say, adding part of an apple or banana. Their juiciness comes from a high water and fibre content, so they're low in calories, yet the intense colour of the skins and juice is also the focus of much of the research into the benefits of the compounds that make them so attractive.

- **Calorie content** This varies from 32 for 100g of strawberries to 57 for 100g blueberries, so a handful will give you lots of taste without ruining your Fast Day.

- **Glycaemic load** This is an indicator of how much different foods raise your blood sugar, and the glycaemic load of berries is lower than that of many other fruits. This means you won't get the same sugar 'hit', with the accompanying crash or craving that often follows eating sweeter foods.

- **Antioxidant and anti-inflammatory compounds** Berries play a part in helping fight cell damage and reduce the damaging effects of inflammation throughout the body thanks to the antioxidant and anti-inflammatory compounds they contain. A lot of the key compounds relate to the pigments that give the berries their dramatic colours.

- **Vitamin C, folate and anthocyanins** Eating berries can help counteract arthritis, age-related memory loss, cataracts and other eyesight problems, and will help maintain healthy skin and hair, thanks to their vitamin and mineral content.

Berry benefits – and the ketone qustion

Different berries have different properties – and some have been subjected to more research – and marketing – than others. Blueberries have been called 'super berries' (along with more exotic berries like acai) due to their high anthocyanin and antioxidant content, while strawberries may help with inflammatory bowel and joint conditions. Raspberries are in the spotlight because a compound in the fruit known as rheosmin (commonly called raspberry ketone) may help with weight loss. In huge doses, rheosmin has been shown to help rats keep weight off, but no evidence has been seen in humans, and we don't know how safe it may be to consume huge doses of the ketone. Therefore, you should be *very* wary of 'miracle' supplements that have not been tested or verified as effective or safe.

Downsides

- **Allergies** It is possible for children to have allergies to these fruits, but such allergies are uncommon in adults.

- **Pesticide exposure** Because we consume berries whole, it may be better to choose organic fruit.

How to buy and store

All berries are very perishable – strawberries in particular lose their firm texture and potentially a lot of their nutritional benefits just a couple of days after picking.

- Choose firm, plump fruit. Check fruits haven't been crushed together.

- Keep berries in the bottom drawer of the fridge, and remove any mould that may have developed on individual fruits to prevent it affecting others.

- Blueberries and raspberries freeze well – and retain much, if not all, of their nutritional benefits. Strawberries lose their plump texture through freezing, but are still tasty in smoothies or mousses.

How (not) to cook berries

Unlike most of the hero ingredients in this book, berries don't need cooking. Simply wash carefully, hull strawberries or slice off the green tops, and serve as soon after buying or picking as possible.

Recipe Ideas

Berries are delicious served very simply with a little 0% fat crème fraîche

Berry Mint Smoothie page 289

Spiced Raspberry and Apple Yoghurt Ice page 298

Whipped Vanilla Mousse with Red Fruit Ripple page 299

5:2 Foundations

*ESSENTIAL RECIPES FOR GOOD,
HEALTHY FOOD*

This chapter is about the brilliantly healthy building blocks of Fast Day food: often surprising, always tasty, sometimes almost *life changing*. The number of people in the 5:2 Facebook group who've swapped from normal pasta to 'courgetti', or ditched basmati rice in favour of cauliflower, is huge. Both substitutions are light and healthy, and put the focus deservedly back on the main dishes they accompany.

You won't just find side dishes here. We also have snacks, marinades, stocks and pickles.

5:2 Lives

THE MONEY-SAVING DIET THAT CHANGED EVERYTHING

'My confidence? I wouldn't say it's rocketed; I'd say I'm a completely different person!' Jo, 29

For Jo Crompton, the decision to lose weight came just after one of the most stressful periods of her life.

'It was January 2014, two months after a very unexpected breakup with my long-term partner and father of my children. I went clothes shopping. In the previous year I'd lost weight through going to the gym, and managed to get into size 16 jeans. But then this day, I couldn't even do the size 16s up! I refused to buy size 18 again. A friend had previously done 5:2 so I decided that night that I would start the next day and I've not looked back.'

Jo, who is a full-time mum to Leo aged four and Logan, two, weighed herself when she got home and was shocked to find she was 78.5kg (173 lb). 'I gave myself a target of 12kg (26lb), that would take me down to 66.5kg (147 lb). I also worked out that it was 26 weeks until my amazing fourteen-night cruise with my family. That was my target: 12kg (26 lb) in 26 weeks!'

Jo actually knocked her target out of the water, losing 19.5kg (44 lb) in 25 weeks. 'My BMI has gone from bordering on obese at 29.5 down to a healthy 22.5. I was a size 18 when I started and now an 8 on top and 10 on bottom! My confidence? I wouldn't even say it's rocketed, I'd say I'm a completely different person!'

As well as the confidence boost, 5:2 has been an education when it comes to good food. 'I was eating two to three times more than I actually needed to out of pure greediness! I eat it slower and really enjoy the taste of it.

'I like to cook healthier dinner options for my boys and me: I've learnt to find healthier alternatives rather than depriving myself of something I want. I have discovered Quorn and also fish, two things I never really would have eaten but both are great options for Fast Days.'

Life with her two energetic young boys is so much easier: 'I can walk anywhere without a struggle and play with the kids without feeling out of breath. I also know my loss has changed the path of certain health issues I might have developed in the future.'

Jo's Fast Day diary

I'm maintaining now, so do 6:1: a fasting day is like a detox.

8 a.m. Black coffee with sweeteners

12 p.m. Black coffee

4–5 p.m. Ready meal with 300–350 calories

I try to drink lots of water and in the evening will have some Coke Zero.

Jo's non-fasting day diary

I found tracking my calorie intake on feast days helped me understand what I was really eating. I would eat normally but within reason. I also allow myself to eat out on occasions and enjoy a glass of wine in an evening.

Favourite foods

I wouldn't say I really have favourite dishes or foods but I do like chicken and trying different dishes with chicken.

Best thing about 5:2?

For me 5:2 is so easy to stick to because I always know you're 'back to normal' tomorrow. 5:2 also doesn't cost anything. Yes, I buy some ready meals for my Fast Days but I was no longer buying crisps and chocolate so my shopping bill has come down. Had I chosen a different way of eating, it would have cost me around £100 in weekly meetings to date and to be honest I don't think I'd have had results even close to those on 5:2. I've started to love my body, including my curves. I can't believe I've achieved this!

Jo's top tip

Don't give up! It's only two days. Two days out of each week is so doable!

CAULIFLOWER RICE
Calories per serving: 25

Vegetarian/gluten free/nut free/dairy free

I don't know how many calories this one dish has saved 5:2 people, but it must run into the millions. It seems weird the first time you do it, but it's very easy and makes a great replacement for rice or couscous: it's lighter, lower in calories, and you are getting a portion of vegetables. It doesn't taste of much on its own, but that's the point: you want it to soak up any sauce or juice from your main dish. You can keep the second portion, covered, in the fridge to eat later the same day.

Serves 2
Preparation and cooking time: 5–10 minutes

> 200g cauliflower florets 50 cals
> salt and pepper

1. Grate or finely chop cauliflower florets until they resemble rice grains. The fastest way to do this is to pulse the cauliflower florets in a food processor, which gives a finer texture.

2. Place the cauliflower into a loosely covered microwaveable dish. Don't add water: there's already enough in the cauliflower to stop it drying out. Place in the microwave and cook on full power for 2 minutes. If you are only cooking one portion, reduce the time to 60 seconds.

3. Or you can stir-fry the grated cauliflower. Add a splash of water to or spray a saucepan with 1-cal cooking spray to prevent it from sticking and set over a high heat. When hot, add the cauliflower and fry for 2–3 minutes, or until softened. If you are using spray, the rice may caramelise a little, adding a little nutty flavour.

4. Season and serve alongside curries, stews and other main dishes.

More ideas from the 5:2 Kitchen I like to add herbs or spices to the mixture when I process it or during cooking. You could try cumin, ginger, fresh chillis or dried chilli flakes or fresh herbs like parsley or basil. You can freeze individual portions, too, which generally won't take much longer to re-heat than fresh.

EGG-FRIED CAULIFLOWER RICE

Calories per serving: 182 for 1 main course servings,
91 cals as a side dish for 2

Vegetarian/gluten free

This is the more souped up version of cauliflower rice that makes a great main meal or side dish. It's infinitely variable, depending on what you've got in the fridge or spice rack.

Serves 1 as a main course or 2 as a side dish
Preparation time: 5 mins
Cooking time: 8–10 minutes

½ medium cauliflower, around 200g of florets 50 cals
½ tsp coconut or sesame oil, 22 cals
½ tsp whole or ground spices e.g. garam masala, five-spice, cumin or spice paste, 3–10 cals
2 medium spring onions, finely chopped, 4, or ½ an onion, 19 cals
150g vegetables e.g. sliced mushrooms, chopped pepper or carrot, frozen or fresh peas, 25–50 cals
1 medium egg, 78 cals
½ small chilli, seeds removed, finely chopped (optional) 2–4 cals
splash of soy sauce, tamari or sweet chilli sauce

1. Prepare the cauliflower as for the basic rice above.

2. Heat half the oil in the largest frying pan or wok you have. Add the spices, onion and vegetables and cook over a high heat for 2 minutes.

3. Add the cauliflower and the other half of the oil: cook for 2 more minutes and allow the 'rice' and vegetables to brown but move in the pan before they burn.

4. Beat the egg. Lower the heat in the pan slightly, move the vegetables to one side of the pan and pour in the egg into the other half. Stir as they scramble, for 1–2 minutes.

5. Mix the eggs and 'rice' together in the pan then serve. Add a splash of soy, tamari or chilli sauce to serve.

More ideas from the 5:2 Kitchen Add chopped cashew or peanuts in place of the eggs plus some cubed tofu for a vegan version. A splash of coconut milk at the end of cooking is yummy too.

COURGETTI
Per serving 34; 37 using frying method

Vegetarian/vegan/gluten free/low carb

This dish has probably done more for sales of julienne slicers than any recipe before or since. Mine cost under £6 and I use it all the time to transform slightly bland courgettes into light, gluten-free noodles that are perfect for the richest of sauces (like the truffle mushroom sauce on page 173). You can steam or blanch it, though I think frying gives the best results.

Serves 1 as a main dish, with sauce added, or serves 2 as a side
    vegetable
Preparation time: 3 minutes
Cooking time: 1–2 minutes

> 170g courgette 34 cals
> salt and pepper
> 1-cal cooking spray or a few drops of oil applied to the pan with kitchen paper
>   around 10 cals

1. Wash the courgette. For ribbons, cut off the stem and base and use either a sharp knife or a potato peeler (pressing harder than you would normally so the peelings are thicker) to cut thin 'noodles'. Go from top to bottom, moving the vegetable round as you slice, to get a nice green strip on each 'noodle'.

2. Alternatively, use a julienne peeler or spiraliser gadget that cuts spaghetti-like strands (you can use this gadget for carrot salad, too). It's easier to leave the stem on to hold the courgette by. Watch your fingers as the blades of the gadget are very sharp. You'll have a little courgette left over, which you can use in soup or stock.

3. Gently press out any moisture using kitchen paper. You can prepare everything to this stage in advance and keep in the fridge or on the worktop for a couple of hours, to help the 'pasta' dry out.

4. To cook, spray a non-stick frying pan with 2–3 pumps of 1-cal cooking spray and place the pan over a high heat. Toss the ribbons or noodles into the pan and keep them moving for 1–2 minutes until they are cooked and even a little browned in places, if you prefer. Remove from the heat, season to taste and serve.

More ideas from the 5:2 Kitchen Add ripe chopped tomatoes, basil leaves, toasted pine nuts and a little grated Parmesan cheese for a fresh sauce that complements the lightness of the noodles. You can serve this uncooked, as a salad, with julienned carrot or mooli radish for a crunchy dish. Add thin slices of onion, chopped fresh herbs and a little cider vinegar or white wine vinegar as a dressing.

Mash and chips: alternatives to the humble spud

Potatoes can be delicious, and they're certainly not banned on 5:2 (nothing is!). But they're not always the best choice for Fast Days. This is partly because their high carbohydrate content may mess with your blood sugar and make you hungry sooner than other vegetables and also because when we cook or eat potatoes, fats like oil, butter or cheese often aren't far away as they bring out the best in the vegetable.

But if you want something as satisfying and homely as a spud on a Fast Day, especially in winter, we have some delicious alternatives.

SWEET POTATO CHIPS

Calories per serving: 71–84

Vegetarian/gluten free/dairy free

Sweet potatoes are high in beta-carotene and vitamin A, and higher in fibre than the white ones.

I've used oil in the recipe, becasues it helps the body absorb the nutrients, but 1-cal cooking spray works just as well if you're serving with meat or other dishes that contain fat already.

Serves 2
Preparation time: 3 minutes
Cooking time: 16–18 minutes

140–170g sweet potato 120–146 cals
½ tsp oil 22 cals or 1-cal cooking spray
light sprinkling smoked paprika (optional)
sea salt and ground black pepper

1. Preheat the oven to 200°C/400°F/Gas mark 6.

2. Wash the potato. Cut the very ends off, but don't peel it. Cut the potato in half then cut the halves into long, thin chips, weighing 5–6g each. Spread the chips out on a baking sheet so they're not overlapping, to allow them to brown evenly. Brush with the oil, or spray with 1-cal cooking spray, then sprinkle over spices, if using.

3. Bake for 8–9 minutes then turn the chips over and bake for another 8–9 minutes, or until the flesh is lightly browned but soft.

4. Remove from the oven and season with salt and pepper to serve.

More ideas from the 5:2 Kitchen I like these with a tablespoon of 0% or reduced-fat crème fraîche with some hot chilli sauce spooned through.

WHITE BEAN MASH WITH GARLIC
Calories per serving: 137–149

Vegan/gluten free/nut free

Oh, white bean mash, where have you been all my life? Again, white beans aren't that much lower in calories than potato, but their high fibre content and minerals mean they're a really good option and keep you full for longer. It can easily make up a very significant part of your meal, served with sausages or the truffle sauce on page 173.

Serves 1
Preparation time: 2 minutes
Cooking time: 2–3 minutes

¼ tsp olive oil 11 cals
½ clove garlic, chopped 2–4 cals
120g tinned cannellini beans, rinsed and drained 120 cals
1 dessertspoon 0% fat crème fraîche 6 cals or 30ml almond 4 cals or 30ml
    semi-skimmed milk 14 cals
chopped fresh parsley, to serve

1. Heat the oil in a non-stick saucepan over a low heat. Add the garlic and sauté gently for 2–3 minutes.

2. Add the white beans to the saucepan and warm through. Mash lightly with a fork and stir in the milk or crème fraîche. Remove from the heat, sprinkle with the chopped parsley and serve.

More ideas from the 5:2 Kitchen Omit the garlic and add finely chopped rosemary and a little lemon zest for a fresher taste. For a less creamy flavour, use vegetable or chicken stock instead of milk or crème fraîche.

CAULIFLOWER, MUSTARD AND HERB MASH

Calories per serving: 33 (92 with butter and milk)

Vegetarian/gluten free

Yes, it's our old friend the cauliflower to the rescue again. This is a robustly flavoured mash that goes well with meats and burgers.

Serves 2
Preparation time: 2 minutes
Cooking time: 2–3 minutes

> 200g of cauliflower florets, fresh or frozen 50 cals
> 50ml vegetable stock 2 cals or 50ml almond milk 2 cals or
>   50 ml semi-skimmed milk 25 cals
> 1–2 tsp wholegrain mustard 8–16 cals
> 1 tbsp chopped chives or parsley or a mixture 5 cals
> sea salt and black pepper
> 1 tsp butter (optional) 37 cals

1. Steam or boil the cauliflower florets for 8–10 minutes, or until tender then drain.

2. Return to the saucepan and mash with a fork or potato masher. Add the stock or milk and continue to mash until it has a smooth texture (you can also do this in a food processor). Add the mustard, herbs and mix well.

3. Season and serve with a little butter on top, if using.

More ideas from the 5:2 Kitchen Add Dijon mustard or horseradish for a different flavoured mash, or even a little grated cheese.

Dressings, stock, marinades

The right dressing or sauce can raise a dish from good to *brilliant* and, personally, I love picking the right accompaniment to a meal, whether it's a piquant pickle or a creamy sauce.

There are lots of great sauce, dip and dressing recipes throughout this book, below there's a list, plus a couple of the most versatile recipes from *The Ultimate 5:2 Recipe Book,* which has many, many more ideas!

Recipe	Try with	Page
Sauces		
Mustard Sauce	Eggs/meat/vegetables	43
Home-made Ketchup	Vegetarian or chicken burgers, breakfasts	50
Romesco Sauce	Grilled vegetables and meats, as a dip or sandwich spread in place of mayonnaise	171
Dressings and dips		
Lemon Pesto Dressing	Pasta/'courgetti', grilled vegetables and meats	45
Parmesan and Mustard	Salads, cooked chicken	103
Cocktail Dressing	Little Gem, chicory and other crisp lettuces or leaves; poached or steamed fish	105
Pecorino Pesto	All vegetables, cooked chicken	111
Feta Dip	Crudités, lamb, barbecued meat	133
Raita	Curries, spiced meat	141
Hummus Dressing	Fresh steamed vegetables, sandwich filling	144
Mango Dipping Sauce	Curries, grilled halloumi cheese	178

Sometimes all a salad needs is a little balsamic or cider vinegar, a squirt of lemon, or a few sunflower or pumpkin seeds. The two recipes below are base recipes that you can adapt to your own tastes. Always use dressings sparingly, though. They aren't low in calories, and you still want to be able to taste the leaves and vegetables underneath.

To make, use a clean jam jar with the lid as a shaker and then you can store it in the fridge. Or simply whisk together in a small bowl. Season to taste.

BALSAMIC AND YOGHURT DRESSING
Calories per 150ml: 160–245; per 5ml: 5–8

One of my favourites, this is sweet *and* savoury. Watch the seasoning, as the soy sauce is already salty.

Makes 150ml

> 60ml balsamic vinegar 20–60 cals
> 1 tbsp light soy sauce 6 cals
> 1 tsp Dijon mustard 5 cals
> 1 tbsp runny honey 60 cals
> 3 tbsp 0% fat Greek yoghurt 24 cals
> 1–2 tsp extra virgin olive oil 45–90 cals

CREAMY HERB DRESSING
Calories per 100ml: 96; per 5ml: 5

Adjust the milk quantities, if you like, to make it thicker. You could try sweet chilli-flavoured cream cheese instead of the garlic and herb type for a change.

Makes 100ml

> 50g Philadelphia Light cream cheese with garlic and herbs 73 cals
> 1–2 tbsp finely chopped fresh herbs of your choice 5 cals
> 2 tbsp semi-skimmed milk 14 cals
> juice of ½ lemon 4 cals or ½ tsp bottled lemon juice 10 cals

Stocking up

If you love soup as much as I do, then making your own stock will raise your creations to another level. This is the simplest version for vegetable stock: the calorie count is approximate because the vegetables are infused, not eaten.

BASIC FAST DAY VEGETABLE STOCK
Approximately 26–30 calories

Makes 1–1.25 litres

> ½ tsp olive oil, 22 cals (or coconut oil if you're planning on using the stock in spicy dishes)
> 2 onions, roughly chopped
> 2 leeks, roughly chopped
> 2 carrots, chopped into chunks (no need to peel)
> 2 sticks of celery, chopped into chunks
> 2 bay leaves
> ½ tsp peppercorns
> thyme sprig
> few thicker parsley stems

1. Heat the olive oil in a wide-bottomed saucepan over a medium heat. Add all of the vegetables and fry for approximately 2–3 minutes, or until they're lightly browned.

2. Add enough water to cover (approximately 1.5 litres should do it). Increase the heat and bring to the boil then simmer on a low heat. After 30–45 minutes, turn off the heat but leave the vegetables to sit in the liquid for as long as possible, or 1 hour at a minimum, before straining through a sieve.

3. The liquid will keep for several days in the fridge, or you can freeze soup-sized portions for up to a year. You can melt the frozen stock straight into the saucepan. If the stock is very intensely flavoured, you can freeze it in ice-cube trays and transfer the cubes to a container once frozen, then use as many as you need at a time.

JAM JAR MARINADE MIX

Calories per serving: 5

Gluten free/nut free

Sometimes you don't want to have to think too much about dinner and, if you've got a jar full of these spices in your cupboard, you won't have to. It's a simple mix but so adaptable, and can be used to perk up meat, tofu or fish. Once you've tried this one, play with the flavours to create your own.

Makes 6 portions
Preparation time: 5 minutes

> 2 tsp ground cumin 10 cals
> 2 tsp ground coriander 10 cals
> 1 tsp dried thyme 5 cals
> 1 tsp smoked paprika 5 cals

1. Mix all the spices together in a jar, seal and store in a cool cupboard away from direct sunlight.

How to use

Mix 1 teaspoon spice mix with one of the following combinations, then use it as marinade for your chosen ingredient. Use one pump of oil spray in a dry frying pan and fry until cooked through.

For chicken, pork or tofu

> ½ tsp olive oil, zest and juice of ¼ lemon for an extra 30 calories

For fish and beef

> ½ tbsp tomato ketchup and ½ tbsp water for an extra 9 calories

For lamb

> 1 tbsp natural yoghurt (around 4% fat) and 1–2 tsp water for an extra 12 calories

Other ways to use the Jam Jar Marinade Mix

- Add to rice or cauliflower rice before stir-frying

- Sprinkle on flatbreads or pittas with ¼ teaspoon oil then warm in the oven

- Mix 1 teaspoon with 3 tablespoons of 0% fat crème fraîche or yoghurt for a great dip

- Sprinkle on vegetables before roasting.

In a pickle

I think pickles and chutneys are heavenly, and making fresh ones is easy and cheap. Here are two easy recipes that work as side dishes to add flavour on a Fast Day.

ALMOST INSTANT HOME-SPICED PICKLES
Calories per serving: 25 as a pickle; 50 as a side vegetable

Vegetarian/dairy free

These are so simple and so good. You can either microwave them to soften the vegetables a little, or simply serve cold as they come. Choose vegetables you can eat raw. Fabulous with Indian dishes, or just as a snack.

Serves 4 (or 2 as a side vegetable)
Preparation time: 3 minutes
Cooking time: 3–5 minutes

250g mixed vegetables, including cauliflower, carrot or cucumber, radishes
   and red onion 23–46 cals
5g root ginger, finely chopped 4 cals
1 clove garlic, finely chopped 4 cals
1 small fresh green chilli, deseeded, core removed, thinly sliced 5 cals
100ml water
100ml white wine vinegar 16 cals or 100ml cider vinegar 18 cals
1 tsp sugar or equivalent in sweetener (optional) 15 cals
1 tsp salt
½ tsp black or white mustard seeds 5 cals
¼ tsp each whole coriander and cumin seeds 5 cals
good pinch dried chilli flakes (optional)

1. Slice or snap the vegetables into bite-size pieces and place in a large microwaveable dish. Add all of the remaining ingredients and cover the bowl with a plate.

2. Microwave on full power for 3–4 minutes, depending on how crunchy you like the vegetables. Or, heat everything in a large saucepan over high heat for 5 minutes. You can skip the heating if you prefer a really crunchy salad pickle to eat on the day.

More ideas from the 5:2 Kitchen The pickles will keep, covered in the fridge for at least one week, though some colour will leach so don't be surprised if your cauliflower florets turn pink from the red onions. Vary the spicing according to what you like: try bay leaves, dried chilli flakes, peppercorns, and other whole spices.

CHILLI BEETROOTS

Calories per serving: 37

Vegetarian/dairy free/nut free

I love chilli and I love beetroot. So this is definitely for me. It's much cheaper to do this than buy the pre-made 'sweet fiery' beetroots from the supermarket, and you can adjust the heat to suit your palate.

Makes 3 x 80g servings
Preparation time: 4 minutes plus at least 60 minutes to marinate

250g beetroots cooked in water 108 cals
2 tbsp cider vinegar 2 cals or wine vinegar 2–3 cals
2 slices bottled jalapeño pepper, finely chopped or good pinch dried chilli flakes 2 cals
few drops chilli or sriracha sauce

1. Slice the beets in half, or into bite-sized pieces, then place in a plastic container with the rest of the ingredients. Shake well, and leave to marinate in the fridge for at least an hour: it gets better with age! Keeps for up to a week, covered, in the fridge.

Salt and Pepper Edamame; Kale Crisps; Designer Popcorn

The search for a great 5:2 snack food is one of the things that comes up a lot on Facebook. Snacking may not always be the right thing (see page 148 for why), but if you're craving a little something to keep you going, these are healthy, tasty options.

Snap: the edamame pods
Crackle: the crunchy kale crisps
Pop: corn at home and add healthy, tasty flavourings

SALT AND PEPPER EDAMAME
Calories per serving: 67

Vegetarian/dairy free/gluten free/nut free

This is as simple as it gets, but really good. Most of the salt we eat comes from processed foods and while we shouldn't go overboard, a little sea salt and pepper will give your taste buds a treat. Edamame are soya beans and are 11 per cent protein. They're satisfying *and* tasty. I buy the ones in their pods, so you get the fun of using your teeth to snap them and then taste the flavouring on the outside. A little sriracha sauce is excellent with these, too.

Serves 1
Preparation time: 1 minute
Cooking time: 3 minutes

    50g frozen edamame in their pods 67 cals
    Sea salt and freshly ground black or mixed pepper

1. Rinse the frozen pods. Microwave or boil them according to pack instructions: the quickest way is usually to microwave them for about 90 seconds. They're nicer warm.

2. Drain any excess water, place in a small bowl and add a good pinch of sea salt then grind over fresh pepper, to taste. They're really good with a wasabi dip: mix a tiny amount (less than ¼ teaspoon) of the hot mustard with a tablespoon of 0% fat crème fraîche or a tablespoon of rice vinegar.

KALE CRISPS

Calories per serving: 21

Vegetarian/dairy free/gluten free/nut free

Kale is very trendy right now, on account of its nutritional profile. This dish is very much like the deep-fried crispy seaweed you get in Chinese restaurants, except it's not deep-fried, and it's made with kale. The trick is to use a low oven temperature, so that the kale dries out, rather than bakes: leaving the oven door very slightly ajar helps any steam escape. I like it with the gochugaru chilli flakes used for kimchi, or any other chilli powder.

Serves 1
Preparation time: 3 minutes
Cooking time: 3–5 minutes

> 50g curly kale, washed, dried well and chopped 18 cals
> ½ tsp ground spices, such as garam masala, paprika or ras al 'hanout 3 cals
> 1-cal cooking spray (optional)

1. Pre-heat the oven to 120°C/250°F/Gas mark ½. Remove any particularly thick stalks from the chopped kale.

2. Lay the kale out in a single layer on a baking sheet and spray it with the 1-cal cooking spray, if desired, then sprinkle over the spices.

3. Cook for 9–10 minutes, or until the kale has dried out and turned golden brown at the edges.

DESIGNER POPCORN

Calories per serving: 56, plus flavouring & oil if using

Vegetarian/dairy free/gluten free/nut free

I love popcorn. It's high in antioxidants and easy to pop on the stovetop or in the microwave: I find popping on the hob gives slightly more reliable results. Carly on the 5:2 group suggested spicemountain.co.uk for some amazing powdered natural flavour including salt and vinegar!

Serves 1
Preparation time: 1 minute
Cooking time: 2–4 minutes

> 1-cal spray or a ¼ tsp of coconut, olive or flavoured oil, (optional) 11 cals
> 15g unpopped popcorn kernels 56 cals

1. Flavouring of your choice: see below for suggestions. Allow 5 calories for ½–1 teaspoons ground or whole spices, or check labels for pre-made commercial seasonings.

2. If using oil, add to pan or popcorn maker, then use kitchen paper to spread over base. Place the corn in the saucepan or popcorn maker and *cover the pan with a lid that has a vent/ gap to allow some air to escape*. On the hob, gently heat the saucepan and keep shaking the pan. The kernels will begin to pop after around 1 minute, and it'll take up to 3 for them to finish: never remove the lid till you haven't heard popping for at least 30 seconds (a glass lid makes this easier!).

3. In the microwave, cover pan or popcorn maker but ensure there's a gap to allow steam to escape. Heat on full for 2 minutes at first. Wait 30 seconds for any corn to stop popping before opening. Tip out the popped corn into a large bowl and return unpopped kernels to the microwave for 45 seconds at a time. There'll always be a few hulls that don't pop.

4. Add the flavouring of your choice, dry ingredients are best. Sprinkle over the top and then use your hands or a spatula to reach the bottom.

   • **Savoury** Many spice blends will work, such as Cajun, Five Spice Powder, salt and vinegar seasoning, or garam masala. Or mix your own favourite spices; celery, truffle or garlic salt, freshly ground mixed pepper with sea salt.

- **Sweet** Try cinnamon, or cinnamon and salt for a sweet and salty combination; a little ground ginger; unsweetened cocoa powder; crushed freeze-dried raspberries and strawberries; ground almonds or finely crushed walnuts; or try sprinkling ground almond or desiccated coconut with vanilla.

5. You can store popcorn with dry flavourings for 24 hours in an airtight plastic container.

Windowsill garden: sprouting your own beans and seeds

My final 'recipe' isn't a recipe at all: it's a suggestion involving seeds, a jam jar and an elastic band.

I've sprouted beans and seeds before, but have been doing it with a vengeance lately, to create healthy, nutritious nibbles that don't ruin my fast but make me feel very slightly like an earth mother. Sprouting makes the nutrients in the beans and seeds much easier for the body to digest, and they have a peppery, spicy taste. Here is my 5:2 guide to becoming a self-sprouter.

You will need

1 clean jam-jar, washed in very hot soapy water and then dry thoroughly
1 thick elastic band
1 square of thin fabric, such as muslin, that will just fit over the mouth of the jar
mesh sieve

1. Buy some beans or seeds from your local health food shop. They will cost you around £2 at the most. Choose either mung or alfalfa or a 'gourmet mix'. Later, you can try wheat, quinoa, China rose radish, or any other that strikes your fancy. Just make sure they're organic, as you'll be eating the whole seed.

2. Rinse your seeds in the sieve (not a colander, they'll fall through), then place them in the jam jar and half-fill with water (filtered is nice). Stretch the fabric over the open mouth of the jar and secure round the rim with the elastic band.

3. Place in a dark place and let the beans or seeds soak, either overnight, or following the instructions in the packet.

4. Drain the original water from the seeds through the fabric without removing the elastic band. Depending on the seeds/beans, you might see tiny white shoots as the skins break. Don't panic if not.

5. Rinse the seeds at least twice a day, preferably more, simply by pouring water gently through the fabric, shaking through the sprouts, and letting it drain out again. Keep the jar on the worktop, but out of sunlight, to remind you.

6. Enjoy your harvest after 4–5 days, when the sprouts are the right size, though they may be a little slower in cold weather. You can store them in the fridge if you want to start a new supply, but do eat as fresh as possible. There's a small risk of contamination with sprouts so do throw them out if they don't smell right, and avoid eating them raw if you're immune-compromised. Enjoy them in salads, sandwiches, in stir-fries or just as a nibble. They're incredibly nutritious and there's something very exciting about home-grown.

If you want to get more sophisticated, there's a cool Biosnacky Germinator, which cost me under £5 and replaces the muslin with a plastic lid that doesn't go brown. But I wouldn't bother with the multi-tiered ones, they're tricky to clean.

I warn you – it *is* addictive. Before long, you'll be trying to sprout anything that moves.

Making sense of... eating for long life and good health

From scares about sweeteners, to hunger hormones, trying to make sense of food can be enough to make your head spin. But as I hope my recipes show, food *isn't* scary. It's delicious, nourishing, exciting, soothing, sociable, and one of life's great pleasures.

The point of these *Making sense of...* sections is to show we have choices. With common sense and a bit of research, we can 'keep calm and dine on.'

Ready for the next scare – or superfood?

Whether it's a miracle supplement that will turn you into a supermodel, or a study insisting water will kill you, do a bit of detective work before acting.

1. **Read the detail.** Who is making this claim? What might their motives be for pushing the story? Could they be selling a product or a newspaper, or even simply creating mischief?

2. **Go back to the original source** and read exactly what is written (studies may not always publish the whole paper but will usually have a summary). Then search online for alternative views: www.snopes.com is great for ruling out hoaxes, the NHS site does balanced analyses of health stories, and even the often-criticised Wikipedia has thorough and useful explanations of human biology.

3. **Discuss with friends and family**, and **then decide** if it's something you want to act upon.

I am naturally sceptical, but sometimes research or science makes you take a second look at something you took for granted. I genuinely thought I had no chance of maintaining a healthy weight till I watched a documentary about intermittent fasting – and here I am, so much happier, and 13.5kg (30 lb) lighter.

Kate's Food Commandments

Here are my 'Food Commandments', based on the topics we've explored. But, remember to treat these with the same 'trust your instincts' scepticism as you'd treat anything else you read.

1. **Never trust a headline** Do your research before changing your behaviour

2. **Tune into your appetite** Respond to its signals and treat it with respect.

3. **Experiment with eating times** Learn what works best for your body.

4. **Listen to advice from good sources** but consider if there's an alternative that's best for you.

5. **Shop wisely** Learn to use your consumer power to influencethe causes that matter to you.

6. **Understand your body's strengths and weaknesses** Nurture it with the right foods for you.

7. **Eat mindfully and gratefully** Forgive yourself the occasional slip-up.

8. **Look for balance in your diet** Appreciate what different foods can do for you and avoid fads. Be creative!

9. **Enjoy treats and know what they do to you** Make choices based on understanding how sugar and high-fat foods affect the body.

10. And above all **Keep it real** Eat and cook real food that is as whole and unprocessed as possible. It's cheaper, better for you and much, much more delicious.

5:2 Food Heroes

CAULIFLOWER AND CHUMS

Once you couldn't get anyone to eat cabbage, including me. Now kale, broccoli and cauliflower are getting their highly deserved moment in the sun, as this group of nutritious and delicious vegetables is in vogue. Treat them right, and you'll banish soggy cauliflower forever.

About cruciferous vegetables

The 'cruciferous' vegetables get their name from the cross, or crucifer, shape of their flowers. They are also part of the brassica or 'mustard' family of plants. Cabbage is the daddy of them all, and has been used for 4,000 years or more, while broccoli and cauliflower came from the Middle East, Brussels sprouts are the newcomers and, as the name suggests, were grown in Belgium in the eighteenth century.

Nutrition

Nutritionally speaking, these vegetables are truly heroic: low in calories, but packed with vitamins, fibre, and nutrients. On a Fast Day, they're filling and also incredibly versatile, making brilliant replacements for starchier foods.

- **Beneficial nutrients and compounds** In this group of vegetables, these are too numerous to mention, but they include high levels of vitamin A, C and K, B-vitamins, minerals, iron/folate and fibre. They also contain some protein and omega-3 fatty acids.

- **Glucosinates** Many of the potential cancer- and inflammation-fighting elements are linked to glucosinates, the same compounds that give them their spicy, almost bitter taste. This family of vegetables offers protection against numerous cancers, including breast, lung, colon, liver, cervix and prostate. The plant compounds that give the vegetable its bitterness and sulphurous smell when overcooked can help reduce the toxicity of cancer-causing substances, and help the body fight back.

- **Reduced oxidative stress and other benefits** This stress is caused by 'free radicals' and reducing them may also cut the risk of certain cancers: one study showed that eating these vegetables daily cuts the stress, especially if they're eaten raw or lightly steamed or cooked (which, luckily, is when they're at their tastiest).

Downsides

- **Bitterness** These vegetables taste much more bitter to some people than others, and it's all down to genes. 'Tasters' may eat less of this kind of veg and so miss out on the benefits. If you've experienced this, try blending or pairing with milder vegetables or ingredients.

- **Thyroid problems** In some animal studies, heavy consumption of cruciferous vegetables has been linked to insufficient thyroid production, so check with your doctor if you have thyroid issues.

How to buy and store

Buy in season if you can. Frozen vegetables are an option but they do lose their crunchiness.

- **Broccoli and cauliflower** Choose vegetables with bright leaves or stalks and tightly packed florets that aren't discoloured. Store in an open plastic bag in the fridge. It'll keep for around 10–14 days, but always tastes better fresher!

- **Cabbage and kale** Avoid limp leaves or discolouration.

Cooking with brassicas

- **Chopping or mincing** This actually helps release the beneficial compounds, so preparing vegetables this way can help make nutrients more available to the body. There are also benefits in letting them 'sit' for several minutes once chopped and before cooking.

- **Avoid boiling** Boiling is bad news, both for the nutrients and for your kitchen. Those sulphurous smells, and soggy textures, are unpleasant.

- **Cook lightly** Serving them raw, steamed, microwaved or stir-fried preserves the nutrients. In fact, steaming can actually make the nutrients more available to your body.

- **Soup** Preparing vegetables at a simmer or lower in soups may also be a good way to maximise the benefits you'll get.

- Adding lemon (or other vegetables with vitamin C) to brassicas helps the body absorb iron from the vegetables. And one study showed broccoli and tomato are a particularly good combination for reducing the risk of prostate cancer.

Recipe Ideas

Cauliflower and mustard soup with melted cheese crispy
crumbs page 81

Home-made pizza with cauliflower base and blue cheese
topping page 165

Kale crisps page 335

3

5:2
RESOURCES

This part of the book contains tools and resources to help you plan your meals, understand your calorie needs and help you discover more about 5:2.

Recipes listed by calorie count per serving

The recipes are listed in the order they appear in the book, with two listings under different categories if there's a lower and higher-calorie option.

Dishes under 100 calories

Cheddar and Apple 'Ploughman's Brunch' Mini-Muffins (see page 48) 44 calories each

Apricot and Coconut Energy Bites (see page 55) 73 cals

Freshly Minted Green Soup with Goat's Cheese Floats (see page 73) 84 cals

Speedy Virgin Mary Soup (with Bloody Mary option for non-fasting days) (see page 74) 44 cals

Cauliflower and Mustard Soup with Melted Cheese Crispy Crumbs (see page 81) 83–101 cals

Calming Apple, Celery and Fennel Seed Soup with Waldorf Topping (see page 84) 67–91 cals

Mushroom and Herb Paté with Melba Toast (see page 107) 72 cals

Buckwheat Pancakes with Breton Toppings (see page 259) 67 cals

Berry Mint Smoothie (see page 289) 31 cals

Black Forest Yoghurt Drink (see page 290) 92 cals

Beetroot and Ginger Booster (see page 291) 60 cals

Infusions: Hot and Cold Drinks from the Garden (see page 293) 0–10 cals

Affogato: Instant Espresso Sundae (see page 297) 24–60 cals

Spiced Raspberry and Apple Yoghurt Ice (see page 298) 63 cals

Whipped Vanilla Mousse with Red Fruit Ripple (see page 299) 52 cals

Prune and Chocolate Nut Truffles (see page 300) 27 cals each

Cauliflower Rice (see page 320) 25 cals
Courgetti (see page 322) 34 cals
Sweet Potato Chips (see page 324) 71–84 cals
Cauliflower Mash (see page 326) 33–92 cals
Almost Instant Home-Spiced Pickles (see page 331) 25 cals
Chilli Beetroots (see page 333) 37 cals
Salt and Pepper Edamame (see page 334) 67 cals
Kale Crisps (see page 335) 21 cals
Designer Popcorn (see page 336) 56–67 cals

Dishes under 200 calories

Eggs 'Benefit' with Mustard Sauce (see page 43) 189–220 cals
Noosa-style Mushrooms and Goat's Cheese with Lemon Pesto
    Dressing (see page 45) 178 cals
Pick 'n' Mix Chilled-Out Magic Muesli (see page 52) 85–190 cals
The World's Easiest Chocolate and Almond Pancakes (see page 56)
    109–125 cals
Coconut and Chicken Thai Broth (see page 76) 179 cals
Creamy Chicken and Tomato Soup (see page 77) 135 cals
Mexican Tortilla Soup (see page 78) 127 cals
Vegan Mulligatawny (see page 80) 164 cals
Fennel and Tomato-Flavoured Fish Broth (see page 83) 148 cals
Romaine 'Tacos' with Fresh Sprouts, Avocado, and Cheese
    (see page 106) 122 cals
Quick and Easy Chilli Omelette Roll with Tomato and Ricotta
    Filling (see page 108) 139 cals
Crostini with Fresh Toppings: Melon and Goat's Cheese/ Broad
    Bean and Feta (see page 112) 168–180 cals
Griddled Red Chicory with Blue Cheese and Walnut Melt
    (see page 169) 158 cals
Chargrilled Vegetable Platter with Smoky Romesco Sauce
    (see page 171) 148–155 cals
Two-colour Courgetti with Truffled Mushroom Cream Sauce
    (see page 173) 132–171 cals

Korean Kimchi Pickle with Tofu Stir-fry (see page 175) 154–270 cals
Chilli Chickpea Nuggets with Mango Dipping Sauce (see page 178)
    140–170 cals
Cured Salmon Fishcakes (see page 202) 199 cals
Lamb Lollies with Popped-Spice Carrot Salad (see page 203) 180 cals
Sweet and Sour Five-Spice Tofu (see page 204) 154 cals
Plaice, Lemon and Capers with Courgette Frites (see page 230)
    216 cals
Chilli-Spiced Chicken Burger on a Mushroom 'Bun' (see page 231)
    150 cals
Pizza Omelette Popovers (see page 261) 105 cals each
Meatloaf 'Muffins' with Super-Greens (see page 264) 177 cals
Black Bean Stew with Creamy Cheese Topping (see page 265)
    155 cals
Mango Smoothie (see page 292) 171–207 cals
Egg-Fried Cauliflower Rice (see page 321) 182 cals
White Bean Mash with Garlic (see page 325) 137–149 cals

Dishes under 300 calories

Baked Haddock Smokie Pot (see page 47) 205–285 cals
Mediterranean-style Quinoa Cakes with Home-Made Ketchup
    Salsa (see page 50) 214–263 cals
Vegan option: Portobello Mushrooms with Mediterranean Quinoa
    Stuffing (see page 52) 229 cals
Mulligatawny with Shredded Beef (see page 80) 253 cals (vegan
    option, 164 cals)
Tex-Mex Beef Salad (see page 101) 246 cals
'Coronation' Quinoa with Asparagus and Almonds (see page 102)
    285 cals
Crunchy Chicken Salad with Parmesan and Mustard Dressing
    (see page 103) 271 cals
Warm Prawn Cocktail Salad (see page 105) 217 cals
Smoked Mackerel with Crisp Vegetable Remoulade (see page 110)
    223 cals

White Bean and Spinach Salad with a Pecorino Pesto (see page 111) 120–200 cals

Crostini with Fresh Toppings: Pear and Blue Cheese (see page 112) 242 cals

Vegetarial Thali: Mushroom and Green Bean Korma, Raita, Pickles (see page 141) 241 cals

Great Big Veggie Burrito Bowl (see page 163) 262 cals

Home-made Pizza with Cauliflower Base and Blue Cheese Topping (see page 165) 296–326 cals

Imam Bayildi (rich stuffed aubergines) (see page 167) 205–225 cals

Savoury Summer Crumble with Tomato and Herbs (see page 170) 224 cals

Sri Lankan Triple Coconut Vegetable Curry (see page 200) 241–269 cals

Smoky Spanish Mussels (see page 205) 287 cals

Chicken Sausage Roll with Leek, Mushroom and Thyme (see page 228) 289 cals

Two-Cheese Soufflé Omelette with Rocket and Onion Salad (see page 235) 230–293 cals

Grilled Red Pepper Stuffed with Millet and Chicken (see page 236) 214 cals

Chicken Chili with Creamy Avocado Topping (see page 256) 205–239 cals

Polenta triangles with Rich Sausage Ragù (see page 257) 209–273 cals

Country-Style Rabbit Stew with Beans, Barley and Gremolata (see page 262) 252 cals

Rich Pork Lasagne with Lucky-Seven Vegetables (see page 267) 289 cals

Best-Ever Beef and Bay Casserole with Chestnuts (see page 269) 264 cals

Dishes Under 400 calories

Sunshine Mezze: Feta Dip, Aubergines with Tahini, Pitta Chips
(see page 133) 303 cals

Spanish Tapas: Asparagus Tortilla, Catalan Roast Vegetables,
Nibbles (see page 135) 340–392 cals

Italian Antipasti: Fiery Mozzarella, Tomato and Courgette
Bruschetta, Salad (see page 137) 319 cals

Smorgasbord with Home-Cured Fish, Salad and Rye (see page 139)
333 cals

Asian-Spiced Fish Parcels With Fennel, Onion and Celery
(see page 142) 374 cals with rice

Moroccan Lamb with Cauliflower 'Couscous' and Hummus Dressing
(see page 144) 337 cals

Star Anise Duck with Coriander Slaw (see page 199) 316 cals

Lemongrass and Ginger Pork with Noodles (see page 206) 356 cals

Pearl Barley Risotto with Sherried Mushrooms, Cavalo Nero and
Sage (see page 227) 328 cals

Prawn Jambalaya (see page 232) 358 cals

Spring Fish Pie (see page 234) 310 cals

One-Pan Pork with Sage and Roasted Vegetables (see page 238)
329 cals

Dishes under 500 calories

Indulgent Salmon and Gnocchi Bake (see page 146) 449 cals

Vegetarian option: Vegetable and Mozzarella Gnocchi Bake (see
page 146) 432 cals

'Bibimbap' Korean Rice and Fresh Pickles (see page 208) 423 cals

5:2 Good Food Kitchen

MENU IDEAS

5:2 gives you so much freedom that it can be overwhelming – so here are some sample meal plans. Each week has one meal for women at around 500 calories, and one for men with 100 more – but they're just suggestions. Do your own thing – whatever works for you!

Week 1 (three meals a day)

1: (for women: 485 calories)
Breakfast: Black Forest Yoghurt Drink, 92 cals
Lunch: Romaine 'Tacos' with Fresh Sprouts, Avocado, and Cheese, 122 cals
Dinner: Crunchy Chicken Salad with Parmesan and Mustard Dressing, 271 cals

2: (for men: 583 calories)
Breakfast: 2 x Cheddar and Apple 'Ploughman's Brunch' Mini-Muffins, 88 cals
Lunch: Smoked Mackerel with Crisp Vegetable Remoulade, 223 cals
Dinner: Polenta Triangles with Rich Sausage Ragù, 272 cals

Week 2
(breakfast and dinner plus 1 snack)

1: (for women: 461 calories)
Breakfast: Pick 'n' Mix Chilled-Out Magic Muesli, 85 cals
Snack: Apricot and Coconut Energy Bites, 73 cals
Dinner: Sunshine Mezze: Feta Dip, Aubergines with Tahini, Pitta Chips, 303 cals

2: (for men: 606 calories)
Breakfast: Eggs 'Benefit' with Mustard Sauce and Smoked Salmon, 220 cals
Snack: Mushroom and Herb Paté with Melba Toast, 72 cals
Dinner: Chicken Sausage Roll with Leek, Mushroom and Thyme, 289 cals

Week 3 (lunch and dinner)

1: (for women: 501 calories)
Lunch: Imam Bayildi (rich stuffed aubergines), 207 cals

Dinner: Home-Made Pizza with Cauliflower Base and Blue Cheese
   Topping, 296 cals

2: (for men: 620 calories)
Lunch: Tex-Mex Beef Salad, 246 cals
Dinner: Asian-Spiced Fish Parcels with Fennel, Onion and Celery,
   374 cals with rice

Week 4 (1 main meal)

1: (for women: 463 calories)
Main meal: Speedy Virgin Mary Soup (with Bloody Mary option
   (for non-fasting days), 44 cals
Lemongrass and Ginger Pork with Noodles, 356 cals
Spiced Raspberry and Apple Yoghurt Ice, 63 cals

2: (for men: 571 calories)
Main meal: Freshly Minted Green Soup with Goat's Cheese Floats,
   70 cals
Indulgent Salmon and Gnocchi Bake, 449 cals
Whipped Vanilla Mousse with Red Fruit Ripple, 52 cals

Calorie counter

Many of the ingredients in this book are listed below, with both
calories per 100g/ml and also calories in an average portion or
serving. These are all actually Kilocalories (kcal on food labels) but
most of us call these calories so that's what we're using.

Where a range of calorie counts is shown, do check the labels to
compare: you're unlikely to go far off course with white wine vinegar,
for example, but higher-fat or higher-calorie products could derail
your Fast Day. We have checked recipes and calorie counts six times,
but it is still possible that errors may have crept in. Do let me know
via the 5:2 website if you spot one!

Food	Calories per 100g/ml	Average serving size	Calories per average portion
Dairy			
Cheeses			
Blue cheese	310–400	25g	78–100
Brie	305	25g slice	76
Cheddar, full-fat mature	400	25g	100
Cheddar, reduced-fat	215–275	25g	54–69
Emmental, reduced-fat	273	25g	68
Feta, full-fat	360	15g	54
Feta-style, light salad cheese	180	15g	27
Fromage frais, fat-free	50	1 tablespoon	8
Goat's cheese	270–330	25g	68–83
Grana Padano (hard Italian cheese)	385	10g	39
Halloumi, reduced-fat	255	50g	128
Lancashire cheese	370	25g	93
Mozzarella, buffalo	288	125g	180
Mozzarella, reduced-fat	174	50g	87
Parmesan	415	10g	42
Pecorino	400	10g	40
Philadelphia Light	146–160	1 tablespoon	22–24
Quark	69	1 tablespoon	10
Ricotta	134	1 tablespoon	20

Food	Calories per 100g/ml	Average serving size	Calories per average portion
Milk and yoghurt/ substitutes			
Almond milk	13	1 tablespoon	2
Coconut milk	233	1 tablespoon	35
Coconut milk, reduced fat	73–210	1 tablespoon	11–32
Coconut (non-dairy) yoghurt	165	1 tablespoon	25
Cow's milk, semi-skimmed	49	1 tablespoon	7
Cow's milk, skimmed	35	1 tablespoon	5
Greek yoghurt, full fat	130	1 tablespoon	20
Greek yoghurt 0% fat	55	1 tablespoon	8
Soya milk, unsweetened	20–34	1 tablespoon	3–5
Yogurt, natural, 4% fat	82	1 tablespoon	12
Eggs			
Egg, medium		1 egg	78
Egg, large		1 egg	100
Egg white		1 egg white	14
Breads and grains (grains all given as dry weight) and baking			
Baking powder		1 teaspoon	5
Barley couscous	340	25g	85
Barley, pearled, uncooked	352	50g	176

Food	Calories per 100g/ml	Average serving size	Calories per average portion
Basmati rice, brown	330	25g	83
Basmati rice, white	355	25g	89
Bread, ciabatta/sourdough	275	1 slice, 25g	69
Bread, rye	212	½ slice	80
Bread, white	220–250	25g slice from smaller loaf	55–63
Bread wholemeal	220–250	25g slice from smaller loaf	55–63
Bulgar wheat	360	25g	90
Couscous	376	25g	94
Egg noodles	220–355	25g	55–89
Filo pastry	355	1 sheet weighing 40–45g	140–160
Flour, white	335	1 teaspoon	17
Flour, wholewheat	310	1 teaspoon	16
Gnocchi	130–160	100g	130–160
Lasagne, raw, spinach	367	1 sheet	84
Millet, raw	378	50g	189
Oatcake biscuit		1 biscuit	40–50
Pasta, white	233–360	25g	58–90
Pasta, wholewheat	330	25g	83

Food	Calories per 100g/ml	Average serving size	Calories per average portion
Polenta	362	25g (baked slice or as a purée)	91
Porridge oats	355	25g	89
Quinoa	365	25g	91
Tortilla, corn	270–340	1 tortilla wrap (varies a lot)	117
Tortilla, white wheat	270–340	1 tortilla wrap (varies a lot)	100–200
Vegetables and salads Given in whole vegetable or portions			
Asparagus	27	4 spears	13
Aubergine	20	1 very small/ baby (60g)	12
		1 medium (200g)	40
Avocado flesh	160	30–40g	48–64
		70–80g	112–128
Baby sweetcorn and sugar snap pea mix	33	50g	17
Beansprouts	34	50g	17
Beetroot	43	5cm diameter	35
Broad beans, fresh	88	50g	44
Broccoli	32	½ small head	32

Food	Calories per 100g/ml	Average serving size	Calories per average portion
Cabbage	26	½ head cabbage (130g)	34
Carrot	34	1 medium (100g)	34
Cauliflower	25	400g (florets only)	100
Celeriac	29	½ celeriac (75g)	
Celery	10	1 medium stick (60g)	6
Chilli, hot	40	1 small (2–5g)	1–2
		1 medium (20–25g)	8–10
Corn	90	1 cob	120
		1 tablespoon kernels	14
Courgette	20	1 medium (170g)	34
Cucumber, with peel	14	½ medium cucumber	15
Edamame beans	130	50g	65
Fennel	31	½ medium fennel	31
Garlic	110	1 clove	4

Food	Calories per 100g/ml	Average serving size	Calories per average portion
Green beans	27	50g	14
Kale	36	25g	9
Leeks, raw	22	1 medium (180g)	40
Lettuce	15	30g	5
Mushrooms, dried	250	5g	13
Mushrooms, fresh	13	100g	13
Mushrooms, portobello	26	1 portobello	18
Mushrooms, shiitake	25	50g	13
Onion, red or white	38	1 medium, peeled	38
Parsnip	75	1 small	110
Peas, fresh and shelled	80	100g	80
Peas, frozen, petit pois/garden peas	50–70	30g	15–23
Peas, sugar snap	35	50g	18
Pepper	30	1 medium red pepper	30
Popping corn, kernels, raw	375	20g	75
Radish	13	3 medium	3
Rocket	24	Handful	2
Runner beans	23	50g	12
Shallots	70	1 medium	7
Spinach	25	30g	8

Food	Calories per 100g/ml	Average serving size	Calories per average portion
Spring onion	32	1 small	1–2
Squash, e.g. butternut	40	50g	20
Swede	38	1 small	70
Sweet potato, uncooked	86	1 small	90–120
Tomatoes	20	1 medium	16
		1 cherry tomato	3–5
Tomatoes, chopped and tinned	18–25	400g tin	72–100
Watercress	26	Handful	3
White potato	77	1 small potato, baked	139
Fruit			
Apple, with skin	47–50	1 medium dessert	60–95
Apricot, fresh	48	1	17
Apricots, dried	180	3 dried, ready-to-eat (about 15g)	27
Banana	105	1 small	89
Blackberries	40	50g	20
Blueberries	57	50g	29
Cherries	60	10 cherries	50
Cranberries, dried	340	15g	51

Food	Calories per 100g/ml	Average serving size	Calories per average portion
Dates, Medjool	287	30g	86
Dried mixed fruit	200–290	10g	20–29
Goji, dried	300	15g	45
Grapes	60	10 grapes	34
Kiwi fruit	55	1 kiwi fruit	42
Lemon, whole	29	juice and zest	19
		squeeze of lemon/a little zest	0
Lemon juice, bottled	24	1 tablespoon	4
Lime	30	1 lime	20
Mango	60	½ medium mango (mango weighing 200–300g total)	60–90
Orange, flesh only	37	1 orange	70
Papaya	39	½ medium (150g)	60
Passion fruit, flesh and seeds	36	1 passion fruit	17
Peach	35	1 medium	51
Pear	40	1 medium	50–90
Pineapple	50	30g	14

Food	Calories per 100g/ml	Average serving size	Calories per average portion
Pomegranate seeds	100	1 tablespoon (15g)	15
Raisins, seedless	300	1 tablespoon	42
Raspberries	52	50g	26
Rhubarb, stewed, no sugar	7	1 tablespoon	1.5
Strawberries	32	50g	16
Sultanas	300	1 tablespoon	42
Tangerine	35	1 tangerine	40
Watermelon	31	1 tablespoon (950g flesh)	5
Proteins			
Baked beans	84	100g	84
Reduced sugar and salt	66	100g	66
Beans, canned, drained, cooked (black beans, cannellini, chickpeas, kidney beans)	90–130	120g (½ large tin, drained)	108–156
Beans, uncooked (black beans, cannellini, chickpeas, kidney beans)	320–350	25g	80–88
Beef, lean	177	100g	177
minced	209	100g	209
minced, extra lean	120–180	100g	120–180
steak, sirloin, lean	200	100g	200
Chicken breast, cooked	160	100g	160

Food	Calories per 100g/ml	Average serving size	Calories per average portion
Chicken breast, skinless	120	100g	120
Chicken thigh, skinless, boneless	115–140	1 small	95–140
Chorizo sausage	495	20g	99
Cod	96	1 fillet	190
Duck fillets	194	100g fillet	194
Haddock, smoked	116	100g fillet	116
Ham, sliced	84–92	1 wafer thin slice	5–19
Ham, tinned	85–116	100g	85–116
Herring	158	184g large fillet	291
Lamb, diced	288	100g	288
Mackerel, raw	153	100g	153
Mackerel, smoked	260	100g	260
Plaice fillet	85	1 small fillet	85
Pollock	81	1 small fillet	81
Pork, lean	182	100g	182
mince	174	100g	174
tenderloin	140	100g	140
Prawns, king	70–80	100g	70–80
Rabbit	114	100g	114
Red lentils, dry	330	25g	82.5
Salmon fillet, skin on	140–200	1 small fillet	100–140

Food	Calories per 100g/ml	Average serving size	Calories per average portion
Salmon, smoked	220	100g	220
Sea bass	160	100g	160
Tofu	85–185	100g	85–185
Tuna, fresh	136	100g	136
Tuna, tinned in brine	99	100g	99
Turkey	155	100g	155
Nuts and seeds			
Almonds, flaked, ground	630	15g	94.5
Almonds, whole, with skin	610	1 almond	7
Brazil nuts	680	1 nut	20–24
Cashew nuts	585	20g serving	117
Chestnuts, vacuum-packed	160	15g	24
Coconut, dried, flaked	616	10g	62
Hazelnuts	668	15g	100
Peanuts, unsalted	564	15g	85
Pecans	698	15g	105
Pine nuts	695	15g	104
Pistachio	594	1 nut	6
Poppy	556	1 teaspoon	28
Pumpkin seeds	582	1 teaspoon	29
Sesame seeds	634	1 teaspoon	32
Sunflower seeds	612	1 teaspoon	30
Walnuts	690	15g	104

Food	Calories per 100g/ml	Average serving size	Calories per average portion
Stocks			
Beef stock	5	500ml	25
Chicken stock	4	500ml	18–20
Marigold stock bouillon powder	240	1 teaspoon	12
Vegetable stock	2.5	500ml	13
Sweeteners			
Agave nectar	300–340	1 teaspoon	15–17
Almond extract	Varies greatly, check label, up to 220	5ml (see packaging)	0–11
Apple juice	42	15ml	6
Cacao powder, raw	269	1 teaspoon	7
Cocoa powder, unsweetened	345	1 teaspoon	5
Honey	300–340	1 teaspoon	20
Maple syrup	255–330	5ml	13–17
Sugar, white/brown	395–400	1 teaspoon	15
Truvia baking blend	200	1 teaspoon	10
Vanilla extract	Varies, check label, up to 288	1 teaspoon	0–15
70% dark chocolate	510–570	1 small square	30

Food	Calories per 100g/ml	Average serving size	Calories per average portion
Flavourings and sauces			
Most ground/whole spices	100		5 per tsp; 0 per pinch
Most leafy fresh herbs	50		0 for a few leaves; 5 per handful/10g/ 1 tablespoon, chopped
Branston pickle	109	1 tablespoon	16
Capers	23	10g	2
Curry pastes	120–260	1 tablespoon	18–39
Gherkins	25	20g	5
Ginger, fresh	80	2cm piece, peeled	4
Ketchup	115	1 tablespoon	17
Mango chutney	200–280	1 tablespoon	30–42
Mayonnaise, low-fat	260	1 tablespoon	40
		I teaspoon	13
Olives, vacuum packed	326	6 olives (15g)	49
Passata	30	1 tablespoon	5
Salsa	30–70	1 tablespoon	5–11
Soy sauce	35–50	1 teaspoon	2–2.5

Food	Calories per 100g/ml	Average serving size	Calories per average portion
Tahini (sesame paste)	595	1 teaspoon	30
Tomato chutney	130–160	1 tablespoon	19.5–24
Tomato purée	75–100	1 tablespoon	10–20
Tomatoes, sun-dried, not in oil	159	3–4 (15g)	24
Worcestershire sauce	113	1 teaspoon	5
Vinegars and mustards			
Balsamic vinegar	54–107	1 tablespoon	5–20
Cider vinegar	18	1 tablespoon	2
Distilled vinegar	16	1 tablespoon	2
Mustard, Dijon	100–150	1 teaspoon	5–10
Mustard, English	175	1 teaspoon	9
Mustard, grain	154	1 teaspoon	8
Mustard powder	520	½ teaspoon	13
Rice vinegar	25–45	1 tablespoon	3–5
Wine vinegar, red or white	22	1 tablespoon	2–3
Drinks			
Ale	25–47	½ pint	71–133
Apple juice	38–49	125ml	48–61
Black coffee	0–2	1 cup	0–5
Black tea	0	1 cup	0
Dry cava/champagne	76	125ml	95
Dry white wine	66	125ml	83

Food	Calories per 100g/ml	Average serving size	Calories per average portion
Gin/vodka/other spirits	222	25ml single measure	56
Lager	29–43	½ pint	82–122
Orange juice	36–43	125ml	45–54
Red wine	68	125ml	85
Stout	21–39	½ pint	60–111
Fats			
Butter	744	1 teaspoon	37
lightest reduced-fat butter	377–570	1 teaspoon	19–29
Oils, all, including coconut, olive and sesame	899	1 teaspoon	45

Glossary

5:2, 6:1, 4:3   Different approaches to fasting or calorie restriction. The second number is usually the number of days you fast or limit your calories.

ADF   Alternate Day Fasting. Cutting down or eating nothing every other day.

Bitly   Nothing to do with fasting, but a very useful way of shortening long web links in the links section that follows. You can type these directly into your browser to find a recommended web page.

BMI   Body Mass Index. Simple height to weight calculation used to gauge whether someone's weight may be putting his or her health at risk.

BMR   Basal Metabolic Rate. This is what your body needs in calorie terms for basic survival, without any activity other than basic functions.

Fast   Fast usually means eating nothing (and, in some religions, not drinking anything either). However, 5:2 dieters often use it as shorthand for days when they eat limited amounts.

IF/ICR   Intermittent Fasting/Intermittent Calorie Restriction. The latter is the more accurate name for the 5:2 approach.

Kcal   Kilocalorie is the accurate name for what most people call 'calories'.

TDEE   Total Daily Energy Expenditure. This is an estimate
of the number of calories you'd need to fulfil your
energy requirements for the day, which factors in
your activity levels as well as age, height and weight.

BMI chart

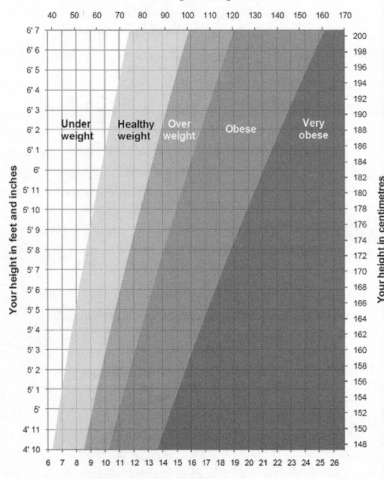

Your weight in kilograms

Your height in feet and inches

Your height in centimetres

Under weight

Healthy weight

Over weight

Obese

Very obese

Your weight in stones

Further reading

I've mainly used shortened bitly links in this list, which are easier to type into your browser. There are general sources of support, plus a list of chapter-by-chapter resources. You can also download a longer resources list with live clickable links from www.the5-2dietbook.com.

The other 5:2 books

My other three books about 5:2 are available as books and e-books, from Orion Publishing. *The 5:2 Diet Book* gives an overview of how to start, and the science, plus my very honest diary of my experiences. *The Ultimate 5:2 Recipe Book* has lots more recipes and case studies, as well as lots of ideas for managing 5:2 on holiday, with the family and on a budget. And *5:2 Your Life: get happy, healthy and slim* is an exciting six-week programme based on using 5:2 principles to become happier with relationships, work and even your sleep. That also has a six-week menu plan with new recipes. I also recommend a well-written and great value e-book, written by one of the first members of the Facebook group, Linda Gruchy, *5:2 Fasting and Fitness: Easy Science in Layman's Terms* (http:amzn.to/1vh8NxG)

Help, support and further information

You can't get much better than our Facebook group when it comes to day-to-day support, tips and encouragement: www.facebook.com/groups/the52diet. There's also a group specifically for the challenges and activities in the *5:2 Your Life* book at www.facebook.com/groups/52YourLife .

Our website, www.the5-2dietbook.com also has a great range of resources, including the Get Started section which includes more food photos, case studies and downloads to help you in your 5:2 journey.

www.myfitnesspal.com has comprehensive calorie listings. However, site users supply these so they are not always reliable. It has a great app for Android and iPhone (free at the time of writing) that helps you track your weight, exercise and calorie consumption.

For more on intermittent fasting research, these two reviews of research (bit.ly/113ykL3 and bit.ly/ShaV4h) are worth downloading to see the positives – as well as the question marks – about human and animal research. And I recommend Mark's Daily Apple for fantastic information about a range of health topics, www.marksdailyapple.com.

Making sense of... research links

The links here are subject to change, and as they're external, I can't be responsible for their contents, but they're a good starting point for your own research.

Making sense of... breakfast

For the heart disease study, compare the BBC report on breakfast skipping: http://bbc.in/1tdjsce and the study itself, Prospective Study of Breakfast Eating and Incident Coronary Heart Disease in a Cohort of Male US Health Professionals, 2013: http://bit.ly/sO02ct with this analysis by author Zoe Harcombe: www.zoeharcombe.com/2013/07/eating-breakfast-can-cut-heart-attack-risk-puh-lease.

Does 'breakfast 'make you brainy?' The *Daily Mail* report suggests it does: http://dailym.ai/1rdDLBL but to find out about the research set-up, see here: http://themindlab.co.uk/services/.

Not eating breakfast may prime your brain to seek out fatty foods later in the day: the BBC report is here: http://bbc.in/1x7OFwo. This is key researcher Dr Goldstone talking more generally about fat in the diet here on a brief BBC video: www.bbc.co.uk/news/health-11158546

The University of Bath study on breakfast and metabolism (The causal role of breakfast in energy balance and health: a randomized controlled trial in lean adults, 2014) is available online: http://bit.ly/1F2CmHE and has been analysed by the NHS site:

http://bit.ly/1yje3AG.

For more on sugar in cereals and cereal bars: http://bit.ly/1lnzLQB and: http://bit.ly/1vLzKKg.

Making sense of... appetite

For a fascinating overview of the complex factors involved in appetite, try: http://ti.me/1Cphia6.

Making sense of... 5 a day (and health by numbers)

On 5-a-day:

'Fruit and vegetable consumption and mortality from all causes, cardiovascular disease, and cancer: systematic review and dose-response meta-analysis of prospective cohort studies', 2014: http://bit.ly/1tZ7m4z.

'Increased fruit and vegetable intake has no discernible effect on weight loss: a systematic review and meta-analysis', 2014: http://bit.ly/1qBcgSs.

On alcohol:

'Lack of international consensus in low-risk drinking guidelines', Drug and Alcohol Review, 2013: http://bit.ly/1yGJ18S.

This NHS overview on research around alcohol is a useful download: http://bit.ly/1fQnmBl.

Or: www.drinkaware.co.uk for information about alcohol and safe drinking.

On water consumption:

BMJ article on water and health marketing, Waterlogged: http://bit.ly/1O1tGBp.

News feature on water and the skin: http://bbc.in/1De25P0.

On waist/height ratio as a health predictor:

There are many studies available but start with: 'Waist-to-height ratio is a better screening tool than waist circumference and BMI for adult cardio metabolic risk factors: systematic review and meta-analysis: http://1.usa.gov/1qBdqx6.

Making sense of... when to eat

There are numerous interesting studies. Start with this general overview: http://bit.ly/1De2i4F and then follow up on the links that interest you. For example, 'Resting energy expenditure in short-term starvation is increased as a result of an increase in serum norepinephrine', 2000: http://bit.ly/11sjH8R.

Meal frequency and energy balance, 1997: http://1.usa.gov1qBeils, and the one study suggesting meal frequency affects metabolism: 'Nibbling versus gorging: metabolic advantages of increased meal frequency', 1989, http://bit.ly/1.usa.gov/1vySttH.

Making sense of... buying good food

For information on ethical and high-welfare products, visit www.ciwf.org.uk www.freedomfood.co.uk www.thegoodshoppingguide.com www.ethicalconsumer.org www.ethical.org.au and www.soilassociation.org/goodfoodforall.

Making sense of... allergies and intolerances

This NHS overview is a good place to start if you want to discover more: http://www.nhs.uk/Conditions/Allergies or www.allergyuk.org have lots of clear, informative downloads.

For more on coeliac disease: www.coeliac.org.uk. This article on resistant starch is also a good starting point for those with digestive issues: http://bit.ly/1cvM7mp. You can read more about FODMAP diets here: http://bit.ly/1yyjRFY but it's recommended you consult a dietician before trying this. To find a dietician in the UK, go to www.bda.uk.com.

Making sense of... emotional eating

The NHS page www.nhs.uk/conditions/Binge-eating has useful tools – including a link to the SCOFF questionnaire if you feel you're eating, or that of someone you know, is out of control. The eating disorders charity www.b-eat.co.uk supports people with all kinds of issues around food, and has extensive information.

Making sense of... carbohydrates, fats, proteins

This is an area where there is a great deal of research, much of it contradictory. Either start with the NHS site, and follow up links from there: http://bit.ly/1dmKRxk. Or go to an original study like 'Association of Dietary, Circulating, and Supplement Fatty Acids With Coronary Risk: A Systematic Review and Meta-analysis', 2014: http://bit.ly/1idxP9u.

'The confusion about dietary fatty acids recommendations for CHD prevention, meta-analysis', 2011: http://1.usa.gov/1sWKCFa.

'Low Protein Intake Is Associated with a Major Reduction in IGF-1, Cancer, and Overall Mortality in the 65 and Younger but Not Older Population', 2014, http://bit.ly/10I1uarm.

The Seven Countries Study, which was launched by Ancel Keys in 1958 and influences government policies world-wide to this day, has its own website: http://sevencountriesstudy.com.

The World Health Organisation also has a site on obesity and healthy diets: http://www.who.int/topics/obesity/en/.

Making sense of... sugar and sweeteners

For a good overview of Glycaemic Index and Glycaemic Load, there's a Q&A here: http://huff.to/1Df0h4X with more detailed information here.

Dr Robert Lustig's *Sugar: The Bitter Truth* has been watched on YouTube over 5 million times: it's a long watch, but worth it if you're interested in the issues: http://bit.ly/1gigkDc.

Making sense of... eating for long life and good health

Whenever you're checking out a scare, a study or a headline, check out www.nhs.uk/news, snopes.com or Wikipedia and a variety of online newspapers to help you make up *your* mind.

Acknowledgements

A cookbook really is a team effort… so thanks to everyone in 'Team 5:2'. As always, the thank you starts with members of the Facebook group all around the world who've been sharing their highs, lows, photos and ideas since Autumn 2012. Particular thanks go to the team who help me run the community and Facebook groups, and especially to Anita, Boo, Elaine, Janine, Julie, Kerry, Linda, Samantha, Sheila, Skids, Tracey, and Wai. Without you, things might go downhill very rapidly on a Fast Day!

Special thanks too to the lovely people who agreed to share *their* stories in this book: Carol and Peter, Elaine, Jo, Louise, Nicky, Pam and Pat, Pippa, Sharon, Susan and Trudie.

Thanks to everyone at LAW but especially Araminta, Elizabeth, Jennifer and Peta.

Thanks also to Belinda at the Byron Beach Café for sharing some of the spice secrets from their Quinoa Salad.

Many thanks to the brilliant team at Orion for making it all come together, and especially for the fantastic photo shoot, to Andrew, Debbie, Helen and Linda. Special 5:2 badges of honour to Amanda and the inestimable Jillian for their poise, unflappability and ability to make it all happen. It was also amazing to meet the fab Hachette Australia team in Sydney during my trip of a lifetime.

Thanks to Linda and Fiona for making sense of *my* making sense of sections – and huge thanks to the terrific Emma Marsden for culinary wisdom, calorie-counting patience and outstanding taste.

As always, my love to Mum, Dad, Toni, Geri, Jenny and Rich. This couldn't happen without you.

Finally, thanks to *you* for buying this book. If you've enjoyed the recipes, do get in touch to share your favourites via www.the5-2dietbook.com – or leave a review for the book on Amazon so other people can find it too! And come and join us in the FB group, too, the more the merrier: www.facebook.com/groups/the52diet.

Index

Recipe and Ingredient Index

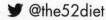